STUDY GUIDE
to accompany

FINANCIAL ACCOUNTING
Tools for Business Decision Making

5th Edition

Paul D. Kimmel PhD, CPA
Associate Professor of Accounting
University of Wisconsin--Milwaukee
Milwaukee, Wisconsin

Jerry J. Weygandt PhD, CPA
Arthur Andersen Alumni Professor of Accounting
University of Wisconsin
Madison, Wisconsin

Donald E. Kieso PhD, CPA
KPMG Peat Marwick Emeritus Professor of Accountancy
Northern Illinois University
DeKalb, Illinois

Prepared by
Cecelia M. Fewox CPA
College of Charleston
Charleston, South Carolina

WILEY
John Wiley & Sons, Inc.

ISBN-13   978-0-470-37976-9

Printed in the United States of America

10 9 8 7 6 5 4 3 2 1

Printed and bound by Bind Rite.

CONTENTS

Specimen Financial Statements: The Bon-Ton Stores, Inc.

CHAPTER 1

Introduction to Financial Statements

CHAPTER OVERVIEW

Chapter 1 introduces you to a variety of financial accounting topics. You will learn about the primary forms of business organization and the three principal types of business activity. You'll also learn about users of accounting information and how that information is delivered. Finally, you'll learn about the basic financial statements and their components as well as items that supplement the financial statements in an annual report.

REVIEW OF SPECIFIC STUDY OBJECTIVES

SO1.   Describe the primary forms of business organization.

△   A **sole proprietorship** is a business owned by one person. It is <u>simple to set up</u>, and the <u>owner has control over the business</u>. Because they are so simple to organize, there are many thousands of sole proprietorships operating in the business world.

△   A **partnership** is a business owned by two or more persons associated as partners. It provides strength in numbers: each <u>partner may bring economic resources</u> or <u>unique talents or skills</u> to the combination.

⋏   A **corporation** is a separate legal entity owned by stockholders. <u>Advantages</u> include shareholders have <u>no personal liability,</u> that <u>ownership is easier to transfer,</u> and that <u>the raising of funds is easier</u>. While there are many more sole proprietorships and partnerships than there are corporations, corporations produce far more revenue.

SO2.   Identify the users and uses of accounting.

⋏   The **purpose of financial information** is to <u>provide inputs for decision making</u>. **Accounting is the information system that identifies, records, and communicates the economic events of an organization to interested users.**

⋏   **Internal users** are people who work for the business, <u>managers who plan, organize, and run a business</u>. Accounting information helps to answer questions such as, "Does the business have enough resources to build a new manufacturing plant?" <u>Internal reports</u> help to provide the required information.

⋏   **External users** work outside of the business and include <u>investors</u> who use accounting information for their stock decisions; <u>creditors</u> who evaluate the risk of lending to and the credit-worthiness of business borrowers; <u>taxing authorities,</u> which review compliance with tax laws; <u>regulatory agencies,</u> which review compliance with prescribed rules; <u>customers;</u> <u>labor unions;</u> and <u>economic planners</u>.

⋏   It is **critical that users trust accounting reports and financial statements**. Concerned about the financial scandals and afraid that users would lose confidence in corporate accounting, United States regulators and lawmakers in 2002 passed the <u>Sarbanes-Oxley Act</u>. Among the provisions of the act are: top management must certify the accuracy of financial information; penalties for fraudulent financial activity are very severe; outside auditors must be more independent; and boards of directors have increased responsibility in their oversight roles.

SO3.   Explain the three principal types of business activity.

⋏   There are **three types of business activity** which the accounting information system tracks: <u>financing</u>, <u>investing</u>, and <u>operating</u>.

⋏   **Financing activities** deal with the ways a business <u>raises funds for operations</u>. The **two primary sources of outside funds** are borrowing money and selling shares of <u>stock</u>.

⋏   A business may **borrow money** by taking out a loan at a bank, issuing debt securities, or purchasing goods on credit. A **creditor** is a person or entity to which a business owes money, and a **liability** is a debt or other obligation that represents creditors' claims on the business. Examples of liabilities are <u>notes payable,</u> resulting from direct borrowing or purchasing on credit and <u>bonds payable,</u> sold to investors and usually due several years in the future. A creditor has a legal right to be paid at an agreed-upon time and must be paid before an owner (stockholder) is paid.

A   A corporation may also **sell shares of stock** to investors. Common stock is the term which describes the total amount paid into the corporation by stockholders for the shares of stock purchased. A stockholder is an owner of the business and receives payments in the form of dividends. (Please note that there are companies which do not pay dividends to stockholders). As noted above, stockholder claims are secondary to creditor claims.

A   **Investing activities** deal with what a corporation does with the financing it receives. Certainly a new business must purchase assets with which to operate. An **asset** is a resource owned by a business. Examples of assets are property, plant, and equipment, such as buildings and trucks. Cash is one of the most important assets owned by a company, and if it has excess cash, it might invest it in debt or equity securities. Such investments are another example of an investing activity.

A   **Operating activities** are just that: operations of the business. Different businesses have different operations, of course. A paper company produces and sells paper while a dairy company produces and sells milk. When a company operates, it earns revenues. **Revenues** are the increase in assets arising from the sale of a product or service. While the purchase of a long-lived asset is an investing activity, operating activities give rise to assets with shorter lives, such as accounts receivable (a customer's promise to pay in the future) and inventory (goods available for future sale). When a company operates, it also incurs costs or expenses. **Expenses** are the cost of assets consumed or services used in the process of generating revenues. Examples of expenses are cost of goods sold, selling expenses, marketing expenses, administrative expenses, and interest expense. Liabilities may arise from these expenses. Examples are accounts payable, interest payable, wages payable, sales taxes payable, property taxes payable, and income taxes payable. If revenues exceed expenses (hopefully!), then a business earns net income. If expenses exceed revenues, then a business incurs a net loss.

SO4.   Describe the content and purpose of each of the financial statements.

A   Various users desire information to help them make decisions, and this financial **information is provided in the form of financial statements**, which form the backbone of financial accounting. There are four financial statements: the income statement, the statement of retained earnings, the balance sheet, and the statement of cash flows.

A   The **income statement** reports the success or failure of the company's operations during the period. Only **revenues and expenses** appear on the income statement, along with their difference, either net income (revenues exceed expenses) or net loss (expenses exceed revenues). Beginning students often want to put the account "Cash" on the income statement, but this is incorrect because cash is an asset (a resource owned by a business). So remember: only revenues and expenses appear on the income statement.

⋏   The **statement of retained earnings** shows the <u>amounts and causes of changes in the retained earnings balance during the period</u>. To beginning retained earnings is added net income (or, if there is a net loss, that amount is deducted), and then dividends are deducted. (Remember that a business will have either net income or a net loss; it can't have both at the same time.) <u>Users of financial statements can find out about management's dividend policy by analyzing this statement</u>. To summarize, the Retained Earnings account is the total of all the net income that the company has earned, all the net losses it has incurred, and all the dividends it has declared. The statement of retained earnings documents this activity.

SO5.   Explain the meaning of assets, liabilities, and stockholders' equity, and state the basic accounting equation.

⋏   The **balance sheet** <u>reports assets and claims to those assets at a specific point in time</u>. There are **two types of claims**: <u>claims of creditors (liabilities)</u> and <u>claims of owners (stockholders' equity)</u>. The balance sheet is an expanded expression of the **basic accounting equation** which is:

$$\text{Assets} = \text{Liabilities} + \text{Stockholders' Equity}$$

Please note that this is a mathematical equation and must be in balance at all times. It can be used to answer questions such as: if assets total $100 and liabilities total $20, then what is the total of stockholders' equity? (Answer: $80 because $20 plus something must equal $100, and the something must be $80.)

Stockholders' equity consists of **two parts**: <u>common stock</u> and <u>retained earnings</u>.

⋏   The **statement of cash flows** <u>provides financial information about the cash receipts and cash payments of a business for a specific period of time</u>. Here a user will find information about the <u>financing, investing, and operating activities</u> of the business.

⋏   Note the **interrelationships between statements**:
1.   Net income or net loss from the income statement appears on the statement of retained earnings.
2.   The ending balance of retained earnings is the same number reported on the balance sheet for retained earnings.
3.   The ending balance of cash must be the same both on the balance sheet and on the statement of cash flows.

⋏   Companies usually present **comparative statements**, which are <u>statements reporting information for more than one period</u>.

⋏   Please be aware of the following when you **prepare financial statements**:
1.   All statements **must have a heading**. The <u>company name</u> appears on the first line, the <u>name of the document</u> appears on the second line, and the <u>date</u> appears on the third line. With respect to **dates**, the **balance sheet date** is for <u>one point in time</u> (June 30, 2010, or December 31, 2010), while

the **date on the income statement, the statement of retained earnings, and the statement of cash flows** is for <u>a period of time</u> ("For the month ended June 30, 2010" or "For the year ended December 31, 2010").

2. The number at the top of a column should have a dollar sign: this indicates that it is the first number in that column. The final number on a statement, such as Net Income or Total Assets, should have a dollar sign and be double-underlined. This indicates that it is the "answer." If there is a negative number, such as Net Loss, then it should be presented in parentheses or brackets. These are part of a type of shorthand used by preparers of statements and understood by users of statements.

SO6. Describe the components that supplement the financial statements in an annual report.

- Companies provide their shareholders with an **annual report**, which includes the <u>financial statements</u>, a <u>management discussion and analysis section</u>, <u>notes to the financial statements</u>, and an <u>independent auditor's report</u>.

- The **management discussion and analysis (MD&A) section** covers **three financial aspects of a company**: its <u>ability to pay near-term obligations</u>, its <u>ability to fund operations and expansion</u>, and its <u>results of operations</u>.

- The **notes to the financial statements** provide <u>additional details about the items presented in the main body of the statements</u>. Examples of notes are one explaining which methods a company uses for its inventory and one explaining the progress of a lawsuit against the company.

- The **independent auditor's report** is prepared by an auditor, a professional who conducts an independent examination of a company's accounting data. Please note that only a certified public accountant (CPA) may conduct an audit. The **most desirable opinion** is the <u>unqualified opinion</u> which states that the financial statements are in accordance with generally accepted accounting principles.

CHAPTER SELF-TEST

As you work the exercises and problems, remember to use the **Decision Toolkit** discussed and used in the text:

1. <u>Decision Checkpoints</u>: at this point you ask a question.

2. <u>Info Needed for Decision</u>: you make a choice regarding the information needed to answer the question.

3. <u>Tool to Use for Decision</u>: at this point you review just what the information chosen in step 2 does for the decision-making process.

4. <u>How to Evaluate Results</u>: you perform evaluation of information for answering the question.

Note: The notation (SO1) means that the question was drawn from study objective number one.

Completion

Please write in the word or words that will complete the sentence.

1. (SO1)　A _____ is a separate legal entity owned by stockholders.

2. (SO1)　A business owned by two or more associated persons is a

    _____ .

3. (SO2)　A manager who plans, organizes, and runs a business is an example of an
    _____ user.

4. (SO2)　A customer is an example of an _____ user.

5. (SO3)　An example of a(n) _____ activity is a corporation's sale of stock to investors.

6. (SO4)　The purpose of the _____ _____ is to report the success or failure of the company's operations during the period.

7. (SO4)　The _____ _____ statement includes an addition of net income and a deduction of dividends.

8. (SO5)　Claims of creditors on the assets of the business are called _____ ; claims of owners are called _____ _____ .

9. (SO5)　If liabilities total $6,000 and stockholders' equity totals $10,000, then assets must total _____ .

10. (SO6)　Only a certified public accountant (CPA) may perform an _____ of a company's financial statements.

Multiple Choice

Please circle the correct answer.

1. (SO1) Which of the following statements is correct?
    a. A sole proprietor has no personal liability for debts of his business.
    b. There are far more corporations than there are sole proprietorships and partnerships.
    c. Revenue produced by corporations is much greater than that produced by proprietorships and partnerships.
    d. It is very difficult for a corporation to raise capital.

2. (SO2) Which of the following is an example of an external user of accounting information?
    a. Marketing manager of the business.
    b. President of the labor union.
    c. Officer of the corporation.
    d. Production supervisor of the business.

3. (SO3) Which of the following is an investing activity?
    a. Borrowing money from a bank.
    b. Earning revenue from the sale of products.
    c. Incurring salaries expense.
    d. The purchase of a delivery truck.

4. (SO3) A business's earning of revenues is considered to be a(n):
    a. operating activity.
    b. investing activity.
    c. financing activity.
    d. balance sheet activity.

5. (SO3) Borrowing money from a bank is considered to be a(n):
    a. operating activity.
    b. investing activity.
    c. financing activity.
    d. balance sheet activity.

6. (SO4) Which of the following accounts will be found on an income statement?
    a. Revenues, expenses, and dividends.
    b. Revenues and expenses.
    c. Revenues, expenses, and cash.
    d. Expenses, dividends, and cash.

7. (SO4) Which of the following accounts will be found on a balance sheet?
    a. Accounts payable, cash, inventory.
    b. Cash, sales revenue, accounts receivable.
    c. Cost of goods sold, notes payable, common stock.
    d. Cash, wages payable, advertising expense.

8.   (SO4) If revenues are $20,000 and expenses are $5,000, then the business:
   a.   incurred a net loss of $25,000.
   b.   earned net income of $20,000.
   c.   earned net income of $15,000.
   d.   incurred a net loss of $15,000.

9.   (SO4) If revenues are $18,000 and expenses are $22,000, then the business:
   a.   incurred a net loss of $4,000.
   b.   incurred a net loss of $40,000.
   c.   earned net income of $4,000.
   d.   earned net income of $18,000.

10.   (SO4) If beginning retained earnings is $10,000, net loss is $3,000, and dividends are $1,000, then the ending retained earnings shown on the statement of retained earnings is:
   a. $14,000.
   b. $12,000.
   c. $ 8,000.
   d. $ 6,000.

11.   (SO4) If beginning retained earnings is $15,000, net income is $6,000, and ending retained earnings is $20,000, how much did the company distribute in dividends?
   a. $6,000.
   b. $5,000.
   c. $4,000.
   d. $1,000.

12.   (SO5) Which of the following is an appropriate date for a balance sheet?
   a.   December 31, 2010.
   b.   For the month ending December 31, 2010.
   c.   For the quarter ending December 31, 2010.
   d.   For the year ending December 31, 2010.

13.   (SO5) Which of the following is the correct expression of the basic accounting equation?
   a.   Liabilities = Assets + Stockholders' Equity.
   h.   Stockholders' Equity = Assets + Liabilities.
   c.   Assets = Liabilities + Stockholders' Equity.
   d.   Assets = Liabilities - Stockholders' Equity.

14.   (SO5) Which of the following is another correct expression of the basic accounting equation?
   a.   Assets – Liabilities = Stockholders' Equity.
   b.   Assets + Liabilities = Stockholders' Equity.
   c.   Assets = Liabilities - Stockholders' Equity.
   d.   Liabilities = Assets + Stockholders' Equity.

15. (SO5) Assets total $14,000, stockholders' equity totals $9,000, and revenues total $6,000. What is the dollar amount of liabilities?
     a. $23,000
     b. $17,000.
     c. $11,000.
     d. $ 5,000.

16. (SO5) Expenses total $6,000, assets total $15,000, and liabilities total $4,000. What is the dollar amount of stockholders' equity?
     a. $19,000.
     b. $11,000.
     c. $ 9,000.
     d. $ 5,000.

17. (SO5) The statement which shows the operating, investing, and financing activities of a business is the:
     a. statement of retained earnings.
     b. statement of cash flows.
     c. income statement.
     d. balance sheet.

18. (SO6) In which section of the annual report does management highlight favorable or unfavorable trends and identify significant events and uncertainties affecting its ability to pay near-term obligations, ability to fund operations and expansion, and results of operations?
     a. Financial statements.
     b. Management discussion and analysis.
     c. Notes to the financial statements.
     d. Auditor's report.

19. (SO6) Which of the following provides additional details about the items presented in the main body of the financial statements?
     a. Management discussion and analysis.
     b. Auditor's report.
     c. Notes to the financial statements.
     d. None of the above is correct.

20. (SO6) Which of the following gives the results of the independent examination of the company's financial data?
     a. Financial statements.
     b. Management discussion and analysis.
     c. Notes to the financial statements.
     d. Auditor's report.

Problems

1. From the appropriate accounts given below, please prepare a balance sheet for Appaloosa Corporation on September 30, 2010 (SO5):

Accumulated Depreciation	$ 4,000
Common Stock	17,000
Service Revenue	20,000
Note Payable	5,000
Salaries Expense	10,000
Accounts Receivable	7,000
Dividends	2,000
Unearned Revenue	3,000
Retained Earnings	26,000
Supplies	2,000
Insurance Expense	1,500
Prepaid Insurance	3,000
Utilities Expense	4,000
Office Equipment	20,000
Accounts Payable	1,000
Cash	24,000

Appaloosa Corporation
Balance Sheet
September 30, 2010

Kimmel Financial Accounting: Tools for Business Decision Making, Fifth Edition

2. Please refer to The Bon-Ton Stores, Inc. financial statements at the end of this study guide for information for answering the following questions. Don't forget to use the Decision Toolkit approach for help in the problem-solving.

    a. What is the total dollar amount of the company's assets on February 2, 2008? What are the two biggest asset classes and their dollar amount on that same date? (SO5)

    b. Which class of liabilities has the largest total dollar amount on February 2, 2008? (SO5)

    c. Was the company profitable in 2007? What has been the trend in company income over the three years shown? (SO4)

    d. What was the company's biggest expense in 2007? (SO4)

    e. What was the company's income tax expense in 2007? (SO4)

SOLUTIONS TO SELF-TEST

Completion

1. corporation

2. partnership

3. internal

4. external

5. financing

6. income statement

7. retained earnings

8. liabilities; stockholders' equity

9. $16,000

10. audit

Multiple Choice

1.	c	Sole proprietors are liable for debts of their businesses, there are more proprietorships and partnerships than there are corporations, and corporations easily raise capital through selling of stock and bonds.
2.	b	The marketing manager, corporation officer, and production supervisor all work for the business and thus are internal users.
3.	d	Borrowing money is a financing activity, and earning revenue and incurring expense are operating activities.
4.	a	Investing activities deal with the purchase of assets, and financing activities deal with the borrowing of money and selling of stock.
5.	c	Operating activities deal with the operations of the business, while investing activities deal with what a company does with the financing it receives. "Balance sheet activity" is not one of the three types of business activities.
6.	b	Dividends appear on the retained earnings statement, and cash is an asset on the balance sheet.
7.	a	Sales revenue, cost of goods sold, and advertising expense are income statement items.
8.	c	$20,000 - $5,000
9.	a	$18,000 - $22,000 = ($4,000)
10.	d	$10,000 - $3,000 - $1,000
11.	d	Retained earnings and net income are added together to arrive at $21,000. Since ending retained earnings is $20,000, dividends must have been $1,000 ($21,000 - $20,000 = $1,000).

12.	a	The balance sheet shows balances on a specific date, not for a period of time.
13.	c	
14.	a	When "Liabilities" is moved to the other side of the equation, the sign changes from positive to negative.
15.	d	$14,000 - $9,000
16.	b	The liabilities + stockholders' equity side of the equation must total $15,000 (total assets). So, $15,000 - $4,000 = $11,000.
17.	b	The retained earnings statement shows changes in the retained earnings account over the period, the income statement summarizes revenue and expense activity, and the balance sheet shows assets, liabilities, and stockholders' equity items.
18.	b	The financial statements report results and balances, the notes give more details about items in the financial statements, and the auditor's report gives the auditor's opinion about whether the statements are presented in accordance with generally accepted accounting principles.
19.	c	Management's discussion and analysis discusses three financial aspects of the operations of the business, while the auditor's report gives the auditor's opinion about whether the statements are presented in accordance with generally accepted accounting principles.
20.	d	The financial statements report results and balances, management's discussion and analysis discusses three financial aspects of the operations of the business, and the notes give more details about items in the financial statements.

Problems

1.

Appaloosa Corporation
Balance Sheet
September 30, 2010

Assets

Cash		$24,000
Accounts Receivable		7,000
Supplies		2,000
Prepaid Insurance		3,000
Office Equipment	$20,000	
Less: Accumulated		
Depreciation	4,000	16,000
Total Assets		$52,000

Liabilities and Stockholders' Equity

Liabilities		
Note Payable	$ 5,000	
Accounts Payable	1,000	
Unearned Revenue	3,000	
Total Liabilities		$ 9,000
Stockholders' Equity		
Common Stock	$17,000	
Retained Earnings	26,000	
Total Stockholders' Equity		43,000
Total Liabilities and Stockholders' Equity		$52,000

2. All numbers are presented in thousands.

   a. $2,067,631

Two asset classes:	Current Assets	$871,908
	Property, Fixtures and Equipment, Net	$885,455

   b. Long-term debt, less current maturities: $1,079,841

   c. To determine whether a company is profitable, you must look at the income statement. Bon-Ton certainly was profitable in 2007: net income was $11,562. Net income increased from 2005 to 2006 but declined from 2006 to 2007.

   d. Cost of Merchandise Sold is the largest expense, at $2,150,131. Remember that Bon-Ton consists of retail stores which buy merchandise from wholesalers and sell that merchandise to retail customers; thus, the fact that Cost of Merchandise Sold is the largest expense is not surprising.

e. This number, $5,945, is found on the income statement and is labeled "Income tax provision."

CHAPTER 2

A Further Look at Financial Statements

CHAPTER OVERVIEW

Chapter 2 looks in depth at the classified balance sheet. You will look further at financial statements, learning how to construct ratios using a company's financial statements and how to use those ratios to analyze the company's strengths and weaknesses. You'll also learn about the standard-setting environment, characteristics of accounting information, and the assumptions, principles, and constraints that underlie accounting standards.

REVIEW OF SPECIFIC STUDY OBJECTIVES

SO1.   Identify the sections of a classified balance sheet.

> ⅄   The **balance sheet** of a company presents a <u>snapshot of its financial position at a point in time</u>. A **classified balance sheet** breaks the statement components into several classifications, usually having <u>four asset categories</u>, <u>two liability categories</u>, and the <u>one stockholders' equity category</u>.

> ⅄   The following are the **four common asset categories**:
> 1.   **Current assets** are those <u>expected to be converted into cash or used in the business within a relatively short period of time</u>, usually within one year. Please note that some companies use a period longer than one year because they have a longer <u>operating cycle</u> (the average time that it takes to spend cash to obtain or manufacture a product to sell, then to sell the product, and then to collect cash from the customer). The operating cycle is

sometimes called the cash-to-cash cycle. Current assets are <u>listed in the order in which they are expected to be converted into cash</u> and include **cash, short-term investments, receivables, inventories, and prepaid expenses.**

2. **Long-term investments** are <u>investments in stocks and bonds of other corporations that are held for more than one year</u> and <u>long-term assets such as land or buildings that a company is not currently using in its operating activities.</u>

3. **Property, plant, and equipment** are <u>assets with relatively long useful lives that are used in the operations of the business.</u> Examples include **land, building, machinery and equipment, delivery equipment, and furniture.** These assets <u>depreciate</u>, or wear out with the passage of time, and their cost must be allocated to expense over the useful life of the asset. On the balance sheet, they are <u>shown at their cost less total accumulated depreciation</u>. (The one exception is land. Instead of depreciating, land normally appreciates.)

4. **Intangible assets** are <u>noncurrent assets that have no physical substance</u>. They are essentially long-lived rights; examples include **goodwill, patents, copyrights, and trademarks or trade names.** Beginning students often want to say that a patent has physical substance, that a piece of paper can be held in a hand. The piece of paper does have physical substance but is not the patent itself. It is only evidence that a patent exists. The patent is protection of invention granted by the federal government for a specified period of time.

The following are the **two common liability categories**:
1. **Current liabilities** are <u>obligations that are to be paid within one year</u>. Examples include **accounts payable, notes payable, salaries payable, interest payable, taxes payable, and current maturities of long-term obligations.** Notes payable is usually listed first, followed by accounts payable and other current liabilities.

2. **Long-term liabilities** are <u>expected to be paid after one year from the balance sheet date</u>. If the balance sheet date is December 31, 2005, and an obligation is due on June 30, 2007, then the obligation is long-term. Examples include **bonds payable, mortgages payable, long-term notes payable, lease liabilities, and pension liabilities.** There is no particular guidance for listing these long-term obligations, and companies simply choose a way of disclosing them that is most useful for the users of their financial statements.

As you learned in chapter 1, **stockholders' equity** has <u>two components: common stock and retained earnings</u>. Common stock consists of stockholders' investments of assets in the business, while retained earnings is just that—earnings, or income, retained for use in the business.

SO2.   Identify and compute ratios for analyzing a company's profitability.

     A   Financial statements are used to gauge the strength or weakness of a company. To make numbers in the statements more useful and meaningful, users conduct **ratio analysis**, a technique for expressing relationships among selected financial statement data. Ratios can be expressed as a percentage, a rate, or a proportion.

     A   **Profitability ratios** measure the operating success of a company for a given period of time. One such ratio is the **earnings per share ratio**.

     A   The **earnings per share ratio** measures the net income earned on each share of common stock. It is computed by dividing earnings available to common shareholders (net income less preferred stock dividends) by the average number of common shares outstanding during the year.

     A   Please note that one ratio by itself does not convey very much information. The ratio must be compared with something, either with the ratios from prior years of the same company, or with the ratios of other companies in the same industry, or with the particular industry's averages.

SO3.   Explain the relationship between a retained earnings statement and a statement of stockholders' equity.

     A   Remember that stockholders' equity consists of two parts, common stock and retained earnings.

     A   The **retained earnings statement** describes the changes in retained earnings for the period. These changes usually involve net income or net loss and dividends.

     A   A **statement of stockholders' equity** is broader, reporting all changes in stockholders' equity accounts, not just in the retained earnings account. If a company has sold or repurchased shares of its stock, then those data will appear in this statement.

SO4.   Identify and compute ratios for analyzing a company's liquidity and solvency using a balance sheet.

     A   Just as you have performed ratio analysis using numbers from the income statement, so, too, can you compute **ratios using numbers from the classified balance sheet**.

     A   **Liquidity** refers to a company's ability to pay obligations expected to come due within the next year or operating cycle.

     A   One measure of liquidity is **working capital**, which is the difference between current assets and current liabilities. It is certainly preferable to have a positive number (current assets exceed current liabilities) because this indicates that a company has a good likelihood of being able to pay its liabilities. If current assets are $300 and current liabilities are $100, then working capital is $200.

⋏ Another measure of liquidity is the **current ratio**, computed by <u>dividing current assets by current liabilities</u>. Referring to the numbers just above, dividing $300 by $100 yields a current ratio of 3:1, meaning that the company has $3 of current assets for every $1 of current liabilities. Remember that a ratio by itself doesn't convey very much information: it must be compared to something.

⋏ **Solvency** deals with a company's <u>ability to survive over a long period of time</u>, with its <u>ability to pay its long-term obligations and the interest due on them</u>.

⋏ The **debt to total assets ratio** is one source of information about a company's solvency and <u>measures the percentage of assets financed by creditors rather than invested by stockholders</u>. It is computed by <u>dividing total debt (both current and long-term) by total assets</u>. The higher the percentage of debt financing, the greater the risk that the company may be unable to pay its debts as they mature. If total debt is $3,000,000 and total assets are $5,000,000, then the ratio is 60%, meaning that of every dollar invested in company assets, $.60 has been provided by creditors. A creditor does not like to see a high debt to total assets ratio for a company.

SO5. Use the statement of cash flows to evaluate solvency.

⋏ The **statement of cash flows** provides <u>financial information about the sources and uses of a company's cash</u>. You learned in chapter 1 that there are three sections to the statement: <u>operating activities, investing activities, and financing activities</u>.

⋏ A **company's source of cash** is very important. There are generally **two sources**: <u>operating activities and financing activities</u>. When a company is well-established it should be able to generate most of its cash from operations, not from financing activities (issuing stock or borrowing money).

⋏ The **statement of cash flows can be used to calculate measures of liquidity and solvency**. **Free cash flow** is <u>cash remaining from operations after adjusting for capital expenditures and dividends</u>.

SO6. Explain the meaning of generally accepted accounting principles.

⋏ **Generally accepted accounting principles** are accounting <u>rules that have substantial authoritative support and are recognized as a general guide for financial reporting purposes</u>. Standard-setting bodies determine these rules. The **Securities and Exchange Commission (SEC)** is <u>a U.S. government agency that oversees U.S. financial markets and accounting standard-setting bodies</u>. In the United States the **Financial Accounting Standards Board (FASB)** is the primary standard-setting body. **The Public Accounting Oversight Board (PCAOB)** determines auditing standards and reviews auditing firms. The **International Accounting Standards Board (IASB)** sets global standards.   The FASB's **overriding**

criterion is that an accounting guideline should <u>generate financial information that is most</u> **useful** <u>for making business decisions</u>.

SO7. Discuss financial reporting concepts.

⋏ To be useful, information should have the following **characteristics**: <u>relevance</u>, <u>reliability</u>, <u>comparability</u>, and <u>consistency</u>.

⋏ Accounting information is **relevant** if it **makes a difference in a business decision**. If relevant, accounting information provides a <u>basis for forecasting</u>, <u>confirms or corrects prior expectations</u>, and is presented on a <u>timely basis</u>.

⋏ Accounting information is **reliable** if it **can be depended on**. If reliable, accounting information is <u>verifiable</u> (free of error), is a <u>faithful representation</u> of what it purports to be, and is <u>neutral</u> (does not favor one set of users over another).

⋏ Accounting information is **comparable** when **different companies use the same accounting principles.**

⋏ Accounting information is **consistent** when **one company uses the same accounting principles and methods from year to year**. This does not mean that a company must use the same principles forever after making the initial selection. If it changes in order to produce more meaningful information, then it must disclose the change in the notes to the financial statements.

⋏ Please note that **comparability** deals with making comparisons <u>between two or more companies</u>, whereas **consistency** deals with making comparisons <u>within one company over several periods</u>.

⋏ The FASB relies on **assumptions and principles** to develop accounting standards.

⋏ The **monetary unit assumption** states that <u>only those things that can be expressed in monetary terms are included in the accounting records</u>. This assumption means that nonfinancial factors like customer satisfaction and the excellence of employees won't be reported in the financial statements.

⋏ The **economic entity assumption** states that <u>every economic entity should be separately identified and accounted for</u>. If Elizabeth decides to start a horse training business, she needs two sets of accounting records: one for her personal affairs and one for the affairs of her business.

⋏ The **time period assumption** states that <u>the life of a business can be divided into artificial time periods and that reports covering those periods can be prepared for the business</u>. Most companies report results at least annually and perhaps at other intervals during the year.

⋏ The **going concern assumption** states that <u>the business will remain in operation for the foreseeable future</u>. If liquidation is imminent, then the business will abandon historical cost and book values and use liquidation value (selling price less cost of disposal).

⋏ The **cost principle** states that assets are recorded at their cost. Cost is used because it is easy to verify. Usually there is documentation when an asset is purchased. In recent years there has been movement away from the cost principle. The FASB has developed some standards requiring that certain assets be recorded at their fair market value. A new standard gives companies the option to use market value to account for a wide range of items, making U.S. standards more similar to international standards.

⋏ The **full disclosure principle** requires that companies must disclose all circumstances and events that would make a difference to financial statement users. If a piece of information is not disclosed in one of the four financial statements, then it should be included to the notes to the statements.

⋏ The accounting profession has agreed upon **constraints** to **ensure that companies apply accounting rules in a reasonable fashion**, from the perspectives of both company and user. The **two constraints** are materiality and conservatism.

⋏ An item is **material** if its size makes it likely to influence the decision of an investor or creditor. It is important to note that what is material for one company may be immaterial for another. Assume that companies A and B each have a $1,000 error in the financial statements. Company A's net income is $10,000 while company B's net income is $100,000. The $1,000 error most likely will be material for A since it is 10% of net income, while it most likely will be immaterial for B since it is only 1% of net income.

⋏ **Conservatism** in accounting means the following: when preparing financial statements, if a company has a choice between or among acceptable methods of accounting, then it should choose the method that is least likely to overstate assets or income. It absolutely does not mean to understate assets or income on purpose. Valuing inventories at the lower of their cost or their market value is an example of conservatism.

CHAPTER SELF-TEST

As you work the exercises and problems, remember to use the **Decision Toolkit** discussed and used in the text:

1. Decision Checkpoints: at this point you ask a question.

2. Info Needed for Decision: you make a choice regarding the information needed to answer the question.

3. Tool to Use for Decision: at this point you review just what the information chosen in step 2 does for the decision-making process.

4. <u>How to Evaluate Results</u>: you perform evaluation of information for answering the question.

Note: The notation (SO1) means that the question was drawn from study objective number one.

Matching

Please write the letters of the following terms in the spaces to the left of the definitions.

a. Conservatism

b. Consistency

c. Current assets

d. Current liabilities

e. Generally accepted accounting principles

f. Intangible assets

g. Long-term assets

h. Materiality

i. Operating cycle

j. Solvency

_____ 1. (SO4) The ability of a company to pay interest as it comes due and to repay the face value of debt at maturity.

_____ 2. (SO7) The constraint of determining whether an item is important enough to influence the decision of a reasonably prudent investor or creditor.

_____ 3. (SO7) The approach of choosing an accounting method, when in doubt, that will least likely overstate assets and net income.

_____ 4. (SO1) Obligations to be paid within the next year or operating cycle, whichever is longer.

_____ 5. (SO6) A set of rules and practices recognized as a general guide for financial reporting purposes.

_____ 6. (SO1) Resources expected to be realized in cash or sold or consumed within one year or the operating cycle, whichever is longer.

_____ 7. (SO1) Resources not expected to be realized or cash within the next year or operating cycle.

_____ 8. (SO7) Use of the same accounting principles and methods from year to year within a company.

_____ 9. (SO1) The average time required to go from cash to cash in producing revenues.

_____ 10. (SO1) Assets that do not have physical substance.

Multiple Choice

Please circle the correct answer.

1. (SO1) Which of the following is considered a current asset on a classified balance sheet?
   a. Marketable securities.
   b. Land.
   c. Building.
   d. Patent.

2. (SO1) Which of the following is not considered a current asset on a classified balance sheet?
   a. Accounts Receivable.
   b. Trademark.
   c. Prepaid Rent.
   d. Inventory.

3. (SO1) Which of the following is considered property, plant, and equipment on a classified balance sheet?
   a. Supplies.
   b. Investment in Intel Corporation stock.
   c. Land.
   d. Copyright.

4. (SO1) Current liabilities are $10,000, long-term liabilities are $20,000, common stock is $50,000, and retained earnings totals $70,000. Total stockholders' equity is:
   a. $150,000.
   b. $140,000.
   c. $120,000.
   d. $ 70,000.

5. (SO1) Total assets are $125,000, total liabilities are $50,000, and common stock is $30,000. Retained earnings is:
   a. $45,000.
   b. $50,000.
   c. $80,000.
   d. $95,000.

6. (SO1) Which of the following is considered a current liability on a classified balance sheet?
   a. Bonds payable.
   b. Pension liabilities.
   c. Mortgage payable.
   d. Salaries payable.

7.   (SO2)   Net income is $200,000, preferred dividends are $20,000, and average common shares outstanding are 50,000. Earnings per share is:
     a. $4.00.
     b. $3.60.
     c. $ .28.
     d. $ .25.

8.   (SO2)   Which of the following ratios measures the net income earned on each share of common stock?
     a.   Current ratio.
     b.   Debt to total assets ratio.
     c.   Earnings per share ratio.
     d.   Free cash flow ratio.

9.   (SO3)   Which of the following items will not appear on a statement of stockholders' equity?
     a.   Common stock.
     b.   Retained earnings.
     c.   Dividends.
     d.   Cash.

10.   (SO3)   Which of the following statements reports all changes in stockholders' equity accounts?
     a.   Statement of retained earnings.
     b.   Statement of stockholders' equity.
     c.   Balance sheet.
     d.   Statement of cash flows.

11.   (SO4)   Which ratio measures the percentage of assets financed by creditors rather than by stockholders?
     a.   Current ratio.
     b.   Debt to total assets ratio.
     c.   Working capital ratio.
     d.   Free cash flow ratio.

12.   (SO4)   The ability to pay obligations that are expected to become due within the next year or operating cycle is called:
     a.   working capital.
     b.   profitability.
     c.   solvency.
     d.   liquidity.

13.   (SO4)   Current assets are $60,000, total assets are $180,000, current liabilities are $30,000, and total liabilities are $50,000. The current ratio is:
     a.   2 to 1.
     b.   1.2 to 1.
     c.   .5 to 1.
     d.   .33 to 1.

14. (SO5) Which of the following statements provides information about the operating, investing, and financing activities of a company?
   a. Statement of cash flows.
   b. Balance sheet.
   c. Income statement.
   d. Statement of stockholders' equity.

15. (SO5) Cash flows from operating activities are $200,000; cash flows from financing activities are $150,000; capital expenditures are $90,000; and dividends are $20,000. Free cash flow is:
   a. $180,000.
   b. $140,000.
   c. $ 90,000.
   d. $ 40,000.

16. (SO6) The primary accounting standard-setting body in the United States is the:
   a. Financial Accounting Standards Board.
   b. American Institute of Certified Public Accountants.
   c. Securities and Exchange Commission.
   d. Accounting Principles Board.

17. (SO6) Accounting rules having substantial authoritative support and recognized as a general guide for financial reporting purposes are called:
   a. general accounting principles.
   b. generally accepted auditing principles.
   c. generally accepted accounting standards.
   d. generally accepted accounting principles.

18. (SO7) Accounting information is _____ if it would make a difference in a business decision.
   a. reliable
   b. relevant
   c. comparable
   d. consistent

19. (SO7) _____ results when different companies use the same accounting principles.
   a. Relevance
   b. Consistency
   c. Comparability
   d. Reliability

20.   (SO7)   An item is _____ if it is likely to influence the decision of an investor or creditor.
    a.   consistent
    b.   reliable
    c.   conservative
    d.   material

21.   (SO7)   The constraint which states "Do not overstate assets and income" is:
    a.   conservatism.
    b.   materiality.
    c.   relevance.
    d.   reliability.

Problems

1.   Consider the following data from Midas Corporation:

	2011	2010
Current assets	$ 61,000	$ 50,000
Total assets	108,000	85,000
Current liabilities	47,000	39,000
Total liabilities	80,000	62,000
Net sales	200,000	180,000
Net income	39,000	28,000

In 2011, the average number of common stock shares outstanding during the year was 20,000 shares.

After computing the following, please explain what the results mean:

a.   Working capital for 2011 and 2010 (SO7).

b.   Current ratio for 2011 and 2010 (SO7).

c.   Debt to total assets ratio for 2011 and 2010 (SO7).

d.   Earnings per share ratio for 2011 (SO5).

2.   Please refer to The Bon-Ton Stores, Inc. financial statements at the end of this study guide for information for answering the following questions. Don't forget to use the **Decision Toolkit** approach for help in the problem-solving.

a.   What classes of assets does Bon-Ton show on its balance sheet? (SO4)

b.   Can the company meet its near-term obligations in 2007 and 2006? Please comment on the trend that you see. (SO7)

c.   Does Bon-Ton present a statement of retained earnings or a statement of stockholders' equity? What is the advantage of the company's choice? (SO6)

d.   What type of activity generated the most cash flow for Bon-Ton in 2007? (SO8)

SOLUTIONS TO SELF-TEST

Matching

1.	j		6.	c
2.	h		7.	g
3.	a		8.	b
4.	d		9.	i
5.	e		10.	f

Multiple Choice

1. a   Land, Building, and Patent are all long-term assets.

2. b   Accounts Receivable, Prepaid Rent, and Inventory are all current assets. A trademark is an intangible asset.

3. c   Supplies is a current asset, Investment is a noncurrent asset, and Copyright is an intangible asset.

4. c $50,000 + $70,000

5. a   Since total assets are $125,000, the total of liabilities and stockholders' equity must be $125,000. Since liabilities total $50,000, total equity must equal $75,000. Equity consists of common stock and retained earnings. If common stock is $30,000, then retained earnings must equal $45,000.

6. d   The other three are all long-term liabilities.

7. b   ($200,000 - $20,000) ÷ 50,000

8. c   The current ratio shows the relationship of current assets and current liabilities; debt to total assets ratio measures the percentage of assets financed by creditors; and free cash flow shows cash remaining from operating activities less capital expenditures and dividends.

9. d   Cash is a current asset.

10. b   The statement of retained earnings reports changes in retained earnings only; the balance sheet reports assets, liabilities, and stockholders' equity items; and the statement of cash flows reports operating, investing, and financing activities.

11. b   The current ratio measures the ability of a company to pay its near-term obligations; working capital (current assets minus current liabilities) is not a ratio; and free cash flow (cash flows from operations less capital expenditures and dividends) also is not a ratio.

12. d   Working capital is the difference between current assets and current liabilities, profitability refers to the operating success of an enterprise during a period, and solvency is the ability of a company to pay interest as it comes due and to repay the face value of the debt at maturity.

13. a $60,000 ÷ $30,000

14. a   The balance sheet reports assets, liabilities, and stockholders' equity items; the income statement reports revenues and expenses; and the statement of stockholders' equity reports changes in all stockholders' equity accounts.

15. c $200,000 - $90,000 - $20,000

16.   a   The American Institute is a national group of certified public accountants; the SEC is a federal government regulatory agency; and the Accounting Principles Board was a committee of the American Institute and a previous, not the current, standard-setting body.

17.   d

18.   b   Reliability means that information can be depended on, comparability results when different companies use the same accounting principles, and consistency means that a company uses the same accounting principles and methods from year to year.

19.   c

20.   d   Conservatism means that when preparing financial statements, a company should choose the accounting method that will be least likely to overstate assets and income.

21.   a   An item is material when its size makes it likely to influence the decision of an investor or creditor.

Problems

1.

a.   Current assets - current liabilities = working capital

     2011: $61,000 - $47,000 = <u>$14,000</u>

     2010: $50,000 - $39,000 = <u>$11,000</u>

     Working capital is a measure of liquidity. Since this company's working capital is positive, there is a greater likelihood that it will pay its liabilities.

b.   Current assets ÷ current liabilities = current ratio

     2011: $61,000 ÷ $47,000 = <u>1.30 (rounded) to 1</u>

     2010: $50,000 ÷ $39,000 = <u>1.28 (rounded) to 1</u>

     The current ratio is another measure of liquidity. In 2011 the company had $1.30 of current assets for every dollar of current liabilities. In 2010 it had $1.28 of current assets for every dollar of current liabilities.

c.   Total debt ÷ total assets = debt to total assets ratio

     2011: $80,000 ÷ $108,000 = <u>74% (rounded)</u>

     2010: $62,000 ÷ $85,000 = <u>73% (rounded)</u>

     This ratio measures the percentage of assets financed by creditors rather than by stockholders. In 2011, $.74 of every dollar invested in assets was provided by creditors. In

2010 $.73 of every dollar was provided by creditors. The higher the percentage of debt financing, the riskier the company.

d.   Net income ÷ average common shares outstanding = earnings per share ratio

2011: $39,000 ÷ 20,000 shares = $1.95

This ratio is a measure of profitability. It shows that each of the company's 20,000 outstanding shares of common stock earned $1.95 of the total net income.

2.

a.   Current assets
Property, fixtures and equipment at cost, net of accumulated depreciation and amortization
Deferred income taxes
Goodwill
Intangible assets, net of accumulated amortization
Other long-term assets

b.   Dollar amounts are presented in thousands.

To answer this question, you need to compute the current ratio for each year.

Current assets ÷ current liabilities = current ratio
2007 $871,908 ÷ $445,457 = 1.96 (rounded) to 1
2006 $914,809 ÷ $512,395 = 1.79 (rounded) to 1

In both years Bon-Ton could pay its short-term obligations had they all come due. Notice that the ratio increased from 2006 to 2007 because current liabilities decreased by 13% while current assets decreased by only 5%.

c.   Bon-Ton presents a Consolidated Statements of Shareholders' Equity; its name for a statement of stockholders' equity. Shareholders', or stockholders', equity is comprised of two parts: retained earnings and common stock. The statement of retained earnings provides information about retained earnings only: to the beginning balance is added net income (or net loss is subtracted), and dividends are subtracted to give the ending balance. The advantage of using a statement of stockholders' equity is that it presents changes in all stockholders' equity accounts, not just changes in retained earnings.

d.   To answer this question, you must look at Bon-Ton's statement of cash flows. Remember that this statement shows the company's operating, investing, and financing activities. One source of cash is operating activities, and in 2007 the company's operating activities provided $135,564 in cash flow. Note that investing activities used cash ($106,914) in 2007, as did financing activities ($32,145).

CHAPTER **3**

The Accounting Information System

CHAPTER OVERVIEW

Chapter 3 shows you how to analyze transactions and their effect on the accounting equation. You will learn about accounts and debits and credits and how to perform the basic steps in the recording process: journalizing, posting transactions to the ledger, and preparing a trial balance.

REVIEW OF SPECIFIC STUDY OBJECTIVES

SO1. Analyze the effect of business transactions on the basic accounting equation.

⅄   The **accounting information system** is the system of collecting and processing transaction data and communicating financial information to decision makers.

⅄   **Accounting transactions** are economic events that require recording in the financial statements. An accounting transaction occurs when assets, liabilities, or stockholders' equity items change as a result of an economic event.

⅄   **Transaction analysis** is the process of identifying the specific effects of economic events on the accounting equation. The **accounting equation must always be in balance** after a transaction is recorded. Remember: It is a mathematical equation. If a stockholder invests cash in the business, then cash on the left side of the equation increases while stockholders' equity on the right side of the equation increases by the same amount.

A   Please remember the following with respect to specific parts of the accounting equation:

1.   If a company receives cash for work to be performed in the future, then it should not record revenue. It records an increase in cash on the left side of the equation and an increase in <u>liabilities</u> on the right side of the equation: It <u>owes</u> performance of that work in the future.
2.   Revenues increase stockholders' equity.
3.   Expenses and dividends decrease stockholders' equity.
4.   Some events in the life of a corporation are not transactions and, thus, are not to be recorded. The hiring of an employee and the beginning of an employees' strike are two such events.
5.   Each transaction has a dual (double-sided) effect on the equation. For example, iff an individual asset is increased, there must be a corresponding:
           a. Decrease in another asset, or
           b. Increase in a specific liability, or
           c. Increase in stockholders' equity.

SO2.   Explain what an account is and how it helps in the recording process.

A   **An accounting information system uses accounts** that are <u>individual accounting records of increases and decreases in a specific asset, liability, or stockholders' equity item.</u>

A   The simplest form of an account is the **T-account**, so called because of its shape. T-accounts have <u>account titles</u>, a <u>left side (called the debit side)</u>, and a <u>right side (called the credit side)</u>.

SO3.   Define debits and credits and explain how they are used to record business transactions.

A   **Debit, abbreviated Dr., means left**, while **credit, abbreviated Cr., means right**. These terms simply denote position: They do not mean good or bad, increase or decrease. The <u>important thing is to know what a debit does to a particular account and what a credit does to that same account.</u>

A   **To debit an account** means to <u>enter a number on the left side of the account</u>. **To credit an account** means to <u>enter a number on the right side of the account</u>. If an account has $300 on the debit side and $100 on the credit side, then that account has a $200 overall debit balance. If an account has $500 on the credit side and $200 on the debit side, then that account has a $300 overall credit balance. **Debits are always added together, and credits are always added together, but a debit and a credit are subtracted one from the other.**

A   The **dollar amount of the debits and the dollar amount of the credits must be equal in each transaction.** This provides the <u>basis of the double-entry accounting system</u>. Double-entry simply means that each accounting transaction has two parts.

⅄ The following is a summary of the **debit/credit procedures for the accounts that you know** ("Inc" means "increase, while "Decr" means "decrease):

	Debit	Credit		Debit	Credit
Assets	Inc	Decr	Liabilities	Decr	Inc
Dividends	Inc	Decr	Equity	Decr	Inc
Expenses	Inc	Decr	Revenues	Decr	Inc

Remember that **stockholders' equity has two components: common stock and retained earnings**. Both follow the procedures indicated for "Equity" above.

⅄ **Dividends**, which are distributions by a corporation to its stockholders in an amount proportional to each investor's percentage ownership, **and expenses both reduce stockholders' equity**; therefore, they follow procedures opposite from those followed by equity. **Common stock, retained earnings, and revenues all increase stockholders' equity**.

⅄ **Common stock and retained earnings** are reported in the stockholders' equity section of the balance sheet. **Dividends** are reported on the statement of retained earnings. **Revenues and expenses** are reported on the income statement.

⅄ Since assets are on the left side of the accounting equation while liabilities and stockholders' equity are on the right side, the procedures for assets are opposite from those for liabilities and equity items.

⅄ The **normal balance** is the balance expected to be in an account. Please note that the normal balance is found on the side that increases a particular account. Dividends are increased by debits, and the normal balance is a debit. Revenues are increased by credits, and the normal balance is a credit. Occasionally, however, an account may have a balance other than its normal balance. As your text points out, the Cash account will have a credit balance when the cash account is overdrawn at the bank.

SO4. Identify the basic steps in the recording process.

⅄ The **recording process begins with a source document**.

⅄ Each **transaction is analyzed and entered in a journal**. Then the **journal information is transferred to** the appropriate accounts in **the ledger**.

SO5. Explain what a journal is and how it helps in the recording process.

⅄ A **journal** is a place where a transaction is initially recorded before it is transferred to the accounts. It may be in the form of paper or may be a file on a computer disk or hard drive. **Transactions are entered in chronological order**.

A   The **journal** makes three significant contributions to the recording process:
1. It discloses in one place the <u>complete effect of a transaction</u>.
2. It provides a <u>chronological record</u> of transactions.
3. It <u>helps to prevent or locate errors</u> because the debit and credit amounts for each entry can be readily compared.

A   **Journalizing** is the <u>process of entering transaction data in the journal</u>. A **complete journal entry** consists of the following:

1. The <u>date</u> of the transaction;
2. The <u>accounts and amounts</u> to be debited and credited; and
3. An <u>explanation</u> of the transaction.

A   A typical journal entry has the following format:

May 12	Supplies	500	
	Cash		500
	(Purchased supplies for cash)		

Please note that the **credit account title is indented**. This decreases the possibility of switching the debit and credit amounts. It also makes its easy to see that the account Cash is credited without having to have eyes glance right to see in which column the Cash amount is residing. It is fatiguing to have your eyes continually scan back and forth across a page.

SO6.   Explain what a ledger is and how it helps in the recording process.

A   The **ledger** is the <u>entire group of accounts maintained by a company</u>. It keeps in one place all the information about changes in specific account balances. A **general ledger** contains all the <u>assets, liabilities, and stockholders' equity accounts</u>.

A   As is true for the journal, a general ledger may be in the form of paper or may be a file on a computer disk or hard drive.

A   The **chart of accounts** is a <u>listing of all ledger accounts used in the business</u>.

SO7.   Explain what posting is and how it helps in the recording process.

A   **Posting** is the <u>procedure of transferring journal entries to ledger accounts</u>. Posting accumulates the effects of journalized transactions in the individual accounts.

A   To **illustrate posting**, consider the entry from study objective 5 above in which Supplies was debited and Cash was credited for $500 on May 12. In the ledger account Supplies, the date is recorded and $500 is written in the debit column. In the ledger account Cash, the date is again recorded and $500 is written in the credit column.

SO8.   Explain the purposes of a trial balance.

      ↗   A **trial balance** is a <u>list of accounts and their balances at a given time</u>. A trial balance is usually prepared at the end of an accounting period. Accounts are listed in their ledger order with the balances listed in the appropriate column, debit or credit. The **dollar amount of the debits must equal the dollar amount of the credits**; otherwise, there is an error that must be corrected. A trial balance <u>proves the mathematical equality of debits and credits in the ledger</u>. It also <u>helps to uncover errors in journalizing and posting</u> and is <u>useful in preparation of financial statements</u>.

      ↗   It is, of course, preferable that **a trial balance have equal debits and credits, but mistakes can still be present**. If a <u>journal entry has not been posted</u>, then an error has occurred, but the trial balance will be in balance. If a <u>journal entry is posted twice</u>, then the same is true. If a <u>journal entry is recorded as $500 instead of $5,000 on both the debit and the credit side</u>, then an error has occurred, but once again, the trial balance will be in balance. If a $200 <u>debit is posted to Cash instead of to another asset</u>, then an error is present, but the trial balance will be in balance.

SO9.   Classify cash activities as operating, investing, or financing.

      ↗   Remember that a **statement of cash flows classifies every transaction of a company as an operating activity** (<u>an activity used by the company to generate profits</u>), **an investing activity** (<u>the purchase or sale of long-lived assets</u>), **or a financing activity** (such as <u>borrowing money or issuing shares of its stock</u>).

CHAPTER SELF-TEST

As you work the exercises and problems, remember to use the **Decision Toolkit** discussed and used in the text:

1. <u>Decision Checkpoints</u>: at this point you ask a question.

2. <u>Info Needed for Decision</u>: you make a choice regarding the information needed to answer the question.

3. <u>Tool to Use for Decision</u>: at this point you review just what the information chosen in step 2 does for the decision-making process.

4. <u>How to Evaluate Results</u>: you perform evaluation of information for answering the question.

Note: The notation (SO1) means that the question was drawn from study objective number one.

Completion

Please write in the word or words that will complete the sentence.

1. (SO1)   Economic events that require recording in the financial statements are called _____ _____.

2. (SO2)   A(n) _____ is an individual accounting record of increases and decreases in a specific asset, liability, or stockholders' equity item.

3. (SO3)   Under the _____ - _____ system, the dual effect of each transaction is recorded in appropriate accounts.

4. (SO3)   A debit _____ the Common Stock account.

5. (SO4)   Evidence of an accounting transaction comes in the form of a _____ _____.

6. (SO5)   A complete journal entry consists of a date, accounts and amounts, and a brief _____.

7. (SO6)   A complete listing of a company's accounts is called a _____ of accounts.

8. (SO7)   The procedure of transferring journal entries to ledger accounts is called _____.

9. (SO8)   A _____ _____ is a list of accounts and their balances at a given time.

10. (SO9)   If a company sells for cash a piece of land it no longer needs, then it has engaged in a(n) _____ activity.

Multiple Choice

Please circle the correct answer.

1.   (SO1)   If a company receives cash from a customer before performing services for the customer, then:
   a.   assets increase and liabilities decrease.
   b.   assets increase and stockholders' equity increases.
   c.   assets decrease and liabilities increase.
   d.   assets increase and liabilities increase.

2.   (SO1)   If a company performs services for a customer and receives cash for the services, then:
   a.   assets increase and liabilities decrease.
   b.   assets increase and stockholders' equity increases.
   c.   assets decrease and liabilities increase.
   d.   assets increase and liabilities increase.

3. (SO3) An account has $600 on the debit side and $400 on the credit side. The overall balance in the account is a:
    a. debit of $200.
    b. credit of $200.
    c. debit of $600.
    d. credit of $400.

4. (SO3) An account has $300 on the debit side and $900 on the credit side. The overall balance in the account is a:
    a. debit of $600.
    b. credit of $600.
    c. credit of $900.
    d. debit of $300.

5. (SO3) Which of the following statements is correct?
    a. A debit decreases an asset.
    b. A credit decreases a liability.
    c. A credit increases Retained Earnings.
    d. A credit decreases a revenue account.

6. (SO3) Which of the following statements is <u>incorrect</u>?
    a. A debit increases the Dividends account.
    b. A debit increases an expense account.
    c. A credit increases a revenue account.
    d. A credit increases the Dividends account.

7. (SO3) Which of the following statements is correct?
    a. A credit increases an asset.
    b. A debit increases a liability.
    c. A credit increases an equity account.
    d. A credit increases an expense.

8. (SO3) For which of the following accounts is a credit the normal balance?
    a. Revenue.
    b. Expense.
    c. Asset.
    d. Dividends.

9. (SO4) Which of the following is the correct sequence of events?
    a. Analyze a transaction; record it in the ledger; record it in the journal.
    b. Analyze a transaction; record it in the journal; record it in the ledger.
    c. Record a transaction in the journal; analyze the transaction; record it in the ledger.
    d. None of the above is the correct sequence.

10. (SO5) Transactions are initially recorded in chronological order in a _____ before they are transferred to the accounts.
      a.   journal
      b.   register
      c.   ledger
      d.   T account

11. (SO5) If a corporation borrows money and issues a 3-month note in exchange, then the journal entry requires a:
      a.   debit to Notes Payable and a credit to Cash.
      b.   debit to Notes Payable and a credit to Unearned Revenue.
      c.   debit to Cash and a credit to Notes Payable.
      d.   debit to Cash and a credit to Unearned Revenue.

12. (SO5) If a company pays its employees their weekly salaries, then the journal entry requires a:
      a.   debit to Unearned Revenue and a credit to Cash.
      b.   debit to Retained Earnings and a credit to Cash.
      c.   debit to Cash and a credit to Salaries Expense.
      d.   debit to Salaries Expense and a credit to Cash.

13. (SO5) If a company performs services for a client and receives cash, then the journal entry requires a:
      a.   debit to Cash and a credit to Service Revenue.
      b.   debit to Cash and a credit to Retained Earnings.
      c.   credit to Cash and a debit to Service Revenue.
      d.   debit to Cash and a credit to Unearned Service Revenue.

14. (SO6) A general ledger of a company contains:
      a.   only asset and liability accounts.
      b.   all the asset, liability, and stockholders' equity accounts.
      c.   only stockholders' equity accounts.
      d.   only asset and stockholders' equity accounts.

15. (SO6) The entire group of accounts maintained by a company is referred to collectively as the:
      a.   ledger.
      b.   journal.
      c.   register.
      d.   T accounts.

16. (SO6) If a corporate accountant wanted to know the balance in the company's Cash account, then she would look in:
      a.   the journal.
      b.   the ledger.
      c.   both the journal and the ledger.
      d.   neither the journal nor the ledger.

17.   (SO7) When an accountant posts, he is transferring amounts from:
a.   the ledger to the journal.
b.   T accounts to the ledger.
c.   the journal to the ledger.
d.   the ledger to T accounts.

18.   (SO7) If an account is debited in the journal entry, then:
a.   that account will be debited in the ledger.
b.   that account will be credited in the ledger.
c.   that account will be both debited and credited in the ledger.
d.   None of the above is correct.

19.   (SO8) Which of the following is the correct sequence of events?
a.   Prepare a trial balance; journalize; post
b.   Journalize; post; prepare a trial balance
c.   Post; journalize; prepare a trial balance
d.   Prepare a trial balance; post; journalize

20.   (SO8) The primary purpose of a trial balance is to:
a.   get a total of all accounts with a debit balance.
b.   get a total of all accounts with a credit balance.
c.   prove the mathematical equality of debits and credits after posting.
d.   provide a list of all accounts used by a company.

Problems

1.   The following is an alphabetical listing of accounts for Penny Corporation. Please prepare a trial balance as of October 31, 2010, assuming that all accounts have their normal balance. List the accounts in their proper order.

Accounts Payable	$ 7,000
Advertising Expense	5,000
Cash	38,000
Common Stock	20,000
Dividends	2,000
Equipment	25,000
Prepaid Insurance	3,000
Rent Expense	6,000
Retained Earnings	30,000
Salaries Expense	9,000
Service Revenue	25,000
Unearned Revenue	6,000

Penny Corporation
Trial Balance
October 31, 2010

2. Please refer to The Bon-Ton Stores, Inc., financial statements at the end of this study guide for information for answering the following questions. Don't forget to use the **Decision Toolkit** approach for help in the problem-solving.

   a. What does Bon-Ton call its equity section on the balance sheet? What does the company call the income retained in the business? (SO3)

b. What are the normal balances of the following accounts Bon-Ton lists on its balance sheet: Merchandise Inventories, Accrued Payroll and Benefits, and Common Stock? What is the normal balance of Obligations under Capital Leases? (SO3)

c. What does Bon-Ton call its income statement? What are the normal balances of the following accounts Bon-Ton lists on this statement: Net Sales, Cost of Merchandise Sold, and Interest Expense, Net? (SO3)

SOLUTIONS TO SELF-TEST

Completion

1.	accounting transactions	6.	explanation
2.	account	7.	chart
3.	double-entry	8.	posting
4.	decreases	9.	trial balance
5.	source document	10.	investing

Multiple Choice

1. d   Cash, an asset, increases, and Unearned Revenue, a liability, increases.
2. b   Cash, an asset, increases, and equity increases because one of its components, revenue, increases.
3. a $600 Dr. - $400 Cr. = $200 Dr.
4. b $900 Cr. - $300 Dr. = $600 Cr.
5. c   A debit increases an asset, a credit increases a liability, and a credit increases a revenue account.
6. d   A debit increases the Dividends account.
7. c   A credit decreases an asset, a debit decreases a liability, and a credit decreases an expense.
8. a   The normal balance is found on the side that increases a particular account, and expenses, assets, and dividends are increased by a debit.
9. b
10. a   The ledger is a collection of accounts, and a T account is a form of account.
11. c   The company receives an asset (Cash is increased by the debit), and its liabilities increase (Notes Payable is increased by the credit).
12. d   Expenses increase with the debit, and cash decreases with the credit to Cash.
13. a   The company receives an asset (Cash is increased by the debit), and its revenues increase because it has performed work for a client (revenues are increased with a credit).
14. b
15. a   The journal is the book of original entry, and T accounts are simply a form of account.
16. b   The easiest place to find the information is the ledger. She could find it in the journal but would have to add and subtract all the entries to Cash, which would be very time-consuming.
17. c

18. a   Whatever is done to an account in the journal entry is done to that account in the ledger.

19. b

20. c   While the trial balance may give a list of all accounts (an account with a zero balance may not be listed) and certainly lists debit and credit balances, these are not the primary purpose of the document.

Problems

1.

Penny Corporation
Trial Balance
October 31, 2010

	Debit	Credit
Cash	$38,000	
Prepaid Insurance	3,000	
Equipment	25,000	
Accounts Payable		$ 7,000
Unearned Revenue		6,000
Common Stock		20,000
Retained Earnings		30,000
Dividends	2,000	
Service Revenue		25,000
Advertising Expense	5,000	
Rent Expense	6,000	
Salaries Expense	9,000	
	$88,000	$88,000

2.

a.   Bon-Ton uses the term "Shareholders' Equity." The company calls the earnings retained in the business "Retained Earnings."

b.   To determine the normal balance of an account, you must know what type of an account it is. The account Merchandise Inventories appears in the current asset section, and assets have a normal debit balance. Accrued Payroll and Benefits appears in the current liabilities section and has a normal credit balance. Common Stock appears in the shareholders' equity section and has a normal credit balance. Because it appears in a section between current liabilities and shareholders' equity accounts, Obligations under Capital Leases must be a long-term liability account and has a normal credit balance. (Another clue is that it appears between Long-term Debt and Other Long-term Liabilities.)

c.   Bon-Ton calls its income statement "Consolidated Statements of Income." Once again, to determine the normal balance of an account, you must know what type of an account it is. Net Sales is Bon-Ton's big revenue account and has a normal credit balance. Cost of Merchandise Sold is an expense account with a normal debit balance. Interest Expense, Net is also an expense account and has a normal debit balance.

CHAPTER **4**

Accrual Accounting Concepts

CHAPTER OVERVIEW

In Chapter 4 you will learn about two generally accepted accounting principles: the revenue recognition principle and the matching principle. You'll learn about differences between the cash basis and the accrual basis of accounting. The chapter will explain what adjusting journal entries are, why they are needed, and how to prepare them. Finally, you will learn how to prepare an adjusted trial balance and closing journal entries, as well as the different steps in the accounting cycle.

REVIEW OF SPECIFIC STUDY OBJECTIVES

SO1.   Explain the revenue recognition principle and the matching principle.

⅄   **Accounting divides the economic life of a business into artificial time periods**; generally, a month, a quarter, or a year. Some business transactions affect more than one accounting period, and it is necessary to consider a transaction's impact on the affected periods.

⅄   The **revenue recognition principle** states that <u>revenue is to be recognized in the accounting period in which it is earned.</u> (To "recognize" means to record an entry in a journal.) For a service firm, revenue is earned <u>at the time that the service is performed,</u> which may or may not be the time at which cash is received. A firm may perform services for a client and receive in return the client's promise to pay the firm in the future.

⅄   The **matching principle** states that <u>expenses (efforts) must be matched with revenues (accomplishments).</u> This means the following: if a company performs services and thus earns revenue in a given accounting period, then any expenses which helped the company earn the revenue must be recorded in that same accounting period. The **critical issue** is <u>determining when the expense makes its contribution to revenue</u>. The principle is easy to state but sometimes difficult to implement.

SO2.   Differentiate between the cash basis and the accrual basis of accounting.

⋏   **Accrual basis accounting**, resulting from application of the revenue recognition and matching principles, means that <u>transactions that change a company's financial statements are recorded in the periods in which the events occur</u>, even if cash is not exchanged.

⋏   With **cash basis accounting**, <u>revenue is recorded only when cash is received, and an expense is recorded only when cash is paid</u>. Because of its potential for violating the revenue recognition and matching principles, the <u>cash basis</u> of accounting <u>does not satisfy generally accepted accounting principles</u>.

⋏   A new business often uses the cash basis of accounting because of its simplicity, but eventually it will have to change to the accrual basis. The change requires extensive adjustment to the business's accounting records.

SO3.   Explain why adjusting entries are needed, and identify the major types of adjusting entries.

⋏   **Adjusting entries** <u>ensure that the revenue recognition and matching principles are followed</u>. Before adjusting entries are recorded, some accounts may have incorrect balances because some events are not journalized daily, some events are not journalized during the accounting period because these costs expire with the passage of time, and some items may simply be unrecorded for a variety of reasons.

⋏   **Adjusting entries** are <u>required every time financial statements are prepared</u>. Sometimes students will comment that adjusting entries are simply "cooking the books," but the opposite is actually true. Because of the reasons noted above, some accounts may have incorrect balances, and adjusting entries will correct them.

⋏   There are **two broad groups of adjusting entries: deferrals and accruals**.

⋏   **Deferrals (or prepayments)** include <u>prepaid expenses</u> (expenses paid in cash and recorded as assets before they are used) and <u>unearned revenues</u> (cash received and recorded as liabilities before revenue is earned). **Accruals** include <u>accrued revenues</u> (revenues earned but not yet received in cash or recorded) and <u>accrued expenses</u> (expenses incurred but not yet paid in cash or recorded).

⋏   There are **two important items** to note before we look at the specifics of adjusting entries:

        1.   The <u>adjusting entries</u> you will learn will always <u>involve one income statement account and one balance sheet account</u>. Please note that this does <u>not</u> say that the income statement account is always increased and the balance sheet account is always decreased, or vice versa. The utility of this fact lies in the

following: if you prepare an adjusting entry and know that the debit to an expense, an income statement account, is correct, then the credit must be to a balance sheet account.

2. The account <u>Cash is never used in an adjusting entry</u>. If cash is involved, then the event is simply a transaction, not an adjustment to the accounts.

SO4. Prepare adjusting entries for deferrals.

- **Prepaid expenses** (or prepayments) are <u>payments of expenses that will benefit more than one accounting period</u>. They are initially recorded as assets and expire either with the passage of time or through use. An adjusting entry for a prepaid expense <u>results in an increase (debit) to an expense account and a decrease (credit) to an asset account</u>. A good general rule to remember is that <u>as an asset is used up or consumed, its cost becomes an expense</u>.

- **Supplies** are one example of a prepaid expense. A company purchases $800 of supplies at the beginning of the accounting period. At the end of the period a physical count shows that only $200 of supplies are left. Therefore, $600 of supplies was used up. The asset account Supplies still has the $800 balance, and if that number is recorded on the balance sheet, then the statement will not be correct. An accountant may not record $200, the correct number, on the balance sheet if the ledger account for Supplies shows a balance of $800. So, an adjusting entry is required:

Supplies Expense   600
      Supplies   600
(To show supplies used)

After the entry is recorded and posted, the Supplies account will show the correct balance, $200, and that number will then correctly be shown on the balance sheet. **If the entry had not been made**, <u>expenses would have been low, net income would have been high, and stockholders' equity would have been high by $600, while assets would have been high by $600</u>.

- **Insurance** and **rent** are two more examples of a prepaid expense. A company pays six months' rent, $2,400, at the beginning of March and wants to prepare financial statements at the end of March. The asset account Prepaid Rent shows a balance of $2,400, but this is no longer correct because the company has used up one month of rent. The balance sheet should show Prepaid Rent of $2,000, but this number may not be recorded if the ledger account for Prepaid Rent shows a balance of $2,400. Again, an adjusting entry is required:

Rent Expense   400
      Prepaid Rent   400
(To record expired rent)

After the entry is recorded and posted, the Prepaid Rent account will show the correct balance, $2,000, and that number will then correctly be shown on the balance sheet. **If**

the entry had not been made, expenses would have been low, net income would have been high, and stockholders' equity would have been high by $400, while assets would have been high by $400.

The adjusting entry for **depreciation** is another example of a prepayment. Long-lived assets, such as vehicles, equipment, and buildings, are recorded at cost. Their acquisition is basically a long-term prepayment for use of an asset. As their useful life progresses, part of the cost should be recorded as an expense. **Depreciation** is the process of allocating the cost of an asset to expense over its useful life in a rational and systematic manner. It is important to remember that **depreciation is an allocation concept, not a valuation concept**. It does not attempt to reflect the actual change in the value of the asset. Assume that depreciation on a vehicle that cost $18,000 is $3,600 per year, or $300 per month. The following entry records one month of depreciation:

Depreciation Expense	300	
Accumulated Depreciation—Vehicle		300
(To record monthly depreciation)		

Accumulated Depreciation--Vehicle is a contra asset account, offset against, or subtracted from, the Vehicle account on the balance sheet. Its normal balance is a credit. The use of this account allows the user to see the original cost of the asset as well as the total cost that has expired to date.

The balance sheet presentation of this vehicle after adjustment is:

Vehicle	$18,000
Less: Accumulated depreciation—Vehicle	300
	$17,700

The $17,700 is the **book value** of the asset. Book value is calculated by subtracting the accumulated depreciation from the cost of the asset.

As was true with Supplies and Prepaid Rent, **failure to record this adjusting entry** for depreciation would have meant that expenses would have been low, net income would have been high, and stockholders' equity would have been high by $300, while assets would have been high by $300.

Unearned revenues occur when cash is received before revenue is earned. Magazine subscriptions and rent are two examples. Unearned revenues are the opposite of prepaid expenses. Unearned revenue on one company's books is a prepaid expense on another company's books. If my company pays your company $6,000 for six months' rent in advance, then my company will have Prepaid Rent of $6,000, while your company will have Unearned Rent of $6,000. After one month has elapsed, your company must write the following adjusting entry to show that it has earned one month of rent revenue:

Unearned Rent   1,000
      Rent Revenue   1,000
(To record revenue earned)

Please note that the entry involves a <u>decrease (debit) to the liability account and an increase (credit) to the revenue account</u>. **If the entry is not recorded**, then <u>revenues, net income, and stockholders' equity will be low by $1,000, while liabilities will be high by $1,000</u>.

Most liabilities are discharged by the payment of money. Note that **unearned revenue, a liability, is discharged by the performance of a service**.

SO5.   Prepare adjusting entries for accruals.

       ⋏   Adjusting entries for **accruals** are required in order to <u>record revenues earned and expenses incurred in the current accounting period that have not been recognized through daily entries and thus are not yet reflected in the accounts</u>. Accruals occur in the form of **accrued revenues** and **accrued expenses**.

       ⋏   The adjusting entry for accruals will **increase both a balance sheet and an income statement account**.

       ⋏   **Accrued revenues** are <u>revenues earned but not yet received in cash or recorded at the financial statement date</u>. Examples are interest, rent, and services. They may accrue with the passage of time or may result from services performed but neither billed nor collected. The adjusting entry for accrued revenue will always involve an **increase in a receivable (debit) and an increase in revenue (credit)**. A company has earned $300 in interest revenue but has not been paid that amount in cash. If financial statements are to be prepared, then an adjusting entry to recognize that revenue is required:

Interest Receivable   300
      Interest Revenue   300
(To record interest revenue)

If this entry is not made, then <u>assets and stockholders' equity on the balance sheet and revenues and net income on the income statement will be low</u>. When the company receives that interest in cash, it will record a debit to Cash and a credit to Interest Receivable, not to Interest Revenue.

       ⋏   **Accrued expenses** are <u>expenses incurred but not yet paid or recorded at the statement date</u>. Examples include interest, rent, taxes, and salaries. The company that owes the $300 of interest in the above example has an accrued expense of $300. The adjusting entry for an accrued expense will always involve an **increase (debit) to an expense account and an increase (credit) to a liability account**. A company borrows $12,000 at 12% interest for six months on November 1. The principal and all the interest are due on May 1. If financial statements are prepared on December 31, then the company must journalize an adjusting entry for the interest owed but not yet paid. <u>Interest is</u>

computed by multiplying the principal by the rate by the time: in our example, $12,000 X .12 X 2/12, or $240. The entry is:

```
Interest Expense                240
        Interest Payable                 240
(To record accrued interest)
```

It is **important to note** that the account Notes Payable is not used in the entry. Notes Payable was credited when the money was borrowed and will be debited when the note principal of $12,000 is repaid. **If this adjusting entry is not made**, then liabilities and interest expense will be low and net income and stockholders' equity will be high.

SO6.   Describe the nature and purpose of the adjusted trial balance.

A   **A trial balance is prepared after many journal entries have been journalized and posted**. Just as a trial balance was prepared after journalizing and posting regular transactions, so an **adjusted trial balance** is prepared after adjusting entries have been journalized and posted. The purpose of an adjusted trial balance is to prove the equality of debits and credits in the general ledger. Since all account balances have been brought up to date, the adjusted trial balance is used in the preparation of financial statements.

A   One **format** is to put two sets of columns side by side: one is for debits and credits before adjustment, and the other is for debits and credits after adjustment. Remember that it is from the adjusted trial balance columns that the financial statements are prepared.

SO7.   Explain the purpose of closing entries.

A   **Temporary accounts** relate to only a given accounting period and include revenues, expenses, and dividends. **Permanent accounts** have balances that carry forward into future accounting periods and include assets, liabilities, and stockholders' equity, the balance sheet accounts.

A   At the end of the accounting period, **temporary account balances are closed, or zeroed out**, transferring their balances to Retained Earnings. **Closing entries** transfer net income or net loss and dividends to Retained Earnings. Revenues and expenses are closed to another temporary account, Income Summary, and the resulting net income or net loss is then transferred to Retained Earnings.

A   So, **closing entries accomplish two things**: they update the Retained Earnings account, and they zero out the balance in the temporary accounts, making them ready to accumulate data in the next accounting period.

⋏ **After closing entries have been journalized and posted, a post-closing trial balance is prepared**. Once again, the purpose is to prove the equality of debits and credits in the ledger. It also helps to show all temporary accounts have been closed. If, for example, the accountant prepares a post-closing trial balance and finds a balance of $5,000 in Salaries Expense, then she will know that a temporary account was improperly excluded when closing entries were prepared. Only permanent accounts should appear on the post-closing trial balance.

SO8. Describe the required steps in the accounting cycle.

⋏ The following are the steps in the **accounting cycle**:

1. Analyze business transactions.
2. Journalize the transactions.
3. Post to ledger accounts.
4. Prepare a trial balance.
5. Journalize and post adjusting entries.
6. Prepare an adjusted trial balance.
7. Prepare financial statements.
8. Journalize and post closing entries.
9. Prepare a post-closing trial balance.

⋏ These steps are repeated in each accounting period.

SO9. Understand the causes of differences between net income and cash provided by operating activities.

⋏ **Net income on a cash basis is referred to as "net cash provided by operating activities,"** and it sometimes differs from accrual-basis net income. For each item in the computation of the net cash number, a company should confirm that cash was either received or paid.

⋏ **For each item included in accrual-basis net income**, a company should confirm that revenue was earned or that an expense was incurred, regardless of whether cash was received or paid.

SO10. Describe the purpose and the basic form of a work sheet.
(This objective is discussed in the appendix to chapter 4 in your text.)

⋏ A **work sheet** is a multiple-column form used in the adjustment process and in preparing financial statements. It may be prepared manually or on the computer with electronic spreadsheet software.

⋏ A **work sheet is not a permanent accounting record**. It is used by accountants to make work easier at the end of the accounting period. A work sheet helps by putting all required information in one place, saving the accountant from having to leaf through pages or to look in multiple places for information. It helps in preparing adjusting entries, closing entries, and financial statements.

A   There are **usually five sets of two columns** on a work sheet. The first two columns are for the trial balance; the next two are for adjustments; the next two are for the adjusted trial balance; the next two correspond to the income statement; and the last two correspond to the balance sheet. <u>Every number in the Adjusted Trial Balance columns is extended either to the Income Statement or to the Balance Sheet columns.</u>

CHAPTER SELF-TEST

As you work the exercises and problems, remember to use the **Decision Toolkit** discussed and used in the text:

1. <u>Decision Checkpoints</u>: at this point you ask a question.

2. <u>Info Needed for Decision</u>: you make a choice regarding the information needed to answer the question.

3. <u>Tool to Use for Decision</u>: at this point you review just what the information chosen in step 2 does for the decision-making process.

4. <u>How to Evaluate Results</u>: you perform evaluation of information for answering the question.

Note: The notation (SO1) means that the question was drawn from study objective number one.

Matching

Please write the letters of the following terms in the spaces to the left of the definitions.

a.	Accrual basis accounting	g.	Closing entries
b.	Accrued expenses	h.	Permanent accounts
c.	Accrued revenues	i.	Post-closing trial balance
d.	Adjusted trial balance	j.	Prepaid expenses
e.	Adjusting entries	k.	Temporary accounts
f.	Cash basis accounting	l.	Unearned revenues

_____ 1.   (SO2) An accounting basis in which revenue is recorded only when cash is received, and an expense is recorded only when cash is paid.

_____ 2.   (SO3) Expenses paid in cash and recorded as assets before they are used or consumed.

_____ 3.   (SO7) A trial balance prepared after closing entries have been journalized and posted.

_____ 4.   (SO7) Asset, liability, and stockholders' equity accounts.

_____ 5.   (SO3) Revenues earned but not yet received in cash or recorded.

_____ 6.   (SO2) Accounting basis in which transactions are recorded in the periods in which the events occur, rather than in the periods in which the company receives or pays cash.

_____ 7. (SO7) Revenue, expense, and dividend accounts whose balances are transferred to retained earnings at the end of an accounting period.

_____ 8. (SO6) A trial balance prepared after adjusting entries have been journalized and posted.

_____ 9. (SO3) Entries made at the end of an accounting period to ensure that the revenue recognition and matching principles are followed.

_____ 10. (SO7) Entries made at the end of an accounting period to transfer the balances of temporary accounts to Retained Earnings.

Multiple Choice

Please circle the correct answer.

1. (SO1) The generally accepted accounting principle which dictates that revenue be recognized in the accounting period in which it is earned is the:
   a. time period principle.
   b. matching principle.
   c. revenue recognition principle.
   d. accrued revenues principle.

2. (SO2) In 2010, Abbott Company performs work for a customer and bills the customer $10,000; it also pays expenses of $3,000. The customer pays Abbott in 2011. If Abbott uses the cash basis of accounting, then Abbott will report:
   a. revenue of $10,000 in 2010.
   b. revenue of $10,000 in 2011.
   c. expenses of $3,000 in 2011.
   d. net income of $7,000 in 2010.

3. (SO2) In 2010, Abbott Company performs work for a customer and bills the customer $10,000; it also pays expenses of $3,000. The customer pays Abbott in 2011. If Abbott uses the accrual basis of accounting, then Abbott will report:
   a. revenue of $10,000 in 2010.
   b. revenue of $10,000 in 2011.
   c. expenses of $3,000 in 2011.
   d. net income of $7,000 in 2011.

4. (SO3) Adjusting journal entries must be prepared:
   a. at the end of every calendar year.
   b. at the end of every month.
   c. when the accountant has time to write them.
   d. whenever financial statements are to be prepared.

5.   (SO3)   Cash received and recorded as a liability before revenue is earned is called:
   a.   an accrued revenue.
   b.   an unearned revenue.
   c.   an unrecorded revenue.
   d.   None of the above is correct.

6.   (SO4)   On October 1, Cynthia Company paid $6,000 for a one-year insurance policy, debiting Prepaid Insurance and crediting Cash. The adjusting entry on December 31 will require a:
   a.   debit to Insurance Expense for $1,500.
   b.   debit to Insurance Expense for $4,500.
   c.   credit to Prepaid Insurance for $4,500.
   d.   credit to Cash for $1,500.

7.   (SO4)   At the beginning of an accounting period, a company purchased $800 of supplies, debiting Supplies and crediting Cash. At the end of the accounting period, a physical count of supplies showed that only $100 of supplies were still on hand. The adjusting entry will require a:
   a.   credit to Supplies Expense for $700.
   b.   debit to Supplies Expense for $100.
   c.   debit to Supplies for $700.
   d.   credit to Supplies for $700.

8.   (SO4)   A company accountant has determined that monthly depreciation on a new company vehicle is $500.   The journal entry to record the first month's depreciation will include a:
   a.   debit to Depreciation Expense for $500.
   b.   credit to Depreciation Expense for $500.
   c.   debit to Accumulated Depreciation for $500.
   d.   debit to Vehicle for $500.

9.   (SO4)   If the cost of the vehicle in number 8 is $30,000, then the book value of the vehicle after the adjusting entry is recorded is:
   a. $30,500.
   b. $30,000.
   c. $29,500.
   d. $ 500.

10.   (SO4)   Little Corporation received $5,000 from a customer for whom it is to perform work in the future, debiting Cash and crediting Unearned Revenue. At the end of the accounting period, Little has earned $2,000 of the revenue. The adjusting entry will require a:
   a.   debit to Cash for $2,000.
   b.   debit to Service Revenue for $2,000.
   c.   credit to Service Revenue for $2,000.
   d.   credit to Service Revenue for $3,000.

11. (SO1) The generally accepted accounting principle which dictates that efforts be matched with accomplishments is the:
    a.   accrued expenses principle.
    b.   matching principle.
    c.   revenue recognition principle.
    d.   time period principle.

12. (SO5) At the end of its accounting period, Pooky Corporation has not billed a customer for $400 of rent. The adjusting entry will require a:
    a.   debit to Cash for $400.
    b.   credit to Accounts Receivable for $400.
    c.   credit to Unearned Revenue for $400.
    d.   credit to Rent Revenue for $400.

13. (SO5) If the adjusting entry for an accrued expense is not written, then:
    a.   liabilities and expenses will be understated.
    b.   liabilities and expenses will be overstated.
    c.   net income will be understated.
    d.   liabilities and stockholders' equity will be overstated.

14. (SO5) Buddy Corporation pays its employees $1,000 per five-day week. The last day of the month falls on a Thursday, and financial statements will be prepared that day. The adjusting entry for salaries will require a:
    a.   debit to Salaries Payable for $200.
    b.   credit to Salaries Expense for $200.
    c.   debit to Salaries Expense for $200.
    d.   debit to Salaries Expense for $800.

15. (SO5) A company borrows $15,000 at 8% interest for 3 months on June 1. If adjusting entries are written on June 30, how much will be credited to Interest Payable?
    a. $ 100.
    b. $ 300.
    c. $ 900.
    d. $1,200.

16. (SO6) Financial statements can be prepared directly from the:
    a.   trial balance.
    b.   adjusted trial balance.
    c.   post-closing trial balance.
    d.   reversing trial balance.

17. (SO7) Which of the following is a temporary account?
    a.   The dividends account.
    b.   An asset account.
    c.   A liability account.
    d.   A stockholders' equity account.

18.   (SO7) Which of the following is true?
    a.   Only permanent accounts are closed.
    b.   Both permanent and temporary accounts are closed.
    c.   Neither permanent nor temporary accounts are closed.
    d.   Only temporary accounts are closed.

19.   (SO7) Which of the following correctly describes the closing process?
    a.   Net income or net loss is transferred to the Cash account.
    b.   Net income or net loss is transferred to Retained Earnings.
    c.   Permanent accounts become ready to accumulate data in the next accounting period.
    d.   Each revenue and each expense account is closed individually to Retained Earnings.

20.   (SO8) Which is the correct order of steps in the accounting cycle?
    a.   Post transactions, journalize transactions, prepare a trial balance, prepare financial statements.
    b.   Journalize and post transactions, journalize and post closing entries, journalize and post adjusting entries.
    c.   Journalize and post transactions, journalize and post adjusting entries, journalize and post closing entries.
    d.   Prepare financial statements, prepare adjusting entries, prepare closing entries, prepare a post-closing trial balance.

21.   (SO9) A company provided $900 of services on account, with cash to be received in 30 days. Which of the following is correct?
    a.   The $900 will be recognized as revenue on the income statement in 30 days when cash is received.
    b.   The $900 is included immediately in the computation of net cash provided by operating activities.
    c.   The $900 is recognized immediately as revenue on the income statement.
    d.   The $900 is included immediately in the Cash account on the balance sheet.

22.   (SO10) A work sheet:
    a.   is not a permanent accounting record.
    b.   is a type of journal.
    c.   is a type of ledger.
    d.   does not contain columns for adjustments.

Problems

1.   Please write for Cassie Company as of June 30 adjusting entries for the following situations (SO4, SO5):

    a. The Supplies account shows a balance of $1,500, but a physical count shows only $300 of supplies.

b. The company purchased a one-year insurance policy for $3,600 on May 1, debiting Prepaid Insurance.

c. On June 1 the company received $1,200 from another company that is renting a small building from Cassie for 6 months. Cassie credited Unearned Rent Revenue.

d. Cassie's accountant discovered that Cassie had performed services for a client totaling $900 but has not yet billed the client or recorded the transaction.

e. Cassie pays employees $2,000 per five-day workweek, and June 30 falls on a Wednesday.

f. The company owns a van that cost $18,000 and has a useful life of 6 years. The company purchased the van in early April this year.

g. What type of an account is the account that you credited in "f"? Please show the balance sheet presentation for the van after you have recorded the depreciation entry.

Date	Account Titles	Debit	Credit

2.   Please refer to The Bon-Ton Stores, Inc., financial statements at the end of this study guide for information for answering the following questions. Don't forget to use the **Decision Toolkit** approach for help in the problem-solving.

   a. Using the consolidated statements of income and consolidated balance sheets, please identify <u>items that may result in</u> adjusting entries for prepayments (SO3).

   b. Using the consolidated statements of income and consolidated balance sheets, please identify <u>accounts which may be involved in</u> adjusting entries for accruals (SO4).

   c. Using the consolidated statements of cash flows, what amount is shown for depreciation and amortization for 2007 and 2006? (SO3)

   d. Using the consolidated statements of income, what has been the trend for interest expense from 2005 to 2007? (SO4)

SOLUTIONS TO SELF-TEST

Matching

1.	f		7.	k
2.	j		8.	d
3.	i		9.	e
4.	h		10.	g
5.	c			
6.	a			

Multiple Choice

1.   c   The time period assumption says that the economic life of a business can be divided into artificial time periods, the matching principle dictates that expenses be matched with revenues, and the accrued revenues principle is a non-existent principle.

2.   b   Revenue can't be reported in 2010 because Abbott did not receive cash. It paid the expenses in 2010 and must report them in that year. Since it recorded no revenue in 2010, it had a net loss of $3,000 (the expenses it paid) in 2010.

3.   a   It reports revenue in the year when the work is performed (2010, not 2011). Expenses are reported in 2010, when incurred, and net income of $7,000 is reported in 2010.

4.   d   If adjusting entries are not made, the balances of some accounts will be incorrect on the financial statements.

5.   b   An accrued revenue arises when money is owed to a company, not when it owes money. "Unrecorded revenue" is an accounting term but is not appropriate in this instance.

6.   a   The journal entry is:

Insurance Expense	1,500	
Prepaid Insurance		1,500

7.   d   The journal entry is:

Supplies Expense	700	
Supplies		700

8.   a   The journal entry is:

Depreciation Expense	500	
Accumulated Depreciation		500

9.   c   The cost of an asset less its accumulated depreciation is the book value. So, $30,000 - $500 = $29,500.

10.   c   The journal entry is:

Unearned Revenue	2,000	
Service Revenue		2,000

11.   b   "Accrued expenses principle" is a nonexistent term. The revenue recognition principle states that revenue must be recognized when it is earned, and the time period assumption says that the economic life of a business can be divided into artificial time periods.

12.   d   The journal entry is:

Accounts Receivable	400	
Rent Revenue		400

13.   a   The journal entry debits an expense and credits a liability, thereby increasing both accounts. If an expense is not recorded, then income will be overstated (as will stockholders' equity), and if a liability is not recorded, then liabilities will be understated.

14.   d   The journal entry is:

Salaries Expense	800	
Salaries Payable		800

15.   a   Interest = Principal X Rate X Time. So, $15,000 X 8% X 1/12 = $100.

16.   b   The trial balance does not have the adjustments updates, the post-closing trial balance has no temporary accounts, and there is no such thing as a reversing trial balance.

17.   a   The other three types of accounts are all permanent accounts.

18.   d   Permanent accounts are not closed.

19.   b   Income and loss are not transferred to the Cash account, permanent accounts are not closed, and revenue and expense accounts are closed first to Income Summary (which is itself closed to Retained Earnings).

20.   c

21.   c   Revenue is recognized on the accrual-basis income statement when services are provided, even if cash is not received. Since cash has not been received, the $900 cannot be included in the computation of net cash provided by operating activities or in the Cash account.

22.   a   It is neither a journal nor a ledger, and it certainly does have adjustments columns.

Problems

1.   a.

Supplies Expense	1,200	
Supplies		1,200
(To record supplies used)		

    b.

Insurance Expense	600	
Prepaid Insurance		600
(To record insurance expired)		

$3,600 ÷ 12 months = $300 per month X 2 months

    c.

Unearned Rent Revenue	200	
Rent Revenue		200
(To record rent earned)		

$1,200 ÷ 6 months = $200 per month

    d.

Accounts Receivable	900	
Service Revenue		900
(To record revenue earned)		

e.   Salaries Expense   1,200
          Salaries Payable   1,200
      (To record accrued salaries)
      $2,000 ÷ 5 days = $400 per day X 3 days

f.   Depreciation Expense   750
          Accumulated Depre-
          ciation—Van   750
      (To record depreciation)
      $18,000 ÷ 6 years = $3,000 per year X 3/12

g.   Accumulated Depreciation is a contra asset account, which is offset against, or subtracted from, the asset account. The advantage of this presentation is that the user sees both the original cost of the asset and the total cost that has expired to date.

      Van $18,000
      Less: Accumulated depreci-
                tion—van   750
                                          $17,250

      The $17,250 is the book value of the asset and has no relationship to the fair market value (what a willing buyer would pay a willing seller) of the asset. Remember that depreciation is an allocation concept, not a valuation concept.

2.   a.   Prepaid expenses and other current assets; and property, fixtures and equipment at cost (some of which must be depreciated).

      b.   Interest expense, accounts payable, accrued expenses, and income taxes payable.

      c.   Amounts are in thousands:
            2007 $121,125
            2006 $103,189

      d.   It increased enormously from 2005 to 2006 and by a much smaller amount from 2006 to 2007. Again, amounts are in thousands:
            Interest expense
            2007 $108,165
            2006 $107,143
            2005 $ 12,052

17

CHAPTER **5**

Merchandising Operations and the Multiple-Step Income Statement

CHAPTER OVERVIEW

Chapter 5 discusses the differences between service firms and merchandising firms. You will learn about the two types of inventory systems used by merchandisers and how to record purchases and sales of inventory using the perpetual inventory system. You'll take a close look at a merchandising firm's financial statements, particularly the income statement, and learn how to compute cost of goods sold under a periodic system. Finally, you will look at factors affecting a firm's profitability and be able to identify a quality of earnings indicator.

REVIEW OF SPECIFIC STUDY OBJECTIVES

SO1.   Identify the differences between a service company and a merchandising company.

      ⋏   **Merchandising companies** buy and sell merchandise as their primary source of revenue. **Retailers** are merchandisers that purchase and sell directly to consumers. **Wholesalers** are merchandisers that sell to retailers.

      ⋏   The **primary source of revenues** for merchandising companies is the sale of merchandise, called sales revenues or sales. **Expenses** are divided into **two categories**: cost of goods sold (the total cost of merchandise sold during the period) and operating expenses. Net income is determined as follows:

          Sales Revenue
      – Cost of Goods Sold
          Gross Profit
      – Operating Expenses
          Net Income

ᐱ The **operating cycle of a merchandising company** is <u>longer than that of a service firm</u> because of the purchase and sale of merchandise inventory. The **flow of costs for a merchandising company is:** <u>beginning inventory is added to the cost of goods purchased, yielding cost of goods available for sale. These available goods are either sold (cost of goods sold) or left on hand for future sale (ending inventory).</u> So, the goods available for sale have two sources (they were left over from last period or purchased this period) and two uses (they are sold or left over to sell in the next period).

ᐱ There are **two systems of inventory** available to a merchandising company: the <u>perpetual inventory system</u> and the <u>periodic inventory system.</u>

ᐱ With a **perpetual system**, <u>detailed records of the cost of each inventory purchase and sale are maintained</u> and show at all times the inventory that should be on hand for every item. <u>Cost of goods sold is determined each time a sale occurs.</u> The use of computer systems, bar codes, and optical scanners makes such a system practicable.

ᐱ With a **periodic system**, <u>detailed records are not kept throughout the period.</u> <u>Cost of goods sold is determined only at the end of the accounting period</u> when a physical count of goods is taken.

ᐱ A **perpetual system** provides <u>better inventory control</u>. Goods can be counted at any time to see if they exist, and shortages can be investigated immediately. The quantity of inventory can be managed so that neither too much nor too little is on hand at a given time.

SO2. Explain the recording of purchases under a perpetual inventory system.

ᐱ **Purchases**, either for cash or on account (credit), are normally <u>recorded when the goods are received from the seller.</u> A business document (a canceled check or a cash register receipt for a cash purchase, or a purchase invoice for a credit purchase) will provide written evidence of the purchase.

ᐱ **A purchase is recorded by a debit to Merchandise Inventory and a credit to Cash or to Accounts Payable.** The <u>Merchandise Inventory</u> account is <u>used only for purchases of goods that will be resold.</u> If the company buys an asset, then the debit will be to the individual asset account.

ᐱ **Purchased goods might be unsuitable** because they are damaged or defective, are of inferior quality, or do not meet the purchaser's specifications. A <u>purchase return</u> occurs when goods are returned to the seller. A <u>purchase allowance</u> occurs when the purchaser keeps the merchandise but is granted an allowance (deduction) by the seller. A **purchase return or allowance is recorded by debiting Cash or Accounts Payable and crediting Merchandise Inventory.**

ᐱ Either the buyer or the seller must pay **shipping charges for the transportation of the merchandise. If the buyer pays (FOB shipping point)**, then the shipping is considered to be part of the cost of purchasing the inventory and is recorded by a debit to Merchandise Inventory and a credit to Cash or Accounts Payable. If the **seller pays (FOB destination)**, then the shipping on the outgoing merchandise is considered to be an operating expense and is recorded by a debit to Freight-out or Delivery Expense and a credit to Cash or Accounts Payable.

⋏ With respect to the **buyer's debit to Merchandise Inventory for shipping charges**, the following is a good rule of thumb to remember: any amount that is paid to get an asset in location and condition for use is debited to the asset account.

⋏ **A seller often offers the buyer of merchandise a cash discount to induce early payment for the goods**. Credit terms are expressed as 1/10, n/30 (the purchaser will receive a 1% cash discount if he pays within 10 days; otherwise, the net amount is due in 30 days) or n/60 (the net amount is due in 60 days). Assume that on May 1 a buyer purchased $5,000 of merchandise on account with terms of 2/10, n/30. If he pays by May 11, then the following entry is required:

Accounts Payable	5,000	
Cash		4,900
Merchandise Inventory		100
(To record payment within the		
discount period)		

If the buyer pays after May 11, then the entry will be:

Accounts Payable	5,000	
Cash		5,000
(To record payment—no discount)		

⋏ It is usually very **advantageous for the buyer to take all cash discounts**. Passing up a 2/10, n/30 discount is the equivalent of paying an annual interest rate of over 36%! Some companies even borrow money at 8% to 12% to take the discount because that is cheaper than paying 36%.

SO3. Explain the recording of sales revenues under a perpetual inventory system.

⋏ **Sales revenues are recorded when earned**, in accordance with the revenue recognition principle. As is true for purchases, sales may be for cash or on account (credit) and should be supported by a business document (a cash register tape for cash sales and a sales invoice for credit sales).

⋏   **Two entries are made for each sale** in the perpetual inventory system. One records the <u>sale</u>, the other records the <u>cost of merchandise sold</u>. If goods costing $200 are sold for cash of $400, then the following entries are required:

Cash	400	
Sales		400
(To record a cash sale)		

Cost of Goods Sold	200	
Merchandise Inventory		200
(To record the cost of merchandise sold)		

If the goods had been sold on account, then the only thing that would have changed in either entry is that the debit in the first entry would have been to Accounts Receivable.

⋏   The **Sales account is used only for sales of merchandise inventory**. If an asset is sold, then the credit is to the asset account. <u>A company may choose to have several Sales accounts</u>, each one dedicated to a type of product. This will <u>help to give management information needed to manage its inventory</u>. Such a company will report only one Sales figure on the income statement. To report many sales accounts would lengthen the income statement and perhaps give too much detail on operating results to competitors. There are many users of a company's financial statements, and one such group of users is a company's competition.

⋏   If **goods that have been sold are returned to the company**, then <u>two entries are required</u>. Assume that the goods sold above are all returned to the company. The required entries are:

Sales Returns and Allowances	400	
Cash		400
(To record return of goods)		

Merchandise Inventory	200	
Cost of Goods Sold		200
(To record cost of goods returned)		

Sales Returns and Allowances is a <u>contra revenue account</u> to Sales. If the debit had been to Sales, then the return would have been buried in that account. Management needs to monitor the amount of returned goods so that it may correct an unsatisfactory situation. The goods it is selling may be of poor quality or defective, and management will have to deal with the supplier of the goods. If the company itself is making mistakes in delivery or shipment of goods, then management will have to deal with this internal problem.

A As noted above, **a seller often offers the buyer of merchandise a cash discount to induce early payment for the goods**. Using the previous example, on May 1 a buyer purchased $5,000 of merchandise on account with terms of 2/10, n/30. If the buyer pays by May 11, then the selling company records the following entry:

Cash	4,900	
Sales Discounts	100	
Accounts Receivable		5,000

(To record collection within the discount period)

If the buyer pays after May 11, then the entry is:

Cash	5,000	
Accounts Receivable		5,000

(To record collection—no discount allowed)

Sales Discounts is another <u>contra revenue account</u> to Sales.

Account Name	Account Type	Normal Balance
Sales	Revenue	Credit
Sales Returns and		
Allowances	Contra Revenue	Debit
Sales Discounts	Contra Revenue	Debit

SO4. Distinguish between a single-step and a multiple-step income statement.

A A **single-step income statement** works in the following way: all <u>revenues are totaled</u>, all <u>expenses are totaled</u>, and <u>expenses are then subtracted from revenues</u> to determine net income or net loss. (The subtraction gives the name "single-step" to this income statement.) This form is simple and easy to read and understand.

A A **multiple-step income statement** breaks net income (or loss) into several components which financial statement users find useful.

1. <u>Gross sales revenues are shown</u>. Any **sales returns and allowances** and **sales discounts are deducted from gross sales**; the resulting <u>difference is called net sales</u>.

2. <u>Net sales less cost of goods sold</u> yields **gross profit or gross margin**. This is merchandising profit, the difference between what the company paid for its inventory and what it received when it sold the inventory. Gross profit should be large enough to cover operating expenses and leave something for net income.

3. <u>Gross profit less operating expenses</u> yields **income from operations**. Operating expenses are often divided into two categories: <u>selling expenses</u>, associated with making sales, and <u>administrative expenses</u>, related to the general operation of the company. The former include advertising expense and shipping expense, and the latter include expenses such as those related to human resources management and accounting.

4. <u>Income from operations less nonoperating activities</u> yields **net income (or loss)**. Nonoperating activities are revenues, expenses, gains, and losses unrelated to a company's main operations. Examples include interest revenue, dividend revenue, interest expense, and loss on the sale of piece of machinery.

⋏ **Operating income** is considered <u>sustainable and long-term</u>, while **nonoperating income** is considered <u>nonrecurring and short-term</u>. It is obviously important for a company to derive the bulk of its income from its main line of operations and not from peripheral activities, such as the sale of factories and equipment.

To recap, if there are no nonoperating activities:

    Sales Revenue
 − Cost of Goods Sold
    Gross Profit
 − Operating Expenses
    Net Income

SO5.   Determine cost of goods sold under a periodic system.

⋏ To **determine cost of goods sold** (done only at the end of the period under a periodic system), it is necessary to <u>record merchandise purchases</u>, <u>determine the cost of goods purchased</u>, and <u>determine both beginning and ending inventory</u>. The cost of the ending inventory must be determined by a physical count and by application of the cost to the items counted in the inventory.

⋏ To determine cost of goods sold, it is necessary first to determine the **cost of goods purchased**:

       Gross purchases
Less: Purchase returns and allowances
       Purchase discounts
       Net purchases
Add: Freight-in
       Cost of goods purchased

Cost of goods sold is then <u>computed as follows</u>:

Beginning inventory
<u>Plus: Cost of goods purchased</u>
Cost of goods available for sale
<u>Less: Ending inventory</u>
Cost of goods sold

SO6.   Explain the factors affecting profitability.

   ∧   A **company's gross profit may be expressed as a percentage**: the <u>gross profit rate</u> is computed by <u>dividing gross profit by net sales</u>. This rate is closely monitored. A decline in the rate may result from selling items with lower markup, from having to lower selling prices due to increased competition, or from having to pay higher prices for merchandise without being able to pass those higher costs on to customers.

   ∧   The **profit margin ratio** is computed by <u>dividing net income by net sales</u>. It measures the percentage of each dollar of sales that results in net income and shows the extent by which selling price covers all expenses. To improve this ratio, a company can either increase its gross profit rate or control its expenses and costs.

SO7.   Identify a quality of earnings indicator.

   ∧   **Earnings have high quality if the provide a full, transparent depiction of how a company performed**. To provide this information, analysts sometimes use the **quality of earnings ratio**, computed by <u>dividing net cash provided by operating activities by net income</u>.

   ∧   **A measure significantly less than 1** suggests that <u>a company may be using aggressive accounting techniques,</u> while **a measure significantly greater than 1** suggests that <u>a company is using conservative accounting techniques</u>. As is true with any ratio, the results must be investigated, here by evaluating the causes of the differences between net income and net cash provided by operating activities.

SO8.   Explain the recording of purchases and sales of inventory under a periodic inventory system. (This objective is discussed in the appendix to chapter 5 in your text.)

   ∧   **A periodic inventory system differs from a perpetual inventory system in various ways**, one of which is the time at which cost of goods sold is computed.

   ∧   With a **periodic system**, <u>cost of goods sold is computed only at the end of an accounting period</u>, while with a **perpetual system**, <u>cost of goods sold is computed each time inventory is sold</u>.

⅄ With a **periodic system**, a <u>physical count of inventory must be taken at the end of the accounting period</u> to determine the cost of merchandise on hand and the cost of goods sold during the period. **Purchases of inventory are recorded in a Purchases account**, not in Merchandise Inventory, and there are <u>separate accounts for purchase returns and allowances, purchase discounts, and freight costs on purchases</u>.

Consider the following data. On April 4 Orion Company purchased $5,000 of inventory on account with credit terms of 2/10, n/30. It paid shipping costs of $200 on April 5, and on April 7 it returned $500 of merchandise. It paid the amount due on April 13. The journal entries for these transactions are as follows:

April 4	Purchases	5,000	
	Accounts Payable		5,000
April 5	Freight-in	200	
	Cash		200
April 7	Accounts Payable	500	
	Purchase Returns and		
	Allowances		500
April 13	Accounts Payable	4,500	
	Purchase Discounts		90
	Cash		4,410

Please note the following:
a. **Purchases** is a <u>temporary account</u> (which must be closed) with a <u>normal debit balance</u>.
b. **Purchase Returns and Allowances and Purchase Discounts** are <u>temporary accounts</u> with a <u>normal credit balance</u>.
c. Discounts do not apply to Freight-in charges. **Freight-in is part of cost of goods purchased** and is a <u>temporary account</u> with a <u>normal debit balance</u>.

Sales of merchandise are recorded in the same way as they are recorded in a perpetual system. Sales has a normal credit balance, while the contra revenue accounts, Sales Returns and Allowances and Sales Discounts, have a normal debit balance.

CHAPTER SELF-TEST

As you work the exercises and problems, remember to use the **Decision Toolkit** discussed and used in the text:

1. <u>Decision Checkpoints</u>: at this point you ask a question.

2. <u>Info Needed for Decision</u>: you make a choice regarding the information needed to answer the question.

3. <u>Tool to Use for Decision</u>: at this point you review just what the information chosen in step 2 does for the decision-making process.

4. <u>How to Evaluate Results</u>: you perform evaluation of information for answering the question.

Note: The notation (SO1) means that the question was drawn from study objective number one.

Matching

Please write the letters of the following terms in the spaces to the left of the definitions.

a. Contra revenue account

b. Cost of goods sold

c. Gross profit

d. Net sales

e. Periodic inventory system

f. Perpetual inventory system

g. Purchase discount

h. Sales discount

i. Sales invoice

j. Sales

_____ 1. (SO4)   Sales revenue less sales returns and allowances and sales discounts.

_____ 2. (SO4)   Net sales less cost of goods sold.

_____ 3. (SO1)   An inventory system in which two entries are required each time there is a sale of merchandise.

_____ 4. (SO2)   A cash discount claimed by a buyer for prompt payment of a balance due.

_____ 5. (SO3)   Primary source of revenue for a merchandising company.

_____ 6. (SO1)   An inventory system in which cost of goods sold is determined only at the end of an accounting period.

_____ 7. (SO4)   A reduction given by a seller for prompt payment of a credit sale.

_____ 8. (SO3,4) The total cost of merchandise sold during the period.

_____ 9. (SO3)   A document which provides support for credit sales.

_____ 10. (SO3)   An account subtracted from Sales on a merchandising company's income statement.

Multiple Choice

Please circle the correct answer.

1. (SO1) The operating cycle of a merchandising company is ordinarily _____ that of a service firm.
   a. the same as
   b. shorter than
   c. longer than
   d. four times as long as

2. (SO1) Which of the following statements is correct?
   a. A periodic inventory system gives better control over inventories than does a perpetual inventory system.
   b. A perpetual inventory system gives better control over inventories than does a periodic inventory system.
   c. A periodic inventory system computes cost of goods sold each time a sale occurs.
   d. A perpetual inventory system computes cost of goods sold only at the end of the accounting period.

3. (SO2) Poobah Corporation, which uses a perpetual inventory system, purchased on account $3,000 of merchandise on June 4. What entry is required on June 8 when it returned $500 of the merchandise to the seller?

   a. Accounts Payable   500
        Merchandise Inventory   500
   b. Merchandise Inventory   500
        Accounts Payable   500
   c. Accounts Payable   500
        Purchases Returns   500
   d. Cash   500
        Merchandise Inventory   500

4. (SO2) Cassie Corporation, which uses a perpetual inventory system, purchased on account $2,000 of merchandise on July 5. Credit terms were 2/10, n/30. It returned $400 of the merchandise on July 9. When it pays its bill on July 11, the journal entry will require a:
   a. debit to Accounts Payable for $2,000.
   b. debit to Accounts Payable for $1,600.
   c. credit to Cash for $1,600.
   d. debit to Merchandise Inventory for $32.

5.	(SO2)	Cosmos Corporation, which uses a perpetual inventory system, purchased on account $2,000 of merchandise on July 5. Credit terms were 2/10, n/30. It returned $400 of the merchandise on July 9. When it pays its bill on July 21, the journal entry will require a:
	a.	debit to Accounts Payable for $2,000.
	b.	credit to Accounts Payable for $1,600.
	c.	credit to Cash for $1,600.
	d.	debit to Cash for $1,600.

6.	(SO2)	Elizabeth Company uses a perpetual inventory system and on November 30 purchased merchandise for which it must pay the shipping charges. When it pays the shipping charges of $200, the journal entry will require a debit to:
	a.	Delivery Expense for $200.
	b.	Cash for $200.
	c.	Freight-out for $200.
	d.	Merchandise Inventory for $200.

7.	(SO3)	Which of the following statements is correct?
	a.	A company which uses a perpetual inventory system needs only one journal entry when it sells merchandise.
	b.	A company which uses a perpetual inventory system needs two journal entries when it sells merchandise.
	c.	A company which uses a perpetual inventory system debits Merchandise Inventory and credits Cost of Goods Sold when it sells merchandise.
	d.	None of the above is correct.

8.	(SO3)	Cynthia Corporation, which uses a perpetual inventory system, received $500 of returned merchandise that it had sold a week earlier. When it records the return, the journal entries will require a:
	a.	debit to Sales Returns and Allowances.
	b.	debit to Cost of Goods Sold.
	c.	debit to Accounts Receivable.
	d.	credit to Merchandise Inventory.

9.	(SO3)	Sales Returns and Allowances and Sales Discounts are:
	a.	revenue accounts.
	b.	expense accounts.
	c.	contra revenue accounts.
	d.	contra expense accounts.

10.   (SO3) A company that uses a perpetual inventory system sold $400 of merchandise on July 23 with credit terms of 1/10, n/30. The purchaser paid the amount due on July 30. Which journal entry will the selling company record on July 30?

a.	Cash	400	
	Accounts Receivable		400
b.	Cash	400	
	Sales Discounts		4
	Accounts Receivable		396
c.	Accounts Receivable	400	
	Sales Discounts		4
	Cash		396
d.	Cash	396	
	Sales Discounts	4	
	Accounts Receivable		400

11.   (SO3) Use the same facts as in number 10 above, but assume that the purchaser pays the amount due on August 8. Which journal entry will the selling company record on August 8?

a.	Cash	400	
	Accounts Receivable		400
b.	Cash	400	
	Sales Discounts		4
	Accounts Receivable		396
c.	Accounts Receivable	400	
	Sales Discounts		4
	Cash		396
d.	Cash	396	
	Sales Discounts	4	
	Accounts Receivable		400

12.   (SO4) On its income statement, a company added up all its revenues, added up all its expenses, and then deducted the expense total from the revenue total. Which of the following formats did the company use for its income statement?
    a.   Dual-step.
    b.   Triple-step.
    c.   Single-step.
    d.   Multiple-step.

13.   (SO4) Sales revenues are $10,000, sales returns and allowances are $500, and sales discounts are $1,000. What is the dollar amount of net sales?
    a. $11,500.
    b. $10,500.
    c. $10,000.
    d. $ 8,500.

13

14. (SO4) Gross profit is $50,000, operating expenses are $15,000, and net sales total $75,000. What is cost of goods sold?
 a. $10,000.
 b. $25,000.
 c. $35,000.
 d. $80,000.

15. (SO4) Net sales total $90,000, gross profit is $50,000, and net income is $20,000. The total of operating expenses is:
 a. $ 30,000.
 b. $ 40,000.
 c. $ 70,000.
 d. $110,000.

16. (SO4) Gross profit is $50,000, operating expenses are $15,000, and net sales total $75,000. What is net income?
 a. $10,000.
 b. $25,000.
 c. $35,000.
 d. $80,000.

17. (SO4) Net income is $15,000, operating expenses are $20,000, and net sales total $75,000. What is gross profit?
 a. $60,000.
 b. $40,000.
 c. $35,000.
 d. $15,000.

18. (SO4) Net income is $15,000, operating expenses are $20,000, and net sales total $75,000. What is cost of goods sold?
 a. $60,000.
 b. $40,000.
 c. $35,000.
 d. $15,000.

19. (SO5) Ending inventory is $10,000, beginning inventory is $20,000, the cost of goods purchased is $25,000   The cost of goods sold is:
 a. $45,000.
 b. $35,000.
 c. $25,000.
 d. $15,000.

20. (SO5) Cost of goods sold is $50,000, cost of goods available for sale is $90,000, and cost of goods purchased is $60,000. The beginning inventory is:
 a. $30,000.
 b. $40,000.
 c. $50,000.
 d. $90,000.

21.   (SO6)   Net income is $15,000, operating expenses are $20,000, and net sales total $75,000. What is the gross profit rate?
        a.   20%.
        b.   27%.
        c.   47%.
        d.   75%.

22.   (SO6)   Net income is $15,000, operating expenses are $20,000, net sales total $75,000, and sales revenues total $95,000. What is the profit margin ratio?
        a.   20%.
        b.   16%.
        c.   75%.
        d.   79%.

23.   (SO8)   Which of the following is the correct journal entry to record a return of purchased merchandise for a company which uses a periodic inventory system?
        a.   Debit Purchase Returns and Allowances; credit Accounts Payable.
        b.   Debit Merchandise Inventory; credit Accounts Payable.
        c.   Debit Accounts Payable; credit Merchandise Inventory.
        d.   Debit Accounts Payable; credit Purchase Returns and Allowances.

24.   (SO8)   A company purchased merchandise for $3,000 with credit terms of 2/10, n/30. When it pays the amount due within the discount period, the journal entry will include a debit to:
        a.   Accounts Payable for $3,000.
        b.   Accounts Payable for $2,940.
        c.   Purchase Discounts for $60.
        d.   Cash for $2,940.

25.   (SO7)   Penny Company reports a balance of $15,000 in its Cash account, net income of $50,000, and net cash provided by operating activities of $75,000. Penny Company's quality of earnings ratio is:
        a.   .67.
        b.   1.50.
        c.   3.33.
        d.   5.00.

Problems

1.   From the appropriate accounts below, please prepare a multiple-step income statement for
      Buff Corporation for the year ended January 31, 2010 (SO4).

Cash	$13,000
Utilities expense	15,000
Cost of goods sold	24,000
Insurance expense	2,000
Accounts receivable	12,000
Sales returns and allowances	4,000
Advertising expense	7,000
Merchandise inventory	35,000
Depreciation expense	8,000
Sales revenues	99,000
Freight-out	3,000
Sales discounts	5,000
Salaries expense	28,000
Rent expense	10,000

Buff Corporation
Income Statement
For the Year Ended January 31, 2010

2. Please refer to The Bon-Ton Stores, Inc., financial statements at the end of this study guide for information for answering the following questions. Don't forget to use the **Decision Toolkit** approach for help in the problem-solving.

    a. What is Bon-Ton's gross profit in 2007 and 2006? (SO4)

    b. What form of the income statement does Bon-Ton use? (SO4)

    c. In "a" you solved for the dollar amount of gross profit. Now please express gross profit as a percentage for each year. (SO6)

    d. Please compute for the company in 2007 and 2006 a ratio that shows the percentage of each dollar of sales that results in net income. (SO6)

    e. What do the two ratios tell you about the operations of the business? (SO6)

SOLUTIONS TO SELF-TEST

Matching

1.	d		6.	e
2.	c		7.	h
3.	f		8.	b
4.	g		9.	i
5.	j		10.	a

Multiple Choice

1. c   It is longer because of the purchase and sale of merchandise inventory.

2. b   Periodic systems don't show the quantity of goods which should be on hand, making control more difficult. Cost of goods sold is computed each time a sale occurs under the perpetual system.

3. a   Since the sale was on account, the return entry requires a decrease in the liability, and so Accounts Payable is debited. Since the company uses a perpetual system, all merchandise dollar amounts are recorded in the Merchandise Inventory account. A decrease because of the returned merchandise requires a credit to Merchandise Inventory. Purchases Returns would have been used if the company had used a periodic system.

4. b   The journal entry is:

Accounts Payable	1,600	
Merchandise Inventory		32
Cash		1,568

5. c   The journal entry is:

Accounts Payable	1,600	
Cash		1,600

6. d   The journal entry is:

Merchandise Inventory	200	
Cash		200

7. b   A perpetual inventory system requires two entries when merchandise is sold. One of the entries is a debit to Cost of Goods Sold and a credit to Merchandise Inventory.

8. a   The journal entries are:

Sales Returns and Allowances	500	
Accounts Receivable		500
Merchandise Inventory	300	
Cost of Goods Sold		300

9. c   While these accounts have a normal debit balance, they are not expenses. They are also not revenue accounts: They are subtracted from a revenue account, making them contra revenue accounts.

10. d   The entry requires a debit to Cash but not for $400 since the purchaser receives a $4 discount. Accounts Receivable must be credited for the full amount owed, $400. The $4 difference between the amount owed and the amount of cash received is the debit to Sales Discounts.

11. a   Since the purchaser did not pay within the discount period, the entry simply debits Cash and credits Accounts Receivable for the gross amount.

12. c   A multiple-step income statement shows the intermediate components of net income, and there is no such thing as a dual-step or a triple-step income statement.

13. d $10,000 - $500 - $1,000

14. b $75,000 - $50,000

15. a $50,000 - $20,000

16. c $50,000 - $15,000

17. c $15,000 + $20,000

18. b $15,000 + $20,000 = $35,000 of gross profit;
        $75,000 - $35,000 = $40,000

19. b $20,000 + $25,000 - $10,000

20. a $90,000 - $60,000

21. c $15,000 + $20,000 = $35,000 of gross profit;
        $35,000 ÷ $75,000 = 47% (rounded)

22. a $15,000 ÷ $75,000 = 20%

23. d   Merchandise Inventory is used in a perpetual system. When merchandise is returned, the liability is reduced by debiting, not crediting, Accounts Payable.

24. a   The journal entry is:

Accounts Payable	3,000	
Purchase Discounts		60
Cash		2,940

25. b   The quality of earnings ratio is computed by dividing net cash provided by operating activities by net income ($75,000 ÷ $50,000).

Problems

1.

Buff Corporation
Income Statement
For the Year Ended January 31, 2010

Sales revenues		
Sales		$99,000
Less: Sales returns and allowances	$ 4,000	
Sales discounts	5,000	9,000
Net sales		90,000
Cost of goods sold		24,000
Gross profit		66,000
Operating expenses		
Salaries expense	28,000	
Utilities expense	15,000	
Rent expense	10,000	
Depreciation expense	8,000	
Advertising expense	7,000	
Freight-out	3,000	
Insurance expense	2,000	
Total operating expenses		73,000
Net loss		($ 7,000)

Since total expenses exceeded revenues, Buff Corporation incurred a net loss for the period.

2.   Dollar amounts are in thousands.

a.   2007: $1,215,781   ($3,365,912 - $2,150,131)

        2006: $1,243,517   ($3,362,279 - $2,118,762)

Remember that gross profit is computed by deducting cost of merchandise sold, or cost of goods sold, from net sales.

b.   The company uses the single-step income statement. Four expenses are subtracted from the total of net sales and other income to arrive at income from operations. Remember you had to compute gross profit in "a" above. If the company were using the multiple-step statement, there would have been a line labeled "gross profit."

c.   To express gross profit as a percentage, you must compute the gross profit rate. The rate is calculated by dividing gross profit by net sales.

    2007: $1,215,781 ÷ $3,365,912 = 36.1% (rounded)

    2006: $1,243,517 ÷ $3,362,279 = 37.0% (rounded)

d.   To determine the percentage of each dollar of sales that results in net income, you must compute the profit margin ratio. The ratio is calculated by dividing net income by net sales.

2007: $11,562 ÷ $3,365,912 = 0.3% (rounded)
2006: $46,883 ÷ $3,362,279 = 1.4% (rounded)

e.   The gross profit rate declined from 2006 to 2007 because there was a larger increase in cost of merchandise sold than there was in net sales. The profit margin ratio declined because expenses were higher in 2007, leading to a significantly lower income from operations and net income for the year.

CHAPTER **6**

Reporting and Analyzing Inventory

CHAPTER OVERVIEW

Chapter 6 begins with a discussion of the steps in determining inventory quantities. You will learn about the various ways to assign costs to inventory and about the financial statement and tax effects of the cost flow methods. Valuing inventory at the lower of cost or market is discussed, as are the inventory turnover ratio and LIFO reserve. You will apply inventory cost flow methods to perpetual inventory records, and, finally, you'll see effects of inventory errors on the income statement and the balance sheet.

REVIEW OF SPECIFIC STUDY OBJECTIVES

⅄　A **merchandising firm** has only one inventory account, called Merchandise Inventory. A **manufacturing firm** has three inventory accounts: finished goods inventory, consisting of goods completed and awaiting sale; work in process inventory, consisting of goods partially completed; and raw materials inventory, consisting of materials waiting to be placed into production.

SO1.　Describe the steps in determining inventory quantities.

⅄　Determining inventory quantities involves **two steps**: taking a physical count of goods on hand and determining ownership of goods.

⅄　A **physical count** involves counting, weighing, or measuring each kind of inventory on hand at the end of the accounting period. It can be a time-consuming and formidable task. The quantity of each kind of inventory is **listed on inventory summary sheets** and should be verified by a second employee or supervisor.

⋏   **Determining ownership of goods** can be complex because of situations like the following: inventory in a warehouse does not belong to the owner of the warehouse, and a company's inventory may not be physically present at the time of the physical count.

⋏   If **goods are in transit** at the time of the physical count, then <u>ownership is determined by who has legal title to the goods</u>, and legal title is determined by the <u>terms of the sale</u>. When terms are **FOB (free on board) shipping point**, <u>ownership passes to the buyer when the goods arrive at the public carrier</u>. If goods are being shipped from Atlanta, GA, to Charleston, SC, and terms are FOB shipping point, the buyer in Charleston has legal title to and ownership of the inventory when the seller in Atlanta delivers the goods to the common carrier in Atlanta. When terms are **FOB destination**, <u>ownership of the goods remains with the seller until the goods reach the buyer</u>. In our example, if the goods are shipped FOB destination, the seller in Atlanta has title to the goods until they reach the buyer in Charleston.

⋏   **Consigned goods** pose another problem. Charlie takes goods that he wishes to sell to Barb's place of business. Barb agrees to try to sell them for Charlie, for a commission, of course. Charlie is at all times the owner of the goods until they sell. Even though the goods are physically at Barb's place of business, Barb never has title to the goods. So, at the time of the physical count of the inventory, Charlie must remember to <u>count those consigned goods as part of the inventory</u>.

SO2.   Explain the basis of accounting for inventories and apply the inventory cost flow methods under a periodic inventory system.

⋏   **Cost of goods available for sale must be allocated** to two items: <u>cost of goods sold</u> and <u>ending inventory</u>. Once ending inventory has been determined, it is a simple matter to subtract that number from cost of goods available for sale to determine cost of goods sold.

⋏   There are **four ways of assigning cost to ending inventory**. The first is called <u>specific identification</u> and is used for high-cost, low-volume items such as cars or antiques. Each item has a cost sheet or ticket attached to it, and valuing ending inventory consists of adding up the sheets or tickets of the items in stock. This is not an appropriate method for a hardware store that has many small items in stock or for a retailer with millions of items in the store.

⋏   The other ways of assigning cost are called **cost flow assumptions**, and there are three of these: <u>first-in, first-out (FIFO)</u>, <u>last-in, first-out (LIFO)</u>, and <u>average cost</u>.

⋏   **First-in, first-out** <u>assumes</u> that the <u>earliest ("first") goods purchased are the first sold</u>. FIFO often parallels the actual physical flow of goods: with few exceptions, retailers want to sell the oldest inventory first because of shelf-life or style issues. <u>Ending inventory consists of the most recent purchases</u>.

⋏   **Last-in, first-out** <u>assumes</u> that the <u>most recent ("last") goods purchased are the first sold</u>. This is usually opposite the physical flow of goods, but there is no accounting requirement that the cost flow assumption approximate the physical flow of goods. Ending inventory consists of the oldest purchases.

A   **Average cost** removes the effects of rising or falling prices. An average unit cost is computed by dividing the cost of goods available for sale by the total units available for sale. That unit cost is then applied to the units in ending inventory and the units sold. It is a weighted average cost that is computed.

A   Using the following data, let's compute ending inventory and cost of goods sold under each of the cost flow assumptions.

Date	Units	Unit Cost	Total Cost
Feb. 2	300	$4.00	$ 1,200
Mar. 9	400	5.00	2,000
May 8	600	6.00	3,600
Jun. 3	500	7.00	3,500
	1,800		$10,300

A physical count shows that there are 550 units in ending inventory. The February 2 units are the beginning inventory, and $10,300 is the cost of goods available for sale. Please note that this is a time of rising prices.

FIFO: The most recent purchases are assumed to be in ending inventory; so, to get to 550, begin counting with the June 3 purchase.

June 3   500 X $7.00 = $3,500
May 8   _50_ X   6.00 = _300_
          550              $3,800 ending inventory

Cost of goods available for sale $10,300
Less: Ending inventory   _3,800_
Cost of goods sold $ 6,500

LIFO: The oldest purchases are assumed to be in ending inventory; so, to get to 550, begin counting with the February 2 beginning inventory.

Feb. 2   300 X $4.00 = $1,200
Mar. 9   _250_ X   5.00 = _1,250_
          550              $2,450 ending inventory

Cost of goods available for sale $10,300
Less: ending inventory   _2,450_
Cost of goods sold $ 7,850

Average cost: To compute an average unit cost, divide cost of goods available for sale of $10,300 by the total units available for sale, 1,800. The average unit cost is $5.72 (rounded). This unit cost is applied to the 550 units in ending inventory: 550 X $5.72 = $3,146.

3

Cost of goods available for sale $10,300
Less: ending inventory   3,146
Cost of goods sold $ 7,154

Summarizing these results:

	FIFO	Aver. Cost	LIFO
Cost of goods available	$10,300	$10,300	$10,300
Less: ending inventory	3,800	3,146	2,450
Cost of goods sold	$ 6,500	$ 7,154	$ 7,850

Please note that the results of average cost are between those of FIFO and LIFO: average cost removes the effects of rising, or falling, prices. Please note, too, that the company never paid $5.72 for any units purchased: this is simply a weighted average unit cost.

     All three methods are acceptable, and a <u>company may use more than one method at the same time</u>. It may have two classes of inventories and use LIFO for one and FIFO for the other.

SO3.   Explain the financial statement and tax effects of each of the inventory cost flow assumptions.

     You can see the **income statement effects** of the three methods with the above summarization. Remember that the example shows a period of **rising prices**.

<u>FIFO</u>: lowest cost of goods sold, highest net income.
<u>LIFO</u>: highest cost of goods sold, lowest net income.
<u>Average cost</u>: in the middle for both items.

If this had been a time of **falling prices**, the <u>opposite would have resulted</u>.

     The **tax effects** result from the income statement effects. In a period of rising prices LIFO results in the lowest income taxes because it has the lowest net income. A company using LIFO will be able to conserve cash because it will have a lower tax bill. There is a **LIFO conformity rule** that states that <u>a company using LIFO for tax purposes must also use LIFO for financial reporting purposes</u>.

     The **balance sheet effects** of the three methods can also be seen with the summarization. Remember that <u>results would have been opposite had this been a period of falling prices</u>.

<u>FIFO</u>: highest inventory valuation (because most recent purchases are in ending inventory).
<u>LIFO</u>: lowest inventory valuation (because oldest purchases are in ending inventory). LIFO can produce severe understatement of inventory if inventories contain items purchased in one or more prior accounting periods.
<u>Average cost</u>: in the middle.

      A   While a **company must be consistent in its use of inventory method**, it <u>is</u> <u>allowed to change methods if it will result in better financial reporting</u>. The change and its effects on net income must be disclosed in the notes to the financial statements.

SO4.   Explain the lower-of-cost-or-market basis of accounting for inventories.

      A   **At times companies have in inventory items for which they paid one price but for which they would currently pay a lower price if they were to purchase those same inventory items.**

      A   This situation **requires a departure from the cost principle**, and the inventory will be <u>valued at the lower-of-cost-or-market (LCM)</u>. Market is defined as current replacement cost, used because a decline in the replacement cost usually leads to a decline in the item's selling price.

      A   **LCM is an example of the accounting concept of conservatism**, which states that <u>the best choice among accounting alternatives is the method that is least likely to overstate assets and net income</u>. (Conservatism does <u>not</u> mean that items should be intentionally understated.)

SO5.   Compute and interpret the inventory turnover ratio.

      A   **Managing inventory levels** so that neither too much nor too little is on hand can be complex and is critical to a company's success.

      A   The **inventory turnover ratio** can help in managing inventory levels. It is <u>computed by dividing cost of goods sold by average inventory</u>. (Average inventory is computed by adding together the beginning and the ending inventories of a period and dividing the sum by 2.) If a company's cost of goods sold is $50,000 and its average inventory is $16,000, then its inventory turnover ratio is 3.13 (rounded). This means that the company sells its entire inventory about 3 times every accounting period.

      A   **Days in inventory** is <u>computed by dividing the inventory turnover ratio into 365</u>. Using the same example above, 365 ÷ 3.13 = 116.6 days. This means that it takes the company about 116 days to sell its inventory.

      A   **Both the inventory turnover ratio and days in inventory must be compared with something to be meaningful.** They may be compared with the same company's numbers from prior periods or with numbers of other companies in the same industry.

SO6.   Describe the LIFO reserve and explain its importance for comparing results of different companies.

⋏   **Using different inventory cost flow assumptions complicates analysts' attempts to compare the results of firms that use different inventory methods.**

⋏   **Companies using LIFO** are required to report the amount that inventory would have increased (or occasionally decreased) if the firm had instead been using FIFO. This amount is called the **LIFO reserve.**

⋏   A company using the LIFO method for costing inventories shows inventory of $100,000 in 2011. If by using FIFO the company's inventories would have been higher by $50,000 and $40,000 in 2011 and 2010 respectively, then the adjustment is as follows:

2011 inventory using LIFO	$100,000
2011 LIFO reserve	50,000
2011 inventory assuming FIFO	$150,000

If cost of goods sold in 2011 is $30,000, then the adjustment to cost of goods sold is as follows:

2011 cost of goods sold—LIFO	$ 30,000
Less: increase in 2011 LIFO reserve	10,000 *
2011 cost of goods sold—FIFO	$ 20,000

* $50,000 - $40,000

If the LIFO reserve had decreased from 2010 to 2011, then the amount of the decrease would have been added to the 2011 cost of goods sold—LIFO to determine the 2011 cost of goods sold—FIFO.

SO7.   Apply the inventory cost flow methods to perpetual inventory records.
(This objective is discussed in Appendix 6A in your text.)

⋏   The **cost flow methods you've learned to use with a periodic system of inventory can also be applied to a perpetual system.**

⋏   For **FIFO and LIFO**, it is important to keep each purchase of inventory in a separate layer. Consider the following data:
Purchases

Oct. 10	200 units @ $2.00
Nov. 11	300 units @ $3.00
Dec. 15	400 units @ $4.00

Sales

Nov. 30	300 units
Dec. 20	300 units

FIFO yields the following:

	Purchase	Sales	Balance
Oct. 10	200 @ $2.00		200 @ $2.00
Nov. 11	300 @ $3.00		200 @ $2.00
			300 @ $3.00
Nov. 30		200 @ $2.00	
(Sale)		100 @ $3.00	200 @ $3.00
Dec. 15	400 @ $4.00		200 @ $3.00
(Purchase)			400 @ $4.00
Dec. 20		200 @ $3.00	
		100 @ $4.00	300 @ $4.00

Please note that FIFO always yields the same results regardless of whether a periodic or a perpetual inventory system is used. The same is not true for LIFO.

LIFO yields the following:

	Purchase	Sales	Balance
Oct. 10	200 @ $2.00		200 @ $2.00
Nov. 11	300 @ $3.00		200 @ $2.00
			300 @ $3.00
Nov. 30		300 @ $3.00	200 @ $2.00
(Sale)			
Dec. 15	400 @ $4.00		200 @ $2.00
(Purchase)			400 @ $4.00
Dec. 20		300 @ $4.00	200 @ $2.00
			100 @ $4.00

The **average cost method** when applied to a perpetual inventory system is called the <u>moving average method</u>. **A new average cost is computed after each purchase.** Consider the following data:

Purchases	Balance
	200 units @ $2.00
100 units @ $2.50	300 units @ $2.17 (rounded)*

* (200 X $2.00) + (100 X $2.50) ÷ 300 units = $2.167

SO8.   Indicate the effects of inventory errors on the financial statements.
(This objective is discussed in Appendix 6B in your text.)

⋏   **Inventory errors affect the determination of cost of goods sold and net income in two periods** because the ending inventory of one period becomes the beginning inventory of the next period.

⋏   An **error in beginning inventory** will have a <u>reverse effect on net income of the same accounting period</u> (if beginning inventory is understated, then net income will be overstated). An **error in ending inventory** will have the <u>same effect on net income of the same accounting period</u> (if ending inventory is understated, then net income will be understated, too).

⋏   An **error in ending inventory of the current period** will have a <u>reverse effect on net income of the next accounting period</u>. Even though there is an error, **total net income will be correct over the two periods because the errors offset each other**.

⋏   An **error in beginning inventory** <u>does not result in a corresponding error in the ending inventory for that same period</u>.

⋏   On the **balance sheet**, if <u>ending inventory is overstated, then both assets and stockholders' equity will be overstated. If ending inventory is understated, then both assets and stockholders' equity will be understated.</u>

CHAPTER SELF-TEST

As you work the exercises and problems, remember to use the **Decision Toolkit** discussed and used in the text:

1. <u>Decision Checkpoints</u>: at this point you ask a question.

2. <u>Info Needed for Decision</u>: you make a choice regarding the information needed to answer the question.

3. <u>Tool to Use for Decision</u>: at this point you review just what the information chosen in step 2 does for the decision-making process.

4. <u>How to Evaluate Results</u>: you perform evaluation of information for answering the question.

Note: The notation (SO1) means that the question was drawn from study objective number one.

Completion

Please write in the word or words that will complete the sentence.

1. (SO1)   A company is said to _____ goods if it gives those goods to another party to try to sell them.

2. (SO1)   If merchandise is shipped FOB shipping point, then the goods belong to the _____ while they are in transit.

3. (SO2)   _____ _____ is an appropriate method for costing inventory that is low-volume and high-cost.

4. (SO2)   With _____, the oldest costs remain in ending inventory.

5. (SO2)   In a period of falling prices, _____ will give the highest cost of goods sold.

6. (SO3)   In a period of rising prices, _____ will produce the lowest income tax bill.

7. (SO3)   If a company changes its inventory methods, then it must _____ the change and its effects on net income.

8. (SO4)   In the phrase "lower of cost or market," "market" means _____ _____ _____.

9. (SO5)   If the inventory turnover ratio is 4.5 times, then the days in inventory calculation yields _____ days.

10. (SO6)   Companies using LIFO are required to report the amount, called _____ _____, that inventory would increase (or occasionally decrease) if the firm had instead been using FIFO.

Multiple Choice

Please circle the correct answer.

1.   (SO1)   If goods are shipped FOB destination, then which of the following parties includes in its inventory the goods while they are in transit?
    a.   Shipping company.
    b.   Buyer.
    c.   Seller.
    d.   Both the buyer and the seller include the goods in their inventory.

2. (SO1) Ceil gives goods on consignment to Jerry who agrees to try to sell them for a 25% commission. At the end of the accounting period, which of the following parties includes in its inventory the consigned goods?
   a. Ceil.
   b. Jerry.
   c. Both Ceil and Jerry.
   d. Neither Ceil nor Jerry.

3. (SO2) Beginning inventory is $30,000, ending inventory is $25,000, and cost of goods purchased is $45,000. What is cost of goods sold?
   a. $10,000.
   b. $40,000.
   c. $45,000.
   d. $50,000.

4. (SO2) Beginning inventory is $50,000, cost of goods purchased is $70,000, and cost of goods sold is $90,000. What is ending inventory?
   a. $ 30,000.
   b. $ 50,000.
   c. $ 70,000.
   d. $110,000.

5. (SO2) Cost of goods purchased is $30,000, ending inventory is $20,000, and cost of goods sold is $60,000. What is beginning inventory?
   a. $20,000.
   b. $30,000.
   c. $50,000.
   d. $80,000.

6. (SO2) Cost of goods sold is $80,000, ending inventory is $30,000, and beginning inventory is $20,000. What is cost of goods purchased?
   a. $110,000.
   b. $ 90,000.
   c. $ 70,000.
   d. $ 60,000.

7. (SO2) Which of the following inventory costing methods most often parallels the physical flow of goods?
   a. LIFO.
   b. FIFO.
   c. Average cost.
   d. Lower of cost or market.

Please use the following data for 8, 9, and 10:

Date	Units	Unit Cost	Total Cost
Feb. 5	200	$2.00	$ 400
Mar. 6	500	4.00	2,000
Apr. 9	400	6.00	2,400
Jun. 7	300	7.00	2,100
	1,400		$6,900

On June 30 there are 350 units in ending inventory.

8. (SO2) What is the value of ending inventory using first-in, first-out (FIFO)?
    a. $1,000.
    b. $1,726.
    c. $2,400.
    d. $5,177.

9. (SO2) What is the value of ending inventory using last-in, first-out (LIFO)?
    a. $1,000.
    b. $1,726.
    c. $2,400.
    d. $5,177.

10. (SO2) What is the cost of goods sold using average cost?
    a. $1,000.
    b. $1,726.
    c. $2,400.
    d. $5,177.

Please use the following data for 11, 12, and 13:

Date	Units	Unit Cost	Total Cost
Feb. 2	100	$8.00	$ 800
Mar. 9	400	7.00	2,800
Apr. 3	500	5.00	2,500
Jun. 5	300	3.00	900
	1,300		$7,000

On June 30 there are 400 units in ending inventory.

11. (SO2) What is the value of ending inventory using first-in, first-out (FIFO)?
    a. $1,400.
    b. $2,900.
    c. $4,100.
    d. $5,600.

12. (SO2) What is cost of goods sold using first-in, first-out (FIFO)?
   a. $1,400.
   b. $2,900.
   c. $4,100.
   d. $5,600.

13. (SO2) What is cost of goods sold using last-in, first-out (LIFO)?
   a. $1,400.
   b. $2,900.
   c. $4,100.
   d. $5,600.

14. (SO3) In a period of rising prices, which of the following methods will give the highest ending inventory?
   a. Specific identification.
   b. Average cost.
   c. LIFO.
   d. FIFO.

15. (SO3) In a period of falling prices, which of the following methods will give the highest net income?
   a. Specific identification.
   b. Average cost.
   c. LIFO.
   d. FIFO.

16. (SO4) Using lower of cost or market is an example of the accounting concept of:
   a. revenue recognition.
   b. conservatism.
   c. matching.
   d. full disclosure.

17. (SO5) Net sales are $80,000, cost of goods sold is $30,000, and average inventory is $20,000. The inventory turnover ratio is:
   a. 4.00 times.
   b. 2.67 times.
   c. 1.50 times.
   d. .25 times.

18. (SO5) Net sales are $200,000, cost of goods sold is $90,000, and average inventory is $30,000. Days in inventory is:
   a. 3.0.
   b. 6.7 (rounded).
   c. 54.5 (rounded).
   d. 121.7 (rounded).

19.   (SO6) In 2011 a company shows inventory of $250,000 using LIFO. If the company had used FIFO, its inventories would have been higher by $40,000 and $30,000 in 2011 and 2010, respectively. Its LIFO reserve in 2011, therefore, is:
   a. $10,000.
   b. $30,000.
   c. $40,000.
   d. $70,000.

20.   (SO7) A company shows the following three purchases of inventory:
   January 3   100 units @ $5.00
   February 5   300 units @ $6.00
   March 1   200 units @ $7.00

   On February 24 the company sold 300 units. If the company uses LIFO perpetual, then the dollar amount of ending inventory on March 1 is:
   a. $2,000.
   b. $1,900.
   c. $1,400.
   d. $ 500.

21.   (SO7) Using the data from 20 above, what is the dollar amount of ending inventory on March 1 if the company uses FIFO perpetual?
   a. $2,000.
   b. $1,700.
   c. $1,400.
   d. $ 500.

22.   (SO7) Which of the following inventory methods yields the same results for both the periodic and the perpetual systems of inventory?
   a.   Lower of cost or market.
   b.   Average cost.
   c.   LIFO.
   d.   FIFO.

23.   (SO8) If ending inventory is understated, then:
   a.   the current period's cost of goods sold is understated.
   b.   the current period's net income is overstated.
   c.   the next period's cost of goods sold is overstated.
   d.   the next period's net income is overstated.

24.   (SO8) If beginning inventory is overstated, then the current year's:
   a.   cost of goods sold is overstated.
   b.   cost of goods sold is understated.
   c.   ending inventory is overstated.
   d.   ending inventory is understated.

Problems

1. Below are data for Hattie Corporation for the year ended December 31, 2010. Please use these data to answer the questions.

Sales	$250,000
Purchase discounts	8,000
Sales discounts	40,000
Operating expenses	65,000
Sales returns and allowances	10,000
Freight-in	30,000
Purchase returns and allowances	15,000
Inventory, January 1, 2007	38,000
Inventory, December 31, 2007	32,000
Purchases	102,000

a. What are net sales? (SO3)

b. What is cost of goods purchased? (SO3)

c. What is cost of goods sold? (SO3)

d. What is gross profit? (SO3)

e. What is net income? (SO3)

2. Please refer to The Bon-Ton Stores, Inc. financial statements at the end of this study guide for information for answering the following questions. Don't forget to use the **Decision Toolkit** approach for help in the problem-solving.

a. What type of company is Bon-Ton, a merchandiser or a manufacturer? (SO1)

b. What cost flow methods does Bon-Ton use for its inventories? (SO2, SO4)

c. In 2007 how many days did items remain in inventory? (SO5)

SOLUTIONS TO SELF-TEST

Completion

1.	consign	6.	LIFO
2.	buyer	7.	disclose
3.	Specific identification	8.	current replacement cost
4.	LIFO	9.	81.1 365 ÷ 4.5
5.	FIFO	10.	LIFO reserve

Multiple Choice

1. c   When goods are shipped FOB destination, the seller retains title to the goods until they reach the buyer's place of business. Since the seller has title, he pays the shipping costs.

2. a   Consigned goods are always the property of the person who has put them out on consignment. They are Ceil's; Jerry never has title to the goods.

3. d $30,000 + $45,000 - $25,000

4. a $50,000 + $70,000 - $90,000

5. c $$60,000 + $20,000 = $80,000 - $30,000 = $50,000

6. b $80,000 + $30,000 = $110,000 - $20,000 = $90,000

7. b   LIFO is opposite the physical flow of the goods, and average cost and specific identification do not parallel the physical flow.

8. c
$$
\begin{array}{lrcr}
\text{June 7} & 300 \times \$7.00 & = & \$2,100 \\
\text{Apr. 9} & \underline{50} \times 6.00 & = & \underline{300} \\
& 350 & & \$2,400 \text{ ending inventory}
\end{array}
$$

9. a
$$
\begin{array}{lrcr}
\text{Feb. 5} & 200 \times \$2.00 & = & \$400 \\
\text{Mar. 6} & \underline{150} \times 4.00 & = & \underline{600} \\
& 350 & & \$1,000 \text{ ending inventory}
\end{array}
$$

10. d $6,900 ÷ 1,400 = $4.93 (rounded)/unit X 1,050 units

11. a
$$
\begin{array}{lrcr}
\text{June 5} & 300 \times \$3.00 & = & \$900 \\
\text{Apr. 3} & \underline{100} \times \$5.00 & = & \underline{500} \\
& 400 & & \$1,400
\end{array}
$$

12. d   You can simply subtract the ending inventory of $1,400 (solved for in number 11) from the cost of goods purchased, $7,000, or you can do the following:
$$
\begin{array}{lrcr}
\text{Feb. 2} & 100 \times \$8.00 & = & \$800 \\
\text{Mar. 9} & 400 \times \$7.00 & = & 2,800 \\
\text{Apr. 3} & \underline{400} \times \$5.00 & = & \underline{2,000} \\
& 900 & & \$5,600
\end{array}
$$

Since 1,300 units were available for sale and the ending inventory is 400 units, then 900 units were sold.

13. c   Jun. 5   300 X $3.00 = $ 900
          Apr. 3   500 X $5.00 =   2,500
          Mar. 9   100 X $7.00 =   700
                   900              $4,100

14. d   LIFO gives the lowest ending inventory, and average cost results will be between those of FIFO and LIFO.

15. c   The method with the lowest cost of goods sold will yield the highest net income: this method is LIFO.

16. b   Revenue recognition says that revenue is recognized when it is earned, matching dictates that expenses be matched with revenues, and full disclosure says that circumstances and events that make a difference to financial statement users should be disclosed.

17. c $30,000 ÷ $20,000

18. d   365 ÷ ($90,000 ÷ $30,000)

19. c   The LIFO reserve is the amount by which inventory would have changed had FIFO been used.

20. b   (100 @ $5.00) + (200 @ $7.00)

21. a   (200 @ $7.00) + (100 @ $6.00)

22. d

23. d   Since ending inventory is understated, cost of goods sold is overstated and net income is understated in the current period. Since the ending inventory of one period is the beginning inventory of the next period, then the next year's beginning inventory is understated, yielding an understated cost of goods available for sale and an understated cost of goods sold, which in turn yields an overstated net income.

24. a   An error in beginning inventory does not have an effect on ending inventory of the same year.

Problems

1. a. | Sales | $250,000 |
          |---|---|
          | Sales ret. and allow. | - 10,000 |
          | Sales discounts | - 40,000 |
          | Net sales | $200,000 |

    b. | Purchases | $102,000 |
          |---|---|
          | Purch. ret. and allow. | - 15,000 |
          | Purchase discounts | - 8,000 |
          | Freight-in | + 30,000 |
          | Cost of goods purch. | $109,000 |

    c. | Inventory, Jan. 1 | $ 38,000 |
          |---|---|
          | Cost of goods purch. | +109,000 |
          | Inventory, Dec. 31 | - 32,000 |
          | Cost of goods sold | $115,000 |

d.	Net sales	$200,000
	Cost of goods sold	-115,000
	Gross profit	$ 85,000
e.	Gross profit	$ 85,000
	Operating expenses	- 65,000
	Net income	$ 20,000

2.

a. To determine what type of company Bon-Ton is, you must look at inventory information in the financial statements and/or in the notes to the financial statements. The current assets section of the balance sheet shows "Merchandise Inventories," indicating that the company is a merchandiser. If the company had been a manufacturer, either on the face of the balance sheet or in the notes would have been listed the three types of inventories for such a company: raw materials, work in process, and finished goods.

b. To answer this question, you must read the first note to the financial statements, "Summary of Significant Accounting Policies," found on page F-7 of the company's 2007 10-K on the following Web site: http://investors.bonton.com/annuals.cfm. (The notes begin immediately after the consolidated statements of cash flows.) It mentions that inventories are determined by the retail method and that 32% of inventories were valued using a FIFO cost basis while 68% were valued using LIFO for the year 2007.

c. To compute how many days items remain in inventory, you first must calculate the inventory turnover ratio by dividing average inventory into cost of goods sold. Dollar amounts are in thousands.

2007 inventory turnover ratio:

Average inventory = ($754,802 + $787,487) ÷ 2 = $771,145 (rounded)
$2,150,131 ÷ $771,145 = 2.8 times (rounded)

Then, to determine how many days items remain in inventory, you divide the inventory turnover ratio into 365.

2007 days in inventory:
365 ÷ 2.8 times = 130.4 days

This ratio indicates that items are taking over 4 months to sell. Remember that a ratio by itself doesn't give enough information to be useful: it must be compared either to prior years' ratios for the company or to industry averages. The company wants to monitor these data very carefully. If the inventory turnover ratio has been weakening, then products are remaining unsold for too long a period of time, causing the company revenue problems.

CHAPTER 7

Fraud, Internal Control, and Cash

CHAPTER OVERVIEW

Chapter 7 discusses fraud and the principles of internal control, particularly with respect to cash. You will learn about both the limitations and the strengths of internal control. You'll learn about controls over cash receipts and disbursements, how to prepare a bank reconciliation, and how to report cash on the balance sheet. You will learn the basic principles of cash management and tools for help in managing and monitoring cash. Finally, you'll learn about the operation of a petty cash fund.

REVIEW OF SPECIFIC STUDY OBJECTIVES

SO1. Define fraud and internal control.

> ⋏ A **fraud** is a <u>dishonest act by an employee that results in personal benefit to the employee at a cost to the employer</u>.

> ⋏ **Reasons for the commission of a fraud are described in the fraud triangle:**
> 1. The workplace environment must provide <u>opportunity</u> for the employee to commit fraud.
> 2. Employees may experience <u>financial pressure</u>, personal financial problems caused by too much debt, for instance.
> 3. Employees provide a <u>rationalization</u> for their dishonest actions.

⋏   Under the **Sarbanes-Oxley Act of 2002 (SOX),** all publicly traded U.S. corporations are required to maintain an adequate system of internal control, and independent outside auditors must attest to the system's adequacy. Failure to comply can result in company fines and prison terms for company officers.

⋏   The **Sarbanes-Oxley Act also established the Public Company Accounting Oversight Board (PCAOB)** which establishes auditing standards and regulates auditor activity.

⋏   **Internal control** consists of methods and measures adopted within a business to:
1.   **safeguard its assets** from employee theft, robbery, and unauthorized use;
2.   **enhance the accuracy and reliability of its accounting records** by reducing the risk of errors (unintentional mistakes) and irregularities (intentional mistakes and misrepresentations) in the accounting process;
3.   **increase efficiency of operations**; and
4.   **ensure compliance with laws and regulations**.

⋏   **An internal control system** has five primary components:
1.   A control environment, showing that management values ethics and integrity;
2.   Risk assessment, by which the company determines risk factors and how to manage these factors;
3.   Control activities, policies and procedures designed to address specific risks;
4.   Information and communication, ensuring that important information is communicated both up and down the organization; and
5.   Monitoring, by which the system is checked periodically to ensure adequacy.

SO2. Identify the principles of internal control activities. (This section will focus on the control activities component of an internal control system.)

⋏   There are **six principles of control activities**:
1.   Establishment of responsibility. Control is most effective when only one person is responsible for a given task. This area includes authorization and approval of transactions.

2.   Segregation of duties.
a. The responsibility for **related activities** should be assigned to different individuals: this should decrease the potential for errors and irregularities. Related purchasing activities include ordering merchandise, receiving goods, and paying (or authorizing payment) for merchandise. Related sales activities include making a sale, shipping (or delivering) the goods, and billing the customer.

b. **Record-keeping and physical custody of assets** should be assigned to different individuals. In a corporation the controller is responsible for record-keeping functions, while the treasurer has physical custody of assets.

3. Documentation procedures. Wherever possible, **documents should be prenumbered**, and **all documents should be accounted for** (this includes voided documents). Source documents should be forwarded promptly to the accounting department to ensure accurate and timely recording of a transaction.

4. Physical controls. Their use is essential. Physical controls (such as safes and locked computer rooms) relate to the safeguarding of assets, while mechanical and electronic controls (such as time clocks, television monitors, and computer passwords) safeguard assets and enhance the accuracy and reliability of the accounting records.

5. Independent internal verification. This involves the **review of data prepared by employees**. Verification should be made periodically or on a surprise basis; verification should be done by an employee who is independent of the personnel responsible for the information; and discrepancies and exceptions should be reported to a management level that can take appropriate corrective action. Such verification is often performed by **internal auditors** who are employees of the company who evaluate on a continuous basis the effectiveness of the company's system of internal control.

6. Human resource controls. These include **bonding of employees who handle cash, rotating employees' duties and requiring employees to take vacations, and conducting thorough background checks**. The first involves acquiring of insurance protection against misappropriation of assets by dishonest employees. The second helps to deter employees from attempting theft because the employees know that they cannot permanently conceal their theft. The third should help the company in hiring honest employees to begin with.

⋏ **Internal controls** generally provide reasonable assurance that assets are safeguarded and that the accounting records are accurate and reliable. In constructing the system, a company tries to have the best system at the least cost: It attempts to have the benefits of the system outweigh the costs. There are, however, **limitations of any internal control system**. One involves the human element: a dishonest or careless employee can render the system ineffective, and two or more employees may collude to circumvent the system. (Performing a thorough background check when considering whether to hire a person is crucial.) The size of the company is also a factor. A large company has the resources, both human and financial, to put into place a sophisticated system of internal control. A small company may be very limited in both areas and must do the best it can with what it has.

3

SO3.   Explain the applications of internal control principles to cash receipts.

    ⋏ A company must have effective **internal control over cash receipts**, whether they are over-the-counter or mail receipts. While different size companies may apply them differently, all six internal control principles are important:

1.   Establishment of responsibility. Only designated personnel should be authorized to handle cash receipts.
2.   Segregation of duties. Custody of and record-keeping for cash should be separated.
3.   Documentation procedures. A company must use remittance advices, cash register tapes, and deposit slips.
4.   Physical controls. A company must store cash in secure areas, limit access to storage areas, and use cash registers.
5.   Independent internal verification. Supervisors should count receipts daily, and the treasurer should compare total receipts to bank deposits daily.
6.   Human resource controls. Cash-handling personnel should be bonded and required to take vacations, and background checks should be conducted.

SO4.   Explain the applications of internal control principles to cash disbursements.

    ⋏ A **major internal control over cash disbursements** is to use a voucher system (a network of approvals by authorized individuals, acting independently, to ensure that all disbursements **by check** are proper), except for small amounts that may be disbursed via a petty cash fund. Again, all six internal control principles apply:

1.   Establishment of responsibility. Only authorized personnel should sign checks and approve vendors.
2.   Segregation of duties. Again, custody and record-keeping should be separated: those who make payments should not record the transactions.
3.   Documentation procedures. Checks should be prenumbered and used in sequence, and they should be issued only if an invoice has been approved. Invoices should be stamped "paid."
4.   Physical controls. Blank checks should be secured, and check amounts should be printed with indelible ink.
5.   Independent internal verification. Checks and invoices should be compared, and a monthly bank reconciliation should be prepared.
6.   Human resource controls. Cash-handling personnel should be bonded and required to take vacations, and back ground checks should be conducted.

SO5.   Prepare a bank reconciliation.

    ⋏ The **use of a bank can increase good internal control over cash**. A company may use a bank as a depository and clearinghouse for checks received and written. Use of a bank minimizes the amount of currency that must be kept on hand, and a double record of all transactions is kept.

⋏   A **company receives monthly bank statements** and must reconcile the ending balance on the statement with the ending balance in the general ledger account "Cash." The two numbers are often not the same because of time lags (the bank has recorded something that the company has not, or vice versa) and errors made by either the bank or the company.

⋏   It is **customary to reconcile the balance per books and balance per bank to their adjusted (correct or true) cash balances**. The reconciliation should be prepared by someone who has no other responsibilities for cash.

⋏   The following are **adjustments made to the column called "Balance per bank statement"**:
1.   Deposits in transit (deposits which the company has recorded but the bank has not) are always added to the balance per bank column.
2.   Outstanding checks (checks recorded by the company which have not yet been paid by the bank) are always subtracted from the balance per bank column.
3.   Errors may either be added to or subtracted from the column depending on the nature of the error.

⋏   The following are **adjustments made to the column called "Balance per books"**:
1.   NSF checks (bounced checks) are subtracted from the balance per books column.
2.   Bank service charges are subtracted from the balance per books column.
3.   Note and interest collections are added to the balance per books column.
4.   Errors may either be added to or subtracted from the column depending on the nature of the error.

⋏   The **key question to ask when preparing a bank reconciliation** is "Who knows about the transaction and has already recorded it, and who doesn't yet know about it?" For example, with respect to bank service charges, the bank knows about them and has already subtracted them from the company account, reflecting this on the bank statement, but the company does not know the exact amount of the charges until it receives the statement.

⋏   After the bank reconciliation has been prepared, **each reconciling item in the balance per books column must be recorded by the company in a journal entry.** (Bank personnel record any adjustments in the balance per bank statement column.) It is important to note that an NSF check is debited to Accounts Receivable, signaling the intention of the company to try to collect on the bounced check. After the entries are journalized and posted, the balance in the Cash account should equal the total shown on the bank reconciliation.

⋏   **Electronic funds transfers (EFT)** are disbursement systems that use wire, telephone, or computers to transfer cash from one location to another. Use of EFT is widespread and growing rapidly.

SO6. Explain the reporting of cash.

⋏ **Cash** consists of <u>coins, currency (paper money), checks, money orders, and money on hand or on deposit in a bank or similar depository</u>. If a bank will accept an item at face value for deposit, then it is cash. Because cash is readily convertible into other assets, easily concealed and transported, and highly desired, internal control over cash is absolutely necessary.

⋏ **Cash is reported on the balance sheet and on the statement of cash flows**. On the balance sheet a company usually shows only one Cash account, which can be a combination of cash on hand, cash in banks, and petty cash. <u>Cash is listed first in the current assets section because it is the most liquid of assets.</u>

⋏ Companies often label the first current asset **"Cash and cash equivalents."** A **cash equivalent** is a <u>short-term, highly liquid investment which is readily convertible to cash and so near its maturity that its market value is relatively insensitive to changes in interest rates</u>. Examples include Treasury bills, commercial paper, and money market funds.

⋏ If **cash is restricted for a special purpose**, then it should be <u>reported separately as "restricted cash."</u> If it is to be used within the next year, then it is reported as a current asset; if it is to be used at a time beyond one year, then it is reported as a noncurrent asset.

SO7. Discuss the basic principles of cash management.

⋏ A **company's objective in the management of cash** is to <u>have sufficient cash to meet payments as they come due but to minimize the amount of non-revenue-generating cash on hand</u>. Many companies have employees whose sole job responsibility is to manage cash.

⋏ **Management of cash is the job of a company's treasurer and is critical to a company's success**. There are **five principles of cash management**:
1. <u>Increase the speed of collection on receivables.</u> A company wants to receive cash as speedily as possible so that it can have the use of this money.
2. <u>Keep inventory levels low.</u> There are many so-called "carrying costs" of inventory which a company wants to minimize as much as possible.
3. <u>Delay payment of liabilities.</u> A company wants to pay its bills on time but not too early. It certainly wants to take advantage of all cash discounts offered.
4. <u>Plan the timing of major expenditures.</u> A company tries to make major expenditures when it has excess cash, usually during its off season.
5. <u>Invest idle cash.</u> Cash that does not earn a return does a company little good. Invested cash should be highly liquid (easy to sell) and risk-free (there is no concern that the party will default on its promise to pay principal and interest).

SO8.   Identify the primary elements of a cash budget.

    ⅄   **A cash budget is an important tool in effective cash management**. It helps a company <u>plan its cash needs</u> by showing its anticipated cash flows. The cash budget <u>has three sections: cash receipts, cash disbursements, and financing</u>.

    ⅄   The **cash receipts section** shows all anticipated cash receipts: from cash sales and collections of accounts receivable; from interest and dividends; and proceeds from planned sales of investments, plant assets, and the company's capital stock.

    ⅄   The **cash disbursements section** shows expected payments for direct materials, direct labor, manufacturing overhead, selling and administrative expenses, income taxes, dividends, investments, and plant assets.

    ⅄   The **financing section** shows expected borrowings and the repayment of principal and interest.

    ⅄   The **accuracy of the cash budget** <u>depends on the accuracy of assumptions made by the company</u>. Any significant error in the budget will affect all subsequent cash budgets because the ending balance on one budget is the beginning balance on the next budget.

SO9.   Explain the operation of a petty cash fund.
        (This objective is discussed in the Chapter 7 appendix in your text.)

    ⅄   A **petty cash fund** is <u>used for small disbursements</u>, disbursements for which it would not be economical to write a company check.

    ⅄   To **establish a petty cash fund**, a <u>custodian must be selected</u>, and the <u>size of the fund must be determined</u>. If the company sets up the fund for $200, then it writes a check to the custodian for that amount and records a journal entry <u>debiting Petty Cash and crediting Cash</u> for $200.

    ⅄   **Operation of the fund** should <u>follow established procedures that clearly set out acceptable disbursements</u>. If an employee needs money from the fund for postage, then he should fill out a receipt (or voucher) stating the purpose of the disbursement, the date, and the amount. Both the employee and the petty cash custodian should sign the voucher.

    ⅄   **At all times the total of the cash in the petty cash drawer and the vouchers should equal the total of the petty cash fund**. Periodic surprise counts of the drawer are a good idea to determine whether the fund is being maintained correctly. Mutilation of the paid vouchers so that they cannot be resubmitted is also a good idea.

A   The **fund should be replenished** when it is running <u>low on funds and at the end of every accounting period</u> (so that all expenses will be recorded before financial statements are prepared). Once again, a check is made payable to the custodian for the required amount, and a journal entry is written <u>debiting various expenses and crediting Cash</u> (not Petty Cash). If the total of the receipts does not equal the total cash required, the difference is either debited or credited to <u>Cash Over and Short</u>, a temporary account. If this account has an overall debit balance, then it is reported as a miscellaneous expense on the income statement; if it has an overall credit balance, then it is reported as a miscellaneous revenue on the income statement.

A   Consider the following example. A company has a balance in the Petty Cash account of $300. At the end of the period, there are receipts in the petty cash drawer totaling $225, and there is cash in the drawer of $73. To bring the drawer up to $300, a check must be written for $227 ($300 -$73). When the journal entry is written, various expense accounts will be debited for $225 (the amount of the receipts), Cash will be credited for $227, and the difference of $2 will be debited to Cash Over and Short.

CHAPTER SELF-TEST

As you work the exercises and problems, remember to use the **Decision Toolkit** discussed and used in the text:

1. <u>Decision Checkpoints</u>: at this point you ask a question.

2. <u>Info Needed for Decision</u>: you make a choice regarding the information needed to answer the question.

3. <u>Tool to Use for Decision</u>: at this point you review just what the information chosen in step 2 does for the decision-making process.

4. <u>How to Evaluate Results</u>: you perform evaluation of information for answering the question.

Note: The notation (SO1) means that the question was drawn from study objective number one.

Completion

Please write in the word or words that will complete the sentence.

1. (SO1)   Internal control consists of measures to _____ assets, and _____ the accuracy and reliability of accounting records,

_____ efficiency of operations, and _____

compliance with laws and regulations.

2. (SO1)   The _____ Act requires that all publicly traded U.S. corporations maintain an adequate system of internal control.

3. (SO4)   A company should generally make payments by _____ rather then by cash.

4. (SO5)   A previously deposited check that "bounces" because the company that issued it does not have the money to cover the check is called _____.

5. (SO5)   In its journal entries relating to a bank reconciliation, a company will debit _____ _____ for bank service charges.

6. (SO6)   If a _____ will accept an item at face value for deposit, then it is considered to be _____.

7. (SO6)   _____ and _____ are examples of cash equivalents.

8. (SO7)   Two basic principles of cash management are to increase the speed of collection on _____ and to delay payment of _____.

9. (SO8)   The _____ section of a cash budget shows expected borrowings and repayment of principal and interest.

10. (SO9)   When a company replenishes its petty cash fund, if the debits do not equal the credits in the journal entry, the account _____ is used to balance the journal entry.

Multiple Choice

Please circle the correct answer.

1.   (SO2)   Which of the following statements is correct?
   a.   Control is most effective when two or three people are given responsibility for the same task.
   b.   The person who has custody of assets should not perform the record-keeping for the assets.
   c.   The person who has custody of assets should also perform the record-keeping for the assets.
   d.   It is a waste of company resources to have an employee perform independent internal verification.

2.   (SO2)   Which of the following statements is <u>incorrect</u>?
a.   Related purchasing activities should be assigned to different individuals.
b.   Safeguarding of assets is enhanced by the use of physical controls.
c.   Independent internal verification should be done by an employee independent of the personnel responsible for the information.
d.   The use of prenumbered documents is not an important internal control principle.

3.   (SO3)   Effective internal control over cash receipts includes:
a.   the use of one person to receive and record cash receipts.
b.   leaving cash receipts in an unlocked drawer overnight so that they can be accessed easily and quickly the next morning.
c.   using bonded employees and requiring employees to take vacations.
d.   All of the above are part of effective internal control over cash receipts.

4.   (SO4)   Effective internal control over cash disbursements includes:
a.   the use of prenumbered checks.
b.   the storage of blank checks in a secure place.
c.   the separation of authorization of checks and the actual writing of the checks.
d.   All of the above are part of effective internal control over cash disbursements.

5.   (SO5)   Which of the following is <u>added</u> to the balance per books side of a bank reconciliation?
a.   An outstanding check for $300.
b.   A note of $500 collected by the bank.
c.   A deposit in transit of $150.
d.   A bank service charge for $50 for check printing.

6.   (SO5)   Which of the following is <u>deducted</u> from the balance per bank statement side of a bank reconciliation?
a.   An outstanding check for $300.
b.   A bank service charge for $10.
c.   An NSF check in the amount of $50.
d.   A deposit in transit of $200.

7.   (SO5)   Cooper Corporation showed a balance in its Cash account in its books of $1,250 when it received its monthly bank statement. It found the following reconciling items: deposits in transit, $256; outstanding checks, $375; NSF check in the amount of $102; bank service charges of $27; and note and interest collection by the bank for $850. What is the adjusted cash balance Cooper will show on its bank reconciliation?
a. $1,131.
b. $1,852.
c. $1,971.
d. $1,981.

8.   (SO5)   Cumberland Corporation showed a balance in its Cash account in its books of $1,900 when it received its monthly bank statement. It found the following reconciling items: deposits in transit, $260; outstanding checks, $170; bank service charges, $20; and an NSF check in the amount of $100. It also found an error. A customer's check for $620 was recorded as $260. What is the adjusted cash balance Cumberland will show on its bank reconciliation?
   a. $2,140.
   b. $2,180.
   c. $2,340.
   d. $2,500.

9.   (SO5)   A company's monthly bank statement shows a collection by the bank of a note in the amount of $500 and related interest of $30. The journal entry to record the collection will include a:
   a.   credit to Cash for $530.
   b.   credit to Note Receivable for $500.
   c.   credit to Note Receivable for $530.
   d.   debit to Note Receivable for $500.

10.   (SO6)   Which of the following is not considered cash?
   a.   Coins.
   b.   Money orders.
   c.   Short-term investment in stock.
   d.   Checking account.

11.   (SO6)   A company has the following items: cash on hand, $1,000; cash in a checking account, $3,000; cash in a savings account, $5,000; postage stamps, $50; and Treasury bills, $10,000. How much should the company report as cash on the balance sheet?
   a. $ 9,000.
   b. $ 9,050.
   c. $19,000.
   d. $19,050.

12.   (SO6)   On which two financial statements is Cash reported?
   a.   Balance sheet and statement of cash flows.
   b.   Balance sheet and income statement.
   c.   Balance sheet and statement of retained earnings.
   d.   Income statement and statement of cash flows.

13.   (SO6)   If cash is restricted as to its use and will be used within the next year, then it should be:
   a.   included in the Cash and Cash Equivalents line on the balance sheet..
   b.   reported as a current liability on the balance sheet.
   c.   reported as a noncurrent asset on the balance sheet.
   d.   reported as a current asset separate from Cash and Cash Equivalents on the balance sheet.

14.   (SO6)   Which of the following is not a cash equivalent?
        a.   Money order.
        b.   Money market fund.
        c.   Treasury bill.
        d.   Short-term corporate note.

15.   (SO7)   Keeping inventory levels low and planning the timing of major
        expenditures are two basic principles of:
        a.   internal control.
        b.   cash management.
        c.   inventory management.
        d.   capital stock management.

16.   (SO7)   With respect to cash management, most companies try to:
        a.   keep as much spare cash on hand as possible in case of emergency.
        b.   keep a lot of cash in a non-interest-bearing checking account because that
                type of account has the lowest fees.
        c.   invest idle cash, even if only overnight.
        d.   invest idle cash in illiquid investments because that is where money earns
                the greatest return.

17.   (SO8)   Expected incoming dividends and interest will be listed in the _____
        section of a cash budget.
        a.   cash receipts
        b.   cash disbursements
        c.   cash investments
        d.   financing

18.   (SO8)   Expected payments for direct materials will be listed in the _____
        section of a cash budget.
        a.   cash receipts
        b.   cash disbursements
        c.   cash investments
        d.   financing

19.   (SO9)   The journal entry to establish a petty cash fund involves a:
        a.   debit to Cash and a credit to Petty Cash.
        b.   debit to Accounts Receivable and a credit to Cash.
        c.   debit to Petty Cash and a credit to Cash.
        d.   debit to Petty Cash Expense and a credit to Cash.

20.   (SO9)   The Petty Cash account has a balance of $800. The total of the receipts in
        the petty cash drawer is $608, and the cash in the drawer totals $198. When the
        fund is replenished, the journal entry will include a:
        a.   credit to Cash Over and Short for $6.
        b.   debit to Cash Over and Short for $6.
        c.   debit to Cash for $602.
        d.   credit to Petty Cash for $602.

Problems

1. Please use the following data for J By J Corporation to prepare a bank reconciliation as of June 30, 2010. Remember to prepare any required journal entries.

Balance per bank, June 30	$2,417
Balance per books, June 30	2,151
Outstanding checks	569
Deposits in transit	802
NSF check	56
Bank service charges	35
Note collection	500
Interest on note	90

    J By J Corporation
    Bank Reconciliation
    June 30, 2010

Date	Account Titles	Debit	Credit

2. Please refer to The Bon-Ton Stores, Inc. financial statements at the end of this study guide for information for answering the following questions. Don't forget to use the **Decision Toolkit** approach for help in the problem-solving.

a. What is the name of the first current asset on the company's balance sheet? Please explain the two components. (SO5)

b. On a percentage basis, how much did Cash and Cash Equivalents increase or decrease from 2006 to 2007? (SO5)

c. Does Bon-Ton discuss cash anywhere in the notes to the financial statements? (SO5)

SOLUTIONS TO SELF-TEST

Completion

1. safeguard, enhance, increase, ensure
2. Sarbanes-Oxley Act of 2002
3. check
4. NSF (not sufficient funds)
5. Miscellaneous Expense
6. bank, cash
7. Treasury bills or commercial paper or money market funds
8. receivables, liabilities
9. financing
10. Cash Over and Short

Multiple Choice

1. b   Only one person should have responsibility for a task, and custody and record-keeping should always be separated. Internal verification is a critical function, certainly not a waste of resources.
2. d   The use of prenumbered documents is very important.
3. c   Using one person for record-keeping and physical custody of assets violates segregation of duties, while leaving cash in an unlocked drawer violates physical control of the asset.
4. d
5. b   The outstanding check and the deposit in transit are dealt with on the balance per bank side, and the service charge is subtracted from the balance per books side.
6. a   The bank service charge and NSF check are subtracted from the balance per books side, and the deposit in transit is added to the balance per bank statement side.
7. c $1,250 - $102 - $27 + $850
8. a $1,900 - $20 - $100 + $360 The check should have been recorded as an addition of $620, not $260, and the extra $360 must be added in.
9. b   The journal entry is:

Cash	530	
Note Receivable		500
Interest Revenue		30

10. c
11. a $1,000 + $3,000 + $5,000. Postage stamps are office supplies or are expensed when purchased; Treasury bills are investments.
12. a   Cash does not appear on the income statement or the statement of retained earnings.

13. d   To be included in Cash and Cash Equivalents, cash must be unrestricted. It certainly is not a liability and is not noncurrent since it will be used within the next year.

14. a   A money order is considered to be cash.

15. b

16. c   Keeping spare cash on hand or in a non-interest-bearing account is not taking advantage of cash's interest-earning ability. It is unwise to invest in illiquid investments because they cannot be converted into cash when the need arises.

17. a   The cash receipts section lists receipts from the company's principal sources of revenue, and the cash disbursements section deals with payments, not receipts. There is no cash investments section.

18. b   The question deals with payments, not receipts, and there is no cash investments section. The financing section deals with borrowing money and repaying both principal and interest.

19. c   Accounts Receivable is not involved, and there typically is no "Petty Cash Expense" account.

20. a   The journal entry is:

Various expense accounts	608	
Cash		602
Cash Over and Short		6

Problems

1.

J By J Corporation
Bank Reconciliation
June 30, 2010

Balance per bank statement		$2,417
Add: Deposits in transit		802
		3,219
Less: Outstanding checks		569
Adjusted cash balance per bank		$2,650
Cash balance per books		$2,151
Add: Note collection	$500	
Interest on note	90	590
		2,741
Less: NSF check	56	
Bank service charges	35	91
Adjusted cash balance per books		$2,650

Journal entries are recorded only for the "cash balance per books" side of the bank reconciliation. Bank personnel record journal entries for the "balance per bank" side.

June 30	Cash	590	
	Notes Receivable		500
	Interest Revenue		90
	(To record collection of note and interest)		
	Accounts Receivable	56	
	Miscellaneous Expense	35	
	Cash		91
	(To record NSF check and bank service charges)		

2. All dollar amounts are in thousands.

a. The first current asset on the balance sheet is "Cash and cash equivalents." Cash is, of course, any item that a bank will accept at face value for deposit and includes checking accounts, savings accounts, coins and currency, travelers' checks, and money orders. Cash equivalents are short-term, highly liquid investments that are both readily convertible to amounts of cash and so near their maturity that their market value is relatively insensitive to changes in interest rates.

b. The amount decreased by 14.1% from 2006 to 2007. This is computed in the following way: $24,733 - $21,238 = $3,495 ÷ $24,733 = 14.1\%$ (rounded),

c. There is a brief discussion of "cash equivalents" in the first note to the financial statements, "Summary of Significant Accounting Policies," found on page F-7 of the company's 2007 10-K report on the following Web site: http://investors.bonton.com/annuals/cfm. (The notes are found immediately following the consolidated statements of cash flows.) The company defines cash equivalents as "highly liquid short-term investments with maturities of three months or less at the time of purchase." The note also says that cash equivalents are "generally overnight money market investments."

17

CHAPTER **8**

Reporting and Analyzing Receivables

CHAPTER OVERVIEW

In this chapter you will learn how to recognize and value accounts receivable, including how to record both estimated and actual bad debts. You'll learn about notes receivable, including how to determine the maturity date, how to compute interest, and how to write journal entries for both the honoring and dishonoring of notes. Lastly, you will learn about the issues involved in managing receivables.

REVIEW OF SPECIFIC STUDY OBJECTIVES

SO1. Identify the different types of receivables.

- The term **"receivables" refers to amounts due from individuals and companies**: They are <u>claims expected to be collected in cash</u>. Receivables are often one of the largest assets for a company and are one of the most liquid assets.

- **Accounts receivable** are <u>amounts owed by customers on account</u> and result from the sale of goods and services.

- **Notes receivable** are <u>claims for which formal instruments of credit are issued as evidence of the debt</u>. Unlike accounts receivable, notes receivable involve receipt of interest from the debtor. Notes and accounts receivable resulting from sales transactions are called <u>trade receivables</u>.

A   **Other receivables include non-trade receivables** such as <u>interest receivable, loans to company officers, advances to employees, and income taxes refundable.</u> They are classified separately from accounts and notes receivable on the balance sheet.

SO2.   Explain how accounts receivable are recognized in the accounts.

A   For a **service organization**, accounts receivable are <u>recorded when service is provided on account.</u>

A   For a **merchandiser**, accounts receivable are <u>recorded at the point of sale of merchandise on account.</u>

A   Receivables are **reduced as a result of sales discounts, cash received, and sales returns**.

A   **Some retailers issue their own credit cards**, affording them interest revenue if the card holder doesn't pay the balance due by the payment due date.

SO3.   Describe the methods used to account for bad debts.

A   **Receivables are reported on the balance sheet as a current asset**, but as will be discussed, the amount at which they are reported can be problematic. If a credit customer cannot pay his bill, then the credit loss is recorded as Bad Debts Expense, an income statement account.

A   There are **two methods of accounting for uncollectible accounts**: the <u>direct write-off method</u> and the <u>allowance method.</u>

A   Under the **direct write-off method**, the following entry is written <u>when a specific customer's account is uncollectible:</u>

Bad Debts Expense
      Accounts Receivable
(To write off an uncollectible account)

<u>Bad debts expense will show only actual losses, and accounts receivable will be reported at its gross amount on the balance sheet.</u> Because revenues might be recorded in one period while the expense might be recorded in the next period, the **direct write-off method has the potential for violating the matching principle**. <u>Unless bad debt losses are insignificant, this method is not acceptable for financial reporting purposes.</u>

A   The **allowance method is used when bad debts are material in amount**. A feature of this method is that <u>uncollectible accounts receivable are estimated and matched against sales in the same account period in which the sales occurred.</u>

⅄   The adjusting **journal entry to record estimated uncollectibles** is as follows:

Bad Debts Expense
            Allowance for Doubtful Accounts
(To record estimate of uncollectible accounts)

Bad Debts Expense appears on the income statement as an operating expense (usually as a selling expense). **Allowance for Doubtful Accounts** appears on the balance sheet as a contra account to Accounts Receivable. When it is subtracted from accounts receivable, the difference is the cash (net) realizable value of the accounts receivable.

The number in this journal entry is purely an estimate: At this point the company does not know which customer will not pay his bill. Failure to write the entry would violate the matching principle. Recording this entry keeps the matching principle in operation.

⅄   The **journal entry to record the write-off of an uncollectible account** is as follows:

Allowance for Doubtful Accounts
            Accounts Receivable
(To write off an uncollectible account)

Bad Debts Expense is not used in this entry because it was used in the adjusting journal entry (in order to match revenues of the period to their related expense). The number in this entry is an actual, not an estimated, number: at this point the company knows which customer is not paying his bill and the exact dollar amount of the bill.

Proper authorization of a write-off is critical. The entry to record a cash collection on an account requires a debit to Cash and a credit to Accounts Receivable. If an employee wished to steal money from customers paying on their accounts and to hide it from the company, then the employee could use the write-off entry. In each case, the cash collection and the write-off, the credit is to Accounts Receivable, thereby closing out that account balance. The write-off entry would allow the employee to steal the cash and to close out the customer's account balance.

Cash realizable value is the same after a write-off as it was before a write-off because both accounts receivable and the allowance account are reduced by the same amount.

∧   **Two journal entries are required to record the recovery of an amount previously written off**: The first reinstates the customer's account, and the second records the cash collection.

Accounts Receivable
       Allowance for Doubtful Accounts
(To reverse write-off of an account)
Cash
       Accounts Receivable
(To record collection on account)

The first entry is simply a reversal of the original write-off entry. While the net effect of the two entries is a debit to Cash and a credit to the allowance account, it is important to reinstate the receivable and then show its collection to maintain an information trail on the customer.

∧   **One way to estimate the amount used in the adjusting entry for uncollectible accounts** is the <u>percentage of receivables basis</u> which provides an estimate of the cash realizable value of the receivables as well as a reasonable matching of expense to revenue. The company prepares an <u>aging schedule</u> in which customer balances are classified by the length of time they have been unpaid. A percentage is applied to each class of unpaid receivables: the longer the period unpaid, the higher the percentage. Consider the following example. Edison Company aged its receivables and computed that <u>estimated uncollectible receivables totaled $2,500.</u> At the time the <u>Allowance for Doubtful Accounts had a credit balance of $300.</u> The required adjusting entry is:

Bad Debts Expense   2,200
       Allowance for Doubtful Accounts   2,200
(To record estimate of uncollectible
  accounts)

The Allowance account must have $2,500 in it <u>after</u> the adjusting entry is written. Since there is already a credit balance of $300, $2,200 must be added to the account to bring it up to that balance.

If the <u>Allowance account had had a $400 debit balance</u> in it before adjustment, then the adjusting entry would have been:

Bad Debts Expense   2,900
       Allowance for Doubtful Accounts   2,900
(To record estimate of uncollectible
  accounts)

Remember that the Allowance account must have $2,500 in it <u>after</u> the adjusting entry is written. If there is a debit balance of $400, then the account must be credited for $2,900 in order to have an overall credit balance of $2,500.

SO4.   Compute the maturity date of and interest on notes receivable.

⋏   A **promissory note** is a <u>written promise to pay a specified amount of money on demand or at a definite time</u>. The **maker** of a note is the <u>party making the promise to pay</u>; the **payee** is the <u>party to whom payment is to be made</u>.

⋏   **Notes receivable give the holder a stronger legal claim** to assets than do accounts receivable; both types of receivables can easily be sold to another party. The majority of notes arise from lending transactions.

⋏   The **maturity date of a note** is the date on which the principal and interest (maturity value) are due. If the <u>life of a note is expressed in months</u>, then the due date is found by counting the months from the date of issue. A three-month note issued on September 1 is due on December 1. If the <u>due date is expressed in terms of days</u>, then it is necessary to count the exact number of days to determine the maturity date (this means that you must know how many days are in each month). A 90-day note issued on April 12 is due on July 11. There are 18 days left in April (simply subtract the issuance date, 12, from 30), 31 in May, and 30 in June, giving a total of 79 days. Eleven more days gives the due date of July 11.

⋏   The **due date may be stated in one of three ways**: <u>on a specific date</u>, <u>at the end of a stated period</u>, or <u>on demand</u>.

⋏   The **formula for computing interest** is as follows:

<u>Interest = Principal x Rate x Time</u>

The principal is the face value of the note, the rate is the annual interest rate, and the time is a fraction (in terms of one year). The <u>interest on a $12,000, 90-day note with an interest rate of 10% is $300</u>, computed as follows:

$300 = $12,000 x 10% x 90/360

Although the number of days in a year is 365, the denominator of the fraction is 360 for a variety of reasons, one of which is that the calculation becomes easier. The fraction 90/360 can be reduced to 1/4, which simplifies the computation. Most financial institutions use 365 in the denominator. It is easy to make a calculator mistake when keying in the interest rate. Either key in "10" and then the percent key, or key in ".10."

⋏   A **note receivable** is <u>recorded at its face value</u>, and <u>no interest revenue is recorded when the note is accepted</u>. Interest is a rental charge for the use of money, and only a very immaterial amount of time has elapsed on the day the note is accepted. <u>If a note is exchanged for cash</u>, then the entry is a debit to Notes Receivable and a credit to Cash. <u>If a note is accepted in settlement of an open account</u>, then the entry is a debit to Notes Receivable and a credit to Accounts Receivable.

⋏   **Short-term notes receivable** are <u>reported at their cash (net) realizable value</u>. The notes receivable allowance account is Allowance for Doubtful Accounts. **Long-term notes receivable** pose additional estimation problems; determining the proper allowance is more difficult than it is for short-term notes.

SO5.   Describe the entries to record the disposition of notes receivable.

⋏   **A note may be held until its maturity date**, at which time both principal and interest are due. Occasionally a **maker defaults on a note**. In some cases a **note may be sold by the holder before its maturity date**.

⋏   **A note is honored** if it is <u>paid in full at the maturity date</u>. Consider again the note mentioned above: $12,000, 90-day note with an interest rate of 10%, with total interest due of $300. On the maturity date, the holder records the following journal entry:

Cash	12,300	
Notes Receivable		12,000
Interest Revenue		300
(To record collection of note)		

If the note had been issued on December 1 and the holder had a December 31 year-end, then the holder would have accrued interest earned (though not yet received in cash) on December 31 with the following entry:

Interest Receivable	100	
Interest Revenue		100
(To record accrued interest:		
$12,000 x .10 x 30/360)		

On the maturity date, March 1 (assuming that the year is not a leap year), the following entry would be recorded:

Cash	12,300	
Notes Receivable		12,000
Interest Receivable		100
Interest Revenue		200

⋏   **A note is dishonored** if it <u>is not paid in full at maturity</u>. If the $12,000, 10%, 90-day note had not been paid on March 1, then the following journal entry would have been required:

Accounts Receivable	12,300	
Notes Receivable		12,000
Interest Revenue		200
Interest Receivable		100

While the note no longer has legal validity on the due date, the holder of the note records the entire amount as a receivable, signaling his intention to try to collect from the maker of the note. If the holder later determines that the account is not collectible, then he will write off the account by debiting the Allowance account and crediting Accounts Receivable.

SO6. Explain the statement presentation of receivables.

⋏ **Short-term receivables** are a <u>current asset presented below temporary investments on the balance sheet</u>. They are presented at their cash realizable value. Notes receivable are listed before accounts receivable because they are more liquid (near to cash).

⋏ **Bad Debts Expense** appears <u>on the income statement as an operating expense (in the selling expense section)</u>. **Interest Revenue** is also an <u>income statement item, shown as an Other Revenues and Gains item</u>.

⋏ **A company must disclose any particular problem with receivables, such as significant risk of uncollectible accounts**.

SO7. Describe the principles of sound accounts receivable management.

⋏ **Managing receivables** involves <u>five steps</u>:
1. Determine to whom to extend credit.
2. Establish a payment period.
3. Monitor collections.
4. Evaluate the receivables balance.
5. Accelerate cash receipts from receivables when necessary.

⋏ **Determining who receives credit** is a <u>critical issue for a company</u>. If a credit policy is too generous, then the company may extend credit to risky customers. If the policy is too tight, then it may lose sales. If a **company requires references from new customers**, then it must check out the references before it extends credit and periodically after it extends credit to monitor the financial health of customers.

⋏ When a company **establishes a payment period**, it must make sure to communicate the policy to customers. The payment period should be consistent with the period offered by competitors.

⋏ In order to **monitor collections**, a company should prepare an <u>aging schedule</u> which helps in the following ways: it helps to establish the allowance for bad debts; it aids estimation of the timing of future cash inflows; and it provides information about the collection experience of the company, identifying problem accounts. A company should disclose in the notes to the financial statements a **concentration of credit risk**, which is a <u>threat of nonpayment from a single customer or class of customers that could adversely affect the company's financial health</u>.

SO8.   Identify ratios to analyze a company's receivables.

⋏   To help **evaluate its receivables balance, a company computes the receivables turnover ratio**, computed by <u>dividing net credit sales by average net receivables</u>. (Average receivables are computed by adding together the beginning and ending balances of receivables and dividing the sum by two.) If net credit sales total $25,000 and average receivables total $5,000, then the receivables turnover ratio is 5 times, meaning that the company collects its receivables 5 times during the accounting period.

⋏   This ratio <u>measures the number of times receivables are collected during the period</u>. A decreasing ratio should be of concern to a company, particularly if its competitors' ratios are holding steady or increasing.

⋏   To compute the **average collection period**, the company <u>divides the receivables turnover ratio into 365</u>. Using the numbers above, the average collection period is 73 days (365 ÷ 5). A <u>general rule is that the collection period should not greatly exceed the credit term period</u>.

SO9.   Describe methods to accelerate the receipt of cash from receivables.

⋏   A **company frequently sells its receivables to another company to shorten the operating cycle**. There are <u>three reasons for the sale of receivables</u>: they may be a very large asset that a company wishes to convert to cash; they may be the only reasonable source of cash; and billing and collection are time-consuming and costly for companies.

⋏   A company may sell its receivables to a **factor**, which is a <u>finance company or bank that buys receivables from businesses for a fee and then collects the payments directly from the customers</u>. The factor charges a fee, of course, which reduces the amount that a company receives for its receivables. If a company factors $100,000 of receivables for a service charge of 3%, then the following entry is recorded:

Cash	97,000	
Service Charge Expense	3,000	
Accounts Receivable		100,000
(To record the sale of accounts		
receivable)		

The Service Charge Expense is classified as a selling expense if the company sells receivables frequently; otherwise, it may be reported as an Other Expenses and Losses item.

⋏   A **retailer may allow its customers to use credit cards to charge purchases**, and its acceptance of a national credit card is <u>another form of selling the receivable</u> by the retailer. Use of such credit cards translates to more sales with zero bad debts for the retailer.

⋏ **Sales resulting from the use of VISA and MasterCard are considered cash sales by the retailer**. Issuing banks charge the retailer a fee. If a jewelry store sells $5,000 of jewelry to customers using bank credit cards and its bank charges a fee of 4%, then the jewelry store records the following entry after depositing the credit card slips:

Cash	4,800	
Service Charge Expense	200	
Sales		5,000
(To record credit card sales)		

CHAPTER SELF-TEST

As you work the exercises and problems, remember to use the **Decision Toolkit** discussed and used in the text:

1. Decision Checkpoints: at this point you ask a question.

2. Info Needed for Decision: you make a choice regarding the information needed to answer the question.

3. Tool to Use for Decision: at this point you review just what the information chosen in step 2 does for the decision-making process.

4. How to Evaluate Results: you perform evaluation of information for answering the question.

Note: The notation (SO1) means that the question was drawn from study objective number one.

Matching

Please write the letters of the following terms in the spaces to the left of the definitions.

a. Allowance method
b. Average collection period
c. Cash (net) realizable value
d. Credit risk ratio
e. Direct write-off method
f. Factor

g. Maker
h. Non-trade receivables
i. Notes receivable
j. Payee
k. Receivables turnover ratio

_____ 1. (SO3) Amount expected to be received in cash.

_____ 2. (SO4) The party in a promissory note who has issued the promise to pay.

_____ 3. (SO3) A method of accounting for bad debts that involves expensing accounts at the point they are determined to be uncollectible.

_____ 4. (SO8) A measure of the liquidity of receivables, computed by dividing net credit sales by average net receivables.

_____ 5. (SO9) A finance company or bank that buys receivables from businesses.

_____ 6. (SO1) Receivables that do not result from sales transactions.

_____ 7. (SO3) A method of accounting for bad debts that involves estimating uncollectible accounts at the end of each period.

_____ 8. (SO1) Claims for which formal instruments of credit are issued.

_____ 9. (SO4) The party to whom payment of a promissory note is to be made.

_____ 10. (SO8) The average amount of time that a receivable is outstanding.

Multiple Choice

Please circle the correct answer.

1. (SO1) Accounts and notes receivable that result from sales transactions are called:
   a. other receivables.
   b. non-trade receivables.
   c. trade receivables.
   d. noncurrent receivables.

2. (SO1) Interest receivable and loans to company officers are included in:
   a. non-trade receivables.
   b. trade receivables.
   c. notes receivable.
   d. accounts receivable.

3.   (SO2)   For a service organization, a receivable is recorded when:
    a.   the customer pays the bill.
    b.   when service is provided on account.
    c.   thirty days after service is provided.
    d.   when the bill is sent to the customer one week after service is provided.

4.   (SO3)   If a company uses the allowance method for uncollectible accounts, then the entry to record estimated uncollectibles is:
    a.   Bad Debts Expense
            Accounts Receivable
    b.   Allowance for Doubtful Accounts
            Accounts Receivable
    c.   Accounts Receivable
            Allowance for Doubtful Accounts
    d.   Bad Debts Expense
            Allowance for Doubtful Accounts

5.   (SO3)   If a company uses the allowance method for uncollectible accounts, then the entry to record the write-off of an uncollectible account is:
    a.   Bad Debts Expense
            Accounts Receivable
    b.   Allowance for Doubtful Accounts
            Accounts Receivable
    c.   Accounts Receivable
            Allowance for Doubtful Accounts
    d.   Bad Debts Expense
            Allowance for Doubtful Accounts

6.   (SO3)   If a company uses the allowance method for uncollectible accounts, then the entry to record the reinstatement of an account previously written off will include a:
    a.   debit to Accounts Receivable.
    b.   credit to Accounts Receivable.
    c.   debit to Allowance for Doubtful Accounts.
    d.   debit to Cash.

7.   (SO3)   Before a write-off of an uncollectible account, Accounts Receivable had a $10,000 balance, and the Allowance for Doubtful Accounts had a $500 balance. After a write-off of $100, the cash (net) realizable value is:
    a. $10,000.
    b. $9,500.
    c. $9,400.
    d. $9,300.

8.   (SO3) The Allowance for Doubtful Accounts has a $400 credit balance. An aging schedule shows that total estimated bad debts is $3,600. The adjusting entry will require a debit and a credit for:
a. $4,000.
b. $3,600.
c. $3,200.
d.   some other amount.

9.   (SO3) The Allowance for Doubtful Accounts has a $400 debit balance. An aging schedule shows that total estimated bad debts is $3,600. The adjusting entry will require a debit and a credit for:
a. $4,000.
b. $3,600.
c. $3,200.
d.   some other amount.

10.   (SO4) A 90-day promissory note is issued on September 15. Its maturity date is:
a.   December 16.
b.   December 15.
c.   December 14.
d.   December 13.

11.   (SO5) A 120-day promissory note is issued on April 4. Its maturity date is:
a.   August 1.
b.   August 2.
c.   August 3.
d.   August 4.

12.   (SO4) A company issues a 120-day, 9% note for $30,000. The total interest on the note is:
a. $90.
b. $900.
c. $2,700.
d. $3,000.

13.   (SO4) A company issues a 60-day, 8% note for $18,000. The total interest on the note is:
a. $ 240.
b. $ 480.
c. $1,440.
d. $3,000.

14.   (SO5) The journal entry written on the maturity date by the holder of a 3-month, 12%, $15,000 note, assuming that the note is paid in full, will include a:
a.   debit to Cash for $15,000.
b.   credit to Notes Receivable for $15,450.
c.   debit to Interest Revenue for $450.

d.   debit to Cash for $15,450.

15.   (SO5)   A company holds a 120-day, 10%, $21,000 note which was <u>not</u> paid in full on the maturity date. The journal entry on the maturity date will include a:
a.   debit to Accounts Receivable for $21,700.
b.   credit to Notes Receivable for $21,700.
c.   debit to Cash for $21,700.
d.   debit to Notes Receivable for $21,000.

16.   (SO5)   A company holds a 90-day, 12%, $18,000 note which it received on December 1. The adjusting entry for this note on December 31 includes a:
a.   debit to Interest Receivable for $540.
b.   credit to Notes Receivable for $180.
c.   credit to Interest Revenue for $180.
d.   credit to Interest Revenue for $540.

17.   (SO5)   A company holds a 60-day, 10%, $24,000 note which it received on November 16. The adjusting entry for this note on December 31 includes a:
a.   debit to Notes Receivable for $300.
b.   debit to Interest Receivable for $300.
c.   debit to Interest Revenue for $300.
d.   debit to Interest Receivable for $400.

18.   (SO6)   Which of the following is the correct sequence for receivables on the balance sheet?
a.   Notes receivable, other receivables, accounts receivable
b.   Accounts receivable, notes receivable, other receivables
c.   Notes receivable, accounts receivable, other receivables
d.   Accounts receivable, other receivables, notes receivable

19.   (SO7)   A threat of nonpayment from a single customer or class of customers that could adversely affect the financial health of a company is called:
a.   accounts receivable concentration risk.
b.   notes receivable concentration risk.
c.   credit risk.
d.   a concentration of credit risk.

20.   (SO8)   Net credit sales are $800,000, average net receivables total $150,000, average inventory totals $200,000,and the allowance for doubtful accounts totals $8,000. The receivables turnover ratio is:
a.   100 times.
b.   5.33 times.
c.   4.00 times.
d.   1.33 times.

21.   (SO8)   Please use the information from number 20. The average collection period is:
- a.   100 days.
- b.   75.0 days.
- c.   68.5 days.
- d.   5.33 days.

22.   (SO9)   Kerrison Company sold $6,000 of merchandise to customers who charged their purchases with a bank credit card. Kerrison's bank charges it a 4% fee. The journal entry to record the credit card sales will include a:
- a.   debit to Cash for $5,760.
- b.   credit to Sales for $5,760.
- c.   debit to Cash for $6,000.
- d.   credit to Service Charge Expense for $240.

Problems

1. Morrison Corporation uses the allowance method for estimating uncollectible accounts. Please record journal entries for the following items (all are SO3):

   a. At the end of the accounting period on June 30, Morrison prepares an aging schedule of accounts receivable which shows total estimated bad debts of $5,200. On this date the Allowance for Doubtful Accounts has a debit balance of $300, and Accounts Receivable has a balance of $85,000.

   b. On July 5, Morrison receives word that Sperry Company has declared bankruptcy, and Morrison writes off their account receivable of $800.

   c. On September 12, Sperry Company notifies Morrison that it can pay its $800 debt and includes a check for the entire amount.

Date	Account Titles	Debit	Credit

d. What is the cash (net) realizable value of accounts receivable after the entry in "a" is written? What is the cash realizable value after the write-off in "b"?

2. Please refer to The Bon-Ton Stores, Inc. financial statements at the end of this study guide for information for answering the following questions. Don't forget to use the **Decision Toolkit** approach for help in the problem-solving.

a. What is the dollar amount of receivables on Bon-Ton's 2007 balance sheet? (SO1)

b. Assume that Bon-Ton did have accounts receivable on its balance sheet. If the 2007 balance was $440,500 and the 2006 balance was $400,750, what is the percentage increase or decrease in accounts receivable from 2006 to 2007? (SO1)

c. Using the assumed numbers for accounts receivable in "b," did Bon-Ton collect its receivables in a timely fashion in 2007? (SO8)

SOLUTIONS TO SELF-TEST

Matching

1.	c		6.	h
2.	g		7.	a
3.	e		8.	i
4.	k		9.	j
5.	f		10.	b

Multiple Choice

1. c   Other and nontrade receivables are basically the same thing and arise from such items as interest and loans to company officers. Accounts receivable are always current assets.

2. a   Trade receivables arise from sales transactions, notes receivable are written promises and usually include interest, and accounts receivable are amounts owed by customers on account.

3. b   A receivable is recorded <u>before</u> the customer pays the bill. The receivable should be recorded when the service is performed, not at some other specific date.

4. d   The answer in "a" is the write-off of a debt under the direct write-off method. The answer in "b" is the write-off of a debt under the allowance method. The answer in "c" is the reinstatement of a written-off account under the allowance method.

5. b   The answer in "a" is the write-off of a debt under the direct write-off method. The answer in "c" is the reinstatement of a written-off account under the allowance method. The answer in "d" is the adjusting entry for bad debts under the allowance method.

6. a   The entry is:
        Accounts Receivable
            Allowance for Doubtful Accounts

7. b   The cash realizable value is $9,500 ($10,000 - $500) before the write-off and $9,500 ($9,900 - $400) after.

8. c $3,600 is the amount which must be in the Allowance account after adjustment. Since it already has a credit balance of $400, only $3,200 is needed to raise the balance to $3,600.

9. a $3,600 is the amount which must be in the Allowance account after adjustment. Since it has a debit balance of $400, $4,000 is needed to raise the balance to $3,600.

10. c   September   15 days left
        October   31 days
        November   30 days
        December   <u>14 days</u>
                         <u>90 days</u>

11. b   April   26 days left
        May   31 days
        June   30 days
        July   31 days
        August   <u> 2 days</u>
                         120 days

12. b $30,000 x 9% x 120/360

13. a $18,000 x 8% x 60/360

14.   d   The journal entry is:
Cash   15,450
      Notes Receivable   15,000
      Interest Revenue   450
    ($15,000 x .12 x 3/12 = $450)

15.   a   The journal entry is:
Accounts Receivable   21,700
      Notes Receivable   21,000
      Interest Revenue   700
    ($21,000 x .10 x 120/360 = $700)

1.1.1

16.   c   The journal entry is:
Interest Receivable   180
      Interest Revenue   180
    ($18,000 x .12 x 30/360)

17.   b   The journal entry is:
Interest Receivable   300
      Interest Revenue   300
    ($24,000 x .10 x 45/360)

18.   c
19.   d
20.   b   Net cr. sales ÷ Av. net rec. = $800,000 ÷ $150,000 = 5.33 times
21.   c   365 ÷ rec. turnover ratio = 365 ÷ 5.33 = 68.5 days
22.   a   The journal entry is:
Cash   5,760
Service Charge Expense   240

      Sales   6,000

Problems

1.

a.   June 30   Bad Debts Expense   5,500
      Allowance for Doubtful Accounts   5,500
    (To record the estimate of uncollectible
     accounts: $300 + $5,200)

b.   July 5   Allowance for Doubtful Accounts   800
      Accounts Receivable—Sperry   800
    (To write off the Sperry account)

c.   Sep. 12   Accounts Receivable—Sperry   800
      Allowance for Doubtful Accounts   800
    (To reinstate Sperry account)
         1.1.1.1   <u>Cash 800</u>
      Accounts Receivable—Sperry   800
    (To record collection on Sperry account)

d.

	Before Write-Off	After Write-off
Accounts Receivable	$85,000	$84,200
– Allowance	5,200	4,400
Cash Realiz. Value	$79,800	$79,800

The cash realizable value does not change because both accounts are reduced by the same amount.

2.

a. This is an interesting question because a close inspection of the balance sheet reveals that Bon-Ton has no receivables: neither accounts receivable nor notes receivable. To investigate why this is so, you must read the first note to the financial statements, "Summary of Significant Accounting Policies," found on page F-7 of the company's 2007 10-K on the following Web site: http://investors.bonton.com/annuals/cfm. (The notes begin immediately after the consolidated statements of cash flows.) In the area entitled "Revolving Charge Accounts" is disclosed that in July 2005 the company sold all its proprietary credit card accounts and related receivables.

b. All dollar amounts are in thousands.
There is an increase of 9.9%, computed as follows:
$440,500 – $400,750 = $39,750 ÷ $400,750 = 9.9% (rounded)

c. To answer this question, you must compute the receivables turnover ratio, calculated by dividing net credit sales by average net receivables, and the average collection period, calculated by dividing 365 by the receivables turnover ratio.

To compute average receivables, the 2007 and the 2006 receivables balances are added together and divided by 2. In addition, you need to assume that all sales are on credit.

Average receivables = ($440,500 + $400,750) ÷ 2 = $420,625

$3,365,912 ÷ $420,625 = 8 times

This ratio indicates that Bon-Ton collects its receivables 8 times during the accounting period. To calculate how many days this takes, you compute the average collection period.

Average collection period = 365 ÷ receivables turnover ratio

365 ÷ 8 times = 45.6 days (rounded)

Remember that one ratio by itself is not very helpful. You must compare it either with Bon-Ton's numbers for prior years or with industry averages to see how the company is performing. It would also be useful to compare it to their credit terms.

CHAPTER 9

Reporting and Analyzing Long-Lived Assets

CHAPTER OVERVIEW

In this chapter you will learn how to account for long-lived assets, such as buildings and machinery. You'll learn about the amounts at which they are recorded in the accounting records and how to allocate their cost to expense using periodic depreciation. You'll learn how to dispose of plant assets and methods used by companies for evaluating their use. You will also learn about intangible assets, long-lived assets that have no physical substance, and finally, how all these assets are reported on the balance sheet.

REVIEW OF SPECIFIC STUDY OBJECTIVES

Plant assets are <u>resources that have physical substance, are used in the operations of a business, and are not intended for sale to customers</u>. Other names for these assets are property, plant, and equipment; plant and equipment; and fixed assets. Of the following four classes of these assets, land is the only which does not decline in value (service potential):

1. Land
2. Land improvements, such as driveways and parking lots
3. Buildings, such as offices and factories
4. Equipment, such as office furniture, cash registers, and delivery equipment.

SO1. Describe how the cost principle applies to plant assets.

    ⋏   **Plant assets are recorded at cost**, which consists of <u>all expenditures necessary to acquire the asset and make it ready for its intended use.</u>

⋏   **Revenue expenditures** are <u>costs expensed immediately, not included in the cost of a plant asset</u>.

⋏   **Capital expenditures** are those <u>costs included in a plant asset account, not expensed immediately</u>.

⋏   **Cost** is <u>measured by the cash paid in a cash transaction or by the cash equivalent price paid when noncash assets are used in payment</u>. The **cash equivalent price** is <u>equal to the fair market value of the asset given up or the fair market value of the asset received, whichever is more clearly determinable</u>.

⋏   The **cost of land** includes <u>the cash purchase price, closing costs, real estate brokers' commissions, and accrued property taxes and other liens assumed by the purchaser</u>. All costs incurred in making land ready for its intended use increase the Land account: clearing, draining, filling, grading, and razing old buildings are included.

⋏   The **cost of land improvements** includes <u>all expenditures necessary to make the improvements ready for their intended use</u>. For example, building a parking lot includes paving, fencing, and lighting.

⋏   The **cost of buildings** includes <u>all expenditures relating to the purchase or construction of a building</u>. If a **building is purchased**, then the costs include the purchase price, closing costs, and brokers' commissions, as well as remodeling costs. If a **building is constructed**, then costs include the contract price, architects' fees, building permits, excavation costs, and interest costs incurred to finance the project (the inclusion of the latter is limited to the construction period).

⋏   The **cost of equipment** includes <u>the cash purchase price, sales taxes, freight charges, and insurance during shipping (if paid by the purchaser), as well as assembling, installation of, and testing of the unit</u>. Fees that occur, and recur, after the equipment is operational, such as vehicle licenses and accident insurance, are debited to an expense account or treated as a prepaid asset.

⋏   **Companies often lease assets.** In a lease, a **lessor** agrees to allow another party, the **lessee**, to use the asset for an agreed period of time at an agreed price. Some **advantages of leasing** include <u>reduced risk of obsolescence, low down payment, shared tax advantages, and non-reporting of assets and liabilities</u>. In an **operating lease,** the lessee uses the asset but does not record an asset or a liability. Under a **capital lease**, the lessee uses the asset and does record an asset and a liability.

SO2.   Explain the concept of depreciation.

⋏   **Depreciation** is the <u>process of allocating to expense the cost of a plant asset over its useful (service) life in a rational and systematic manner</u>. It provides a matching of revenues and expenses.

⋏ **Depreciation is a process of cost allocation,** _**not**_ a process of asset valuation. Thus, the book value (cost less accumulated depreciation) may differ significantly from the fair market value of the asset.

⋏ **Land improvements, building, and equipment are depreciable assets,** but land is not a depreciable asset.

⋏ **Depreciable assets lose their utility** because of wear and tear and obsolescence, the process by which an asset becomes out of date before it physically wears out.

⋏ **Depreciation in no way provides cash for the eventual replacement of the asset.**

⋏ **Three factors** affect the computation of depreciation: cost, useful life (an estimate of the productive, or service, life of the asset, expressed in terms of time, units of activity, or units of output), and salvage value (an estimate of the asset's value at the end of its useful life).

SO3. Compute periodic depreciation using the straight-line method, and contrast its expense pattern with those of other methods.

⋏ The **straight-line, declining-balance, and units-of-activity methods** of depreciation are all acceptable under generally accepted accounting principles. Management of a company chooses the method that it feels best measures the asset's contribution to revenue and then applies that method consistently. The straight-line method is the most widely used.

⋏ The **journal entry to record depreciation** is:

Depreciation Expense
  Accumulated Depreciation

Depreciation Expense appears on the income statement, and the Accumulated Depreciation account is a contra-asset account, subtracted from the asset's cost to give its book value.

⋏ Under the **straight-line method**, depreciation is considered to be a function of time, and the same dollar amount of depreciation is taken each full year. Depreciable cost, which is the asset's cost less its salvage value, is divided by the useful life to give the annual depreciation expense. A straight-line rate can also be computed (100% ÷ useful life) and multiplied by the depreciable cost to give the dollar amount of expense.

Consider the **following example**. A company purchased on January 2 for $18,000 a truck with a useful life of 6 years and a salvage value of $3,000. The depreciable cost is $15,000 ($18,000 - $3,000), and annual depreciation is $2,500 (15,000 ÷ 6 years). The straight-line rate is 16.67% (100% ÷ 6 years); multiplying $15,000 by 16.67% also yields $2,500 per year. After 6 years, the total accumulated depreciation is $15,000, and the book value of the asset is $3,000 ($18,000 – $15,000). Note that the book value equals the salvage value after all depreciation is taken. If this asset had been purchased on July 1, then depreciation for the year ended December 31 would have been $1,250 ($2,500 x 6/12).

Л The **declining-balance method** is called an accelerated method because it results in more depreciation in the early years of an asset's life than does the straight-line method. The depreciation expense is lower than under straight-line in the later years of the asset's life. A common way to apply this method is to use a rate that is double the straight-line rate, thus producing double-declining-balance. Just as it is true for straight-line, depreciation under this method is a function of time.

Л With the **units-of-activity method**, useful life is expressed in terms of the total units of production or the use expected from the asset. Units of output, machine hours, miles driven, and hours flown can all be used. This method is excellent for machinery, vehicles, and airplanes.

Л **Under all three methods total depreciation is the same**. The only thing that differs is the timing at which the expense is taken.

Л Computations for declining-balance and units-of-activity are shown in Study Objective 9.

Л For **income tax purposes**, a company may use either straight-line or a method called Modified Accelerated Cost Recovery System (MACRS).

Л A **company must disclose in the notes to the financial statements** its choice of depreciation method.

SO4. Describe the procedure for revising periodic depreciation.

Л **Depreciation must be revised** if wear and tear or obsolescence indicates that annual depreciation is inadequate or excessive.

Л The **change in depreciation** is made in current and future years but not in prior periods. This means that prior years' financial statements do not have to be restated. Continual restatement would undermine confidence in the financial statements.

Л **Significant changes** in estimates must be disclosed in the financial statements or notes to the statements.

Л There are **two possibilities** for how to treat money spent on assets during their useful lives. **Ordinary repairs** are expenditures that maintain the operating efficiency and expected productive life of the asset: they maintain the asset in its current operating condition. These costs are debited to an expense account such as Repair or Maintenance Expense. **Additions and improvements** increase the operating efficiency, productive capacity, or expected useful life of the asset.

Usually material in amount, they improve the asset. These costs are capital expenditures and are debited to the asset account.

⋏ An **impairment** is a permanent decline in the market value of an asset, resulting from obsolescence or market conditions. When this occurs, the asset is written down to its new market value during the year in which the decline in value occurs. The FASB frowns on **earnings management**, which is the practice of delaying recording losses on impairments until a year when the impact on a firm's earnings is minimized. A recent standard requires immediate recognition of a write-down.

SO5.   Explain how to account for the disposal of plant assets.

⋏ Regardless of the method of disposal, **depreciation must be brought up to date, if necessary**. Then, when the disposal journal entry is written, the asset account is credited for its cost, and the related Accumulated Depreciation account is debited.

⋏ If the **disposal is a sale**, then the book value of the asset is compared with the proceeds of the sale. If the proceeds exceed the book value, then there is a **gain on the sale**. If the proceeds are less than the book value, then there is a **loss on the sale**.

Consider the **following example**. A company sells a piece of machinery that cost it $10,000, and which has accumulated depreciation of $6,000, for $5,000. The journal entry to record the sale is as follows:

Cash	5,000	
Accumulated Depreciation	6,000	
Machinery		10,000
Gain on Disposal		1,000

(To record sale of machinery at a gain)

The book value of the asset is $4,000 ($10,000 - $6,000). Since the company received $5,000 for the asset, it sold the asset for a $1,000 gain. **Gain on Disposal** appears in the Other Revenues and Gains section of the income statement.

If the company had sold the asset for $2,000, then it would have incurred a loss of $2,000 ($4,000 book value – $2,000 cash proceeds). The journal entry is as follows:

Cash	2,000	
Accumulated Depreciation	6,000	
Loss on Disposal	2,000	
Machinery		10,000

(To record sale of machinery at a loss)

Loss on Disposal appears in the Other Expenses and Losses section of the income statement.

⋏ If the **disposal is a retirement**, then it is recorded as a sale in which no cash is received. The asset is credited for its cost, Accumulated Depreciation is debited for the proper amount, and a loss is debited for the book value of the asset on the date of retirement. If the asset sold in the two journal entries above is simply retired, then the journal entry is as follows:

Accumulated Depreciation	6,000	
Loss on Disposal	4,000	
Machinery		10,000
(To record retirement of machinery)		

SO6.   Describe methods for evaluating the use of plant assets.

    ⋏   The following are **two measures** used to analyze plant assets.

    ⋏   The **return on assets ratio** is computed by dividing net income by average assets (average assets are calculated by adding the beginning and ending values of assets and dividing by 2). An overall measure of profitability, it indicates the amount of net income generated by each dollar invested in assets. A high ratio is preferable.

    ⋏   The **asset turnover ratio**, computed by dividing net sales by average total assets, indicates how efficiently a company is able to generate sales with a given amount of assets. It shows how many dollars of sales are generated by each dollar invested in assets. The higher the ratio, the more efficiently the company is operating. If the ratio is 1.25 times, then this means that for each dollar invested in assets, the company generates sales of $1.25. Asset turnover ratios vary considerably among industries.

    ⋏   There is an **important relationship between these two ratios and the profit margin ratio** (net income ÷ net sales). Multiplying the profit margin ratio by the asset turnover ratio yields the return on assets ratio.

SO7.   Identify the basic issues related to reporting intangible assets.

    ⋏   **Intangible assets** are rights, privileges, and competitive advantages that result from ownership of long-lived assets that do not possess physical substance. Examples include patents, copyrights, goodwill, franchises, licenses, trademarks and trade names. Intangibles may arise from government grants, purchase of another business, and private monopolistic arrangements.

    ⋏   **Intangible assets are recorded at cost.** If the intangible asset has an indefinite life, its cost should not be amortized. If the intangible asset has a limited life, its cost is amortized in a rational and systematic manner over the useful life of the intangible. The straight-line method is used. The **journal entry to record amortization** includes a debit to Amortization Expense and a credit to the asset account directly: No contra account is used for the credit. The **amortization period** is the shorter of the useful life of the intangible or the legal life of the intangible. If a company purchases a patent with a legal life of 10 years but estimates that the useful life is only 4 years, then the amortization period will be 4 years.

⅄   A **patent** is an exclusive right issued by the United States Patent Office that enables the recipient to manufacture, sell, or otherwise control an invention for a period of 20 years from the date of grant. The **initial cost** of a patent is the cash or cash equivalent price paid to acquire the patent. If the owner of a patent successfully defends the patent in a lawsuit, then the costs of the lawsuit are debited to the Patent account and amortized over the remaining life of the patent.

⅄   **Research and development costs** are expenditures that may lead to patents, copyrights, new processes, and new products. These costs are not intangible assets and are **usually recorded as an expense when incurred**.

⅄   A **copyright** is granted by the federal government, giving the owner the exclusive right to reproduce and sell an artistic or published work. The **legal life** of a copyright is the life of the creator plus 70 years, and the **cost** is the cost of acquiring and defending it.

⅄   A **trademark or trade name** is a word, phrase, jingle, or symbol that distinguishes and identifies a particular enterprise or product. Trademarks and trade names have tremendous value to companies and are vigorously defended. The **legal life** of these intangibles is 20 years, and they may be renewed indefinitely as long as they are in use. If they are **purchased**, then the cost is the purchase price. If they are **developed**, then the cost includes attorney's fees, registration fees, design costs, successful legal defense costs, and other such expenditures. Because trademarks and trade names have indefinite lives, they are not amortized.

⅄   A **franchise** is a contractual agreement under which the franchisor grants the franchisee the right to sell certain products, to render specific services, or to use certain trademarks or trade names, usually within a designated geographic area. Another type of franchise is granted by a governmental body and permits an enterprise to use public property in performing its services. This operating right is called a **license**. Both franchises and licenses may be granted for a definite period of time, an indefinite period, or in perpetuity. **Initial costs associated with the acquisition** are debited to the asset account; after that, annual recurring costs are recorded as operating expenses. In the case of a limited life, a company amortizes the cost of a franchise (or license) as operating expense over the useful life.

⅄   **Goodwill** is recorded only when there is an exchange transaction that involves the purchase of an entire business. In other words, goodwill arises only when one business purchases another. It is the **excess of cost over the fair market value of the net assets (assets minus liabilities) acquired**. Factors giving rise to goodwill include excellent management, employees, customer relations, products, and location. When company A purchases company B, it records the purchased assets and liabilities at their fair market values. Goodwill is not amortized.

SO8.   Indicate how long-lived assets are reported in the financial statements.

⋏ **Plant assets** are shown at their book value in the section entitled <u>Property, Plant, and Equipment</u>. **Intangible assets** appear in a section entitled <u>Intangible Assets</u>.

⋏ There should be **disclosure in the financial statements or in the notes to the statements** of the <u>balances of the major classes of assets and accumulated depreciation by major classes or in total. Depreciation and amortization methods used should be disclosed, as should the amount of expense for the period.</u>

⋏ On the **statement of cash flows**, the <u>investing activities section</u> shows the amount of property, plant, and equipment purchased and the cash received from the sale of such assets during the accounting period.

SO9. Compute periodic depreciation using the declining-balance method and the units-of-activity method. (This objective is discussed in the Chapter 9 appendix in your text.)

⋏ Under the **declining-balance method**, depreciation expense is computed by <u>multiplying the book value of the asset by a rate</u>. **Salvage value is initially ignored in the computations.** Double-declining-balance is one of the forms of this method: the rate is the straight-line rate multiplied by 2. If an asset has a useful life of 5 years, then the straight-line rate is 20% (100% ÷ 5 years). Double that rate is 40%.

Assume that the asset with a 5-year useful life originally cost $50,000 and has a salvage value of $5,000. Depreciation expense for the 5 years will be:

Year	Book Value		Rate		Depr. Exp.
1	$50,000	x	40%	=	$20,000
2	$30,000	x	40%	=	$12,000
3	$18,000	x	40%	=	$ 7,200
4	$10,800	x	40%	=	$ 4,320
5	$ 6,480	x	40%	=	$ 1,480*
					$45,000

* Note that in year 5 only $1,480 of depreciation was taken, even though the book value of $6,480 multiplied by 40% yields $2,592. Remember that book value must equal salvage value at the end of the 5 years, and recording $2,592 of depreciation expense would have violated that. In the final year, a company takes only the dollar amount of depreciation which will make the total depreciation $45,000.

Depreciation under this method is a function of time. Therefore, an asset purchased during the year must have its depreciation prorated. If the asset above had been purchased on April 1, then depreciation for year 1 would have been $15,000 ($50,000 x 40% x 9/12). Book value for year 2 would have been $35,000 ($50,000 – $15,000).

⋏ Under the **units-of-activity method**, a <u>rate per unit is computed and applied to actual units during the accounting period.</u>

A company purchased an asset with a cost of $30,000, a salvage value of $5,000, an estimated useful life of 5 years, and estimated units of output of 50,000. In year 1 the asset produced 12,000 units. Depreciation is computed as follows:

$30,000 – $5,000 = $25,000 depreciable cost
$25,000 ÷ 50,000 units = $.50 per unit
$ .50 per unit x 12,000 actual units = $6,000

Note that the useful life in years is not used in the computation. Note, too, that this method starts with the depreciable cost, just as straight-line depreciation does. Declining-balance, however, ignores salvage value in the initial computation. Since the units-of-activity method is a function of usage and not of time, it is not necessary to prorate depreciation if the asset is purchased at a time other than the beginning of the accounting period.

λ   Remember that **all three methods produce the same total dollar amount of depreciation over the life of an asset**. It is the timing of the expense that differs among the methods.

CHAPTER SELF-TEST

As you work the exercises and problems, remember to use the **Decision Toolkit** discussed and used in the text:

1. Decision Checkpoints: at this point you ask a question.

2. Info Needed for Decision: you make a choice regarding the information needed to answer the question.

3. Tool to Use for Decision: at this point you review just what the information chosen in step 2 does for the decision-making process.

4. How to Evaluate Results: you perform evaluation of information for answering the question.

Note: The notation (SO1) means that the question was drawn from study objective number one.

Completion

Please write in the word or words that will complete the sentence.

1. (SO1)   Costs related to plant assets that are not expensed immediately but are included in a plant asset account are considered _____ expenditures.

2. (SO2)   Depreciation is a process of _____ allocation, not a process of _____ valuation.

3. (SO3)   The cost of an asset less its salvage value is called _____ cost.

4. (SO4) Ordinary   repairs   are   _____   to   a(n)
_____ account.

5. (SO5) If the proceeds from the sale of a plant asset exceed the book value of the asset,
then a _____ on disposal occurs.

6. (SO6) The   return   on   assets   ratio   can   be   computed   by   multiplying   the
_____ _____ ratio   by   the   _____
_____ ratio.

7. (SO7) _____ is the term used to describe the allocation of the cost
of an intangible asset to expense.

8. (SO7) A _____ protects artistic or published work.

9. (SO9) If the useful life of an asset is 8 years, then the straight-line rate is
_____.

10. (SO9) Under the declining-balance method of depreciation, the _____
_____ is initially ignored in determining the amount to which the rate is
applied.

Multiple Choice

Please circle the correct answer.

1. (SO1) Massey Corporation purchased a piece of land for $50,000. It paid
attorney's fees of $5,000 and brokers' commissions of $4,000. An old building on
the land was torn down at a cost of $2,000, and proceeds from the scrap were $500.
The total to be debited to the Land account is:
   a. $61,000.
   b. $60,500.
   c. $59,000.
   d. $50,000.

2. (SO1) Newcome Corporation installed a new parking lot for its employees at a
cost of $10,000. The $10,000 should be debited to:
   a. Repairs and Maintenance Expense.
   b. Land.
   c. Land Improvements.
   d. Parking Lot.

3. (SO1) Luna Company purchased a building for $150,000. Attorneys' fees related
to the purchase were $20,000, while a real estate broker's commission totaled
$9,000. Luna also had to pay $30,000 for remodeling work before the building
could be used. The total to be debited to the Building account is:
   a. $209,000.
   b. $200,000.
   c. $189,000.
   d. $179,000.

4. (SO1)   Oliver Company purchased a piece of equipment for $20,000. It paid sales taxes of $1,200, shipping charges of $500, and insurance during transit of $200. Installation and testing of the new equipment cost $1,000. The total to be debited to the Equipment account is:
   a. $21,200.
   b. $21,900.
   c. $22,200.
   d. $22,900.

5. (SO2)   Which of the following is <u>not</u> a depreciable asset?
   a. Land.
   b. Building.
   c. Driveway.
   d. Equipment.

6. (SO2)   Which of the following is a way to express the useful life of a depreciable asset?
   a. Five years.
   b. Ten thousand machine hours.
   c. Thirty thousand units.
   d. All of the above are expressions of useful life.

7. (SO3)   At the beginning of the year Powers Company purchased a piece of machinery for $50,000. It has a salvage value of $5,000, an estimated useful life of 9 years, and estimated units of output of 90,000 units. Actual units produced during the first year were 11,000. Depreciation expense for the first year under the straight-line method is:
   a. $5,556.
   b. $5,500.
   c. $5,300.
   d. $5,000.

8. (SO3)   Please use the same information from number 7, but assume that Powers Company purchased the equipment on October 1. Using the straight-line method, what will the company record for depreciation expense on December 31?
   a. $5,000.
   b. $2,500.
   c. $1,375.
   d. $1,250.

9. (SO3)   Which of the following statements is correct?
   a. Straight-line depreciation is an accelerated method of depreciation.
   b. The total amount of depreciation for an asset is the same, regardless of the method used.
   c. The total amount of depreciation for an asset differs depending on the method used.
   d. In the later years of an asset's useful life, straight-line depreciation gives lower expense than does declining-balance.

10.   (SO4)   Which of the following statements is correct?
    a.   Once depreciation expense is set, it may never be changed for an asset.
    b.   When a change in estimate for depreciation is required, the change is made to prior periods.
    c.   When a change in estimate for depreciation is required, the change is made in current and future years but not to prior periods.
    d.   When a change in estimate for depreciation is required, the change is made to prior periods and in current and future years.

11.   (SO4)   A permanent decline in the market value of an asset is called:
    a.   an impairment.
    b.   a write-down.
    c.   earnings management.
    d.   a capital expenditure.

12.   (SO5)   A company sold for $3,000 a plant asset that had a cost of $10,000 and accumulated depreciation of $7,500. The company had a:
    a.   loss of $500.
    b.   gain of $500.
    c.   gain of $3,000.
    d.   loss of $7,000.

13.   (SO5)   A company sold for $2,000 a plant asset that had a cost of $10,000 and accumulated depreciation of $7,500. The company had a:
    a.   loss of $500.
    b.   gain of $500.
    c.   gain of $2,000.
    d.   loss of $8,000.

14.   (SO5)   Quick Corporation retired a piece of equipment that had cost $8,000 and had accumulated depreciation of $7,000. The journal entry to record the retirement will include a:
    a.   debit to Gain on Disposal for $1,000.
    b.   credit to Gain on Disposal for $1,000.
    c.   credit to Loss on Disposal for $1,000.
    d.   debit to Loss on Disposal for $1,000.

15.   (SO6)   A company's average total assets are $200,000, net sales is $100,000, and net income is $40,000. The company's return on assets ratio is:
    a.   500%.
    b.   200%.
    c.   50%.
    d.   20%.

16.   (SO6)   A company's average total assets are $200,000, depreciation expense is $10,000, and accumulated depreciation is $60,000. Net sales total $250,000. The asset turnover ratio is:
    a.   .8 times.
    b.   1.25 times.
    c.   3.33 times.
    d.   4.17 times.

17.   (SO7)   Which of the following gives the recipient the right to manufacture, sell, or otherwise control an invention for a period of 20 years?
    a.   Patent.
    b.   Copyright.
    c.   Trademark.
    d.   License.

18.   (SO7)   A company successfully defended its copyright on a piece of literature at a cost of $75,000. The journal entry to record that cost includes a debit to:
    a.   Legal Fees Expense for $75,000.
    b.   Intangible Assets for $75,000.
    c.   Copyright for $75,000.
    d.   Research and Development Expense for $75,000.

19.   (SO7)   At the beginning of the year Righter Company purchased for $10,000 a patent with a legal life of 8 years. Righter estimates that the useful life of the patent will be 4 years. Amortization expense on the patent for the year is:
    a. $2,500.
    b. $1,250.
    c. $588.
    d. $250.

20.   (SO8)   With respect to plant assets, which of the following must be disclosed in the financial statements or notes to the financial statements?
    a.   The balances of major classes of assets.
    b.   Accumulated depreciation by major classes of assets.
    c.   Depreciation methods used.
    d.   All of the above must be disclosed.

21.   (SO9)   On January 3, 2010, Powers Company purchased a piece of machinery for $50,000. It has a salvage value of $5,000, an estimated useful life of 9 years, and estimated units of output of 90,000 units. Actual units produced during the first year were 11,000. Depreciation expense for 2010 under the units-of-activity method is:
    a. $5,556.
    b. $5,500.
    c. $5,300.
    d. $5,000.

22. (SO9) Please use the same information from number 21, but now assume that Powers purchased the machinery on July 1, not at the beginning of the year. On December 31, 2010, what will the company record for depreciation expense if it uses the units-of-activity method and if the machinery produced 6,000 units during the six months?
   a. $3,000.
   b. $1,500.
   c. $5,000.
   d. $2,500.

23. (SO9) On January 4, 2010, Sacks Company purchased a piece of equipment for $20,000. It has a salvage value of $4,000 and an estimated useful life of 8 years. Depreciation expense for 2010 under the double-declining-balance method is:
   a. $5,000.
   b. $4,000.
   c. $2,500.
   d. $2,000.

24. (SO9) Please use the same information from number 23, but now assume that Sacks purchased the equipment on July 1. Depreciation expense for 2010 under the double-declining-balance method is:
   a. $5,000.
   b. $4,000.
   c. $2,500
   d. $2,000.

Problems

1. Townsend Corporation owns a piece of machinery it had purchased 3 years ago for $40,000. The machinery has an estimated salvage value of $5,000 and an estimated useful life of 10 years. At the end of 2009, the Accumulated Depreciation account had a balance of $10,500. On April 1, 2011, the corporation sold the machinery for $27,000. Townsend uses straight-line depreciation for its machinery.

   REQUIRED: Please record the following journal entries:
   a.   The depreciation entry on December 31, 2010.
   b.   The entry or entries to record the sale on April 1, 2011.

Date	Account Titles	Debit	Credit

c.   If Townsend had simply retired the machinery on April 1, then what would the journal entry or entries have been?

Date	Account Titles	Debit	Credit

2. Please refer to The Bon-Ton Stores, Inc. financial statements at the end of this study guide for information for answering the following questions. Don't forget to use the **Decision Toolkit** approach for help in the problem-solving.

a. What line items concerning property, plant, and equipment, intangibles, depreciation, and amortization can be found on Bon-Ton's income statement, statement of cash flows, and balance sheet? (SO 7, 8)

b. In Bon-Ton's 10-K, what does Note 1 disclose about property, plant, and equipment and intangible assets? (SO8)

c. Is there any more information in Bon-Ton's notes concerning property, plant, and equipment and intangible assets? (SO7, 8)

d. In 2007 how successful was Bon-Ton at generating sales from its assets? (SO6)

SOLUTIONS TO SELF-TEST

Completion

1.	capital
2.	cost, asset
3.	depreciable
4.	debited, expense
5.	gain
6.	profit margin, asset turnover
7.	Amortization
8.	copyright
9.	12.5% (100% ÷ 8 years)
10.	salvage value

Multiple Choice

1.	b	$50,000 + $5,000 + $4,000 + $2,000 − $500
2.	c	Using an expense account is incorrect because the parking lot will benefit future periods, and land does not have a limited useful life, as does a parking lot. Typically a company will not call an account "Parking Lot" but will use "Land Improvements."
3.	a	$150,000 + $20,000 + $9,000 + $30,000
4.	d	$20,000 + $1,200 + $500 + $200 + $1,000

5.	a	The other three are depreciable.
6.	d	
7.	d	($50,000 - $5,000) ÷ 9 years = $5,000
8.	d	($50,000 - $5,000) ÷ 9 years = $5,000 x 3/12
9.	b	Straight-line gives an even amount of depreciation for each year of an asset's useful life. In the later year of an asset's useful life, straight-line gives higher expense than does declining-balance.
10.	c	Depreciation methods may be changed. A change in estimate never affects prior periods, only current and future periods.
11.	a	Earnings management involves timing the recognition of gains and losses to achieve certain income results, and a capital expenditure is money spent on an asset after its purchase. A write-down is what is done when there is an impairment.
12.	b	Book value is $2,500 ($10,000 – $7,500). Since the proceeds exceed the book value by $500, there is a gain.
13.	a	Book value is $2,500 ($10,000 – $7,500). Since the book value exceeds the proceeds by $500, there is a loss.
14.	d	Since the book value is $1,000 ($8,000 – $7,000), there is a Loss on Disposal, and losses are always debited.
15.	d	Return on assets = net income ÷ average total assets; $40,000 ÷ $200,000 = 20 %.
16.	b	Asset turnover ratio = net sales ÷ average total assets; $250,000 ÷ $200,000 = 1.25 times.
17.	a	A copyright protects literary and artistic works, and a trademark is a word, phrase, jingle, or symbol that distinguishes or identifies an enterprise or product. A license is an operating right.
18.	c	The money spent for a successful legal defense of an intangible is debited to the asset account. Use of an expense account is inappropriate.
19.	a	$10,000 ÷ 4 years. The shorter period is used.
20.	d	
21.	b	$50,000 – $5,000 = $45,000 ÷ 90,000 units = $.50 / unit $.50 / unit x 11,000 actual units = $5,500
22.	a	($50,000 - $5,000) ÷ 90,000 units = $.50/unit X 6,000 units Because depreciation is a function of usage, not time, with this method, the depreciation is not prorated for a partial year.
23.	a	The double-declining-balance rate is 25% [(100% ÷ 8 years) x 2], and $20,000 x 25% = $5,000.
24.	c	From number 23, $5,000 X 6/12. Depreciation expense must be prorated for a partial year because, with this method, depreciation is a function of time.

Problems

1. a. and b.

Dec. 31, 2010	Depreciation Expense	3,500	
	Accumulated Depreciation		3,500
	(To record annual depreciation)		

$40,000 - $5,000 = $35,000 \div 10$ years $= $3,500

Apr. 1, 2011	Depreciation Expense	875	
	Accumulated Depreciation		875
	(To bring depreciation up to date)		

$3,500 annual depreciation x 3/12

Apr. 1, 2011	Cash	27,000	
	Accumulated Depreciation	14,875	
	Machinery		40,000
	Gain on Disposal		1,875
	(To record disposal at a gain)		

Accumulated Depreciation = $10,500 + $3,500 + $875
Book value = $40,000 – $14,875 = $25,125
Gain = $27,000 – $25,125

   c.

Apr. 1, 2011	Depreciation Expense	875	
	Accumulated Depreciation		875
	(To bring depreciation up to date)		
	$3,500 annual depreciation x 3/12		

Apr. 1, 2011	Loss on Disposal	25,125	
	Accumulated Depreciation	14,875	
	Machinery		40,000

(To record retirement of asset)
Accumulated Depreciation = $10,500 + $3,500 + $875
Book value = $40,000 – $14,875 = $25,125

The loss on disposal equals the book value of the machinery.

2.

a. Income Statement: Depreciation and amortization

   Cash Flows: Depreciation and amortization
   Amortization of lease-related interests
   Loss (gain) on sale of property, fixtures and equipment
   Capital expenditures (possibly on property, fixtures and equipment)

Acquisitions, net of cash acquired
Proceeds from sale of property, fixtures and equipment

Balance Sheet: Property, fixtures and equipment at cost, net of accumulated
depreciation and amortization
Goodwill
Intangible assets, net of accumulated amortization

b.   To answer this question you must read the first note to the financial statements, "Summary
of Significant Accounting Policies," found on pages F-8 and 9 of the company's 2007 10-K
on the following Web site: http://investors.bonton.com/annuals/cfm. The note discloses
that depreciation and amortization are computed using straight-line based on the shorter of
the remaining accounting lease term or the economic life.   It further states that no
depreciation is recorded until the asset is placed into service. It discusses the accounting
for repairs and maintenance, for leasehold improvements, and impairments of assets. In a
following section, the note discusses testing goodwill and other intangible assets for
impairment.

c.   Using the same Web site noted in "b" above, you'll find Note 3 (Property, Fixtures and
Equipment) and Note 4 (Goodwill and Intangibles). Both have a wealth of information
about each asset class in their accompanying tables which give cost and depreciation or
amortization of the assets, resulting in the totals shown on the face of the balance sheet.

d.   Dollar amounts are in thousands.

To answer this question, you must compute the asset turnover ratio, calculated by dividing
net sales by average total assets. Average total assets is computed by adding together 2007
and 2006 total assets numbers and dividing by 2. For 2007, average total assets equals
$2,101,615 [($2,067,631+ $2,134,799) ÷ 2]. Since net sales totals $3,365,912, the ratio is
(rounded) 1.6 times ($3,365,912 ÷ $2,101,615). This means that for every dollar invested in
assets in 2007, Bon-Ton generated sales of $1.60. Remember that the ratio needs to be
tracked over time for the company or compared to industry averages.

CHAPTER 10

Reporting and Analyzing Liabilities

CHAPTER OVERVIEW

Chapter 10 discusses the two basic types of liabilities, current and long-term. In the former category you will learn about notes payable, sales taxes payable, payroll taxes payable, unearned revenues, and current maturities of long-term debt. In the latter category you'll learn about bonds: their issuance, payment of interest and amortization of discount or premium (using both straight-line and effective-interest methods), and their redemption. You will also learn about long-term notes. For both categories you'll learn about financial statement presentation and analysis. Finally, there will be a discussion about off-balance-sheet financing.

REVIEW OF SPECIFIC STUDY OBJECTIVES

SO1.   Explain a current liability and identify the major types of current liabilities.

⋏   A **current liability** is a <u>debt that can reasonably be expected to be paid from existing current assets or through the creation of other current liabilities within one year or the operating cycle, whichever is longer</u>. A debt that does not meet both criteria is a long-term liability.

⋏   **Current liabilities include** <u>notes payable, accounts payable, unearned revenues, and accrued liabilities such as taxes, salaries and wages, and interest</u>. All material current liabilities should be reported on the balance sheet.

SO2.   Describe the accounting for notes payable.

⋏   **Notes payable** are <u>obligations in the form of written notes</u>. They give written documentation of a liability and usually require the borrower to pay interest. If a note is due for payment within one year of the balance sheet, then it is classified as a current liability.

⋏   Consider the **following example**. Robinson Company borrows $20,000 and issues a 3-month, 12% note on May 1. The <u>entry on May 1</u> is:

Cash   20,000
        Notes Payable   20,000
(To record issuance of note)

If Robinson prepares financial statements <u>on June 30</u>, necessitating adjusting entries, then the <u>adjusting entry</u> for accrued interest is:

Interest Expense   400
        Interest Payable   400
(To record accrued interest:
$20,000 X .12 X 2/12)

On the <u>maturity date, August 1</u>, the following entry is recorded:

Notes Payable   20,000
Interest Payable   400
Interest Expense   200
        Cash   20,600
(To record payment of note
 plus interest)

Total interest on the note is $600, and the maturity value is $20,600. The Interest Payable of $400 must be taken off the books since it is no longer payable, and the Interest Expense is the third month's interest ($20,000 X .12 X 1/12).

SO3.   Explain the accounting for other current liabilities.

⋏   There are usually **sales taxes on items sold**. The retailer serves as a collection agent for the taxing authority, usually the state, and must periodically remit to the state the sales taxes collected. <u>Under most state laws, when an item is sold, the amount of the sale and the amount of the sales tax must be rung up separately on the cash register.</u> If $500 of merchandise is sold, and the sales tax percentage is 6%, then the following entry records the sales:

```
Cash                                        530
      Sales                                             500
      Sales Taxes Payable                                30
(To record sales and sales taxes)
```

When the sales taxes are remitted to the state, the entry is:

```
Sales Taxes Payable                         30
      Cash                                              30
(To remit sales taxes to
 tax agency)
```

⋏ If **sales taxes are not rung up separately**, then the retailer must compute the dollar amount of sales taxes on the daily sales. In the above example, if the cash register tape shows $530 of sales, and the sales tax percentage is 6%, then $530 divided by 106% yields $500 of sales. If that amount is deducted from $530, then the sales taxes are $30. Alternatively, the sales of $500 can be multiplied by 6% to yield the same $30 of sales taxes.

⋏ **Every employer incurs liabilities relating to employees' salaries and wages.** Amounts withheld from employees' paychecks, called withholding taxes, must be remitted to the appropriate authorities. Withheld amounts include federal, state, and local income taxes, Social Security taxes, and other amounts specified by employees such as charitable contributions, union dues, and health insurance.

⋏ **Every employer also incurs liabilities to pay various payroll taxes levied upon the employer.** An employer must match Social Security taxes and pay state and federal unemployment taxes.

⋏ **Payroll and payroll tax liability accounts** are classified as current liabilities because they must be paid in the very near term. Employers who do not compute correctly or remit promptly these amounts face stiff fines and penalties.

⋏ **Unearned revenues** arise when cash is received before goods are delivered or services are performed. When the cash is received, Cash is debited and Unearned Revenue is credited. When the goods are delivered or services are performed, then Unearned Revenue is debited and Revenue is credited. Unearned revenues are common in the magazine and newspaper industries, in the sports and entertainment industries, and in the travel industry.

⋏ Companies often have **long-term debt of which a portion is due in the current period**. If a company has a 10-year mortgage, then the portion due in the current period must be classified as current. These items are often identified on the balance sheet as "long-term debt due within one year." No adjusting entry is required: the proper classification is recognized when the balance sheet is prepared.

SO4.   Identify the types of bonds.

A   **Long-term liabilities** are obligations that are expected to be paid after one year. They are often in the form of bonds or long-term notes.

A   **Bonds** are a form of interest-bearing note payable issued by corporations, universities, and governmental agencies. Bonds are used when a corporation or other entity must borrow so much money that one lender does not want to lend the entire amount. Bonds are issued in small denominations ($100 or $1,000) and attract many investors.

A   **Bonds offer advantages over common stock**: stockholder control is not affected because bondholders do not have voting rights; tax savings result because bond interest is tax-deductible; and the earnings per share ratio may be higher because no new shares of common stock are issued.

A   **Disadvantages of bonds** include the fact that interest payments must be made in good times or bad and principal must be repaid at maturity.

A   The following are **types of bonds**:
   a. Secured bonds have specific assets of the issuer pledged as collateral for the bonds.
   b. Unsecured bonds are issued against the general credit of the borrower. These are also called debenture bonds.
   c. Convertible bonds may be converted into common stock at the bondholder's option.
   d. Callable bonds are subject to retirement at a stated dollar amount prior to maturity at the option of the issuer.

A   The **board of directors and shareholders usually must approve issuance of bonds**. The board stipulates the total number of bonds to be authorized, the total face value, and the contractual interest rate.

A   The **face value** is the principal amount due at the maturity date. The **maturity** date is the date of the final payment from the company to the investor. The **contractual interest rate** is the rate used to determine the amount of cash interest the borrower pays and the investor receives. **Bond certificates** are the securities themselves and provide information such as the name of the issuer, the face value, the contractual interest rate, and the maturity date.

A   The **current market value (present value)** of a bond is a function of three factors: the dollar amounts to be received, the length of time until the amounts are received, and the market rate of interest. The **market interest rate** is the rate investors demand for lending funds to the corporation. The process of finding the present value (the value at the present time) is referred to as discounting the future amount. The **current market value** of a bond is equal to the present value of all the future cash payments promised by the bond, the future cash payments being periodic interest payments and the repayment of principal.

SO5. Prepare the entries for the issuance of bonds and interest expense.

⋏   **Bonds may be issued** at face value, at a discount (below face value), or at a premium (above face value).

⋏   **Bond prices** are quoted as a percentage of the face value of the bond, such as 97 or 101. If a $1,000 bond sells at 97, then the issuing corporation receives 97% of the face value, or $970. If the bond sells at 101, then the corporation receives $1,010.

⋏   When a **bond sells at face value (the contractual rate of interest equals the market interest rate)**, the journal entry to record the issuance is a debit to Cash and a credit to Bonds Payable. When **bond interest is paid**, the debit is to Bond Interest Expense, and the credit is to Cash. If **interest is accrued**, then the debit is to Bond Interest Expense, and the credit is to Bond Interest Payable. Bonds Payable is reported as a long-term liability, and Bond Interest Payable is a current liability.

⋏   When a bond is issued, if the **contractual rate of interest exceeds the market rate of interest**, then the bond is issued at a premium. If the **contractual rate of interest is lower than the market rate of interest**, then the bond is issued at a discount.

⋏   Consider the **following example**. A corporation issued $500,000, 5-year, 10% bonds at 96 on January 1, 2010, with interest payable each July and January 1. The **journal entry on January 1, 2010**, is as follows:

Cash	480,000	
Discount on Bonds Payable	20,000	
Bonds Payable		500,000
(To record issuance of bonds)		

Note that Bonds Payable is always credited for the face amount of the bonds. **Discount on Bonds Payable** is a contra account, deducted from Bonds Payable (a credit and a debit are subtracted one from the other). Right after issuance, the balance sheet presentation of the bond is:

Long-term liabilities:

Bonds payable	$500,000
Less: Discount on bonds payable	20,000
	$480,000

The **$480,000 is the carrying (or book) value of the bonds**.

The **discount** is an additional cost of borrowing and should be recorded as bond interest expense over the life of the bonds. This is accomplished by amortizing the bond discount. Amortization of the discount increases the amount of interest expense reported each period. The **total cost of borrowing** in this example can be computed as follows:

Principal at maturity	$500,000
Annual interest payments:	
$500,000 X 10% = $50,000	
$50,000 X 5 years	250,000
Cash paid to bondholders	$750,000
Cash received from bondholders	480,000
Total cost of borrowing	$270,000

Consider the **following example**. A corporation issued $500,000, 5-year, 10% bonds at 102 on January 1, 2010, with interest payable each July and January 1. The **journal entry on January 1, 2010**, is as follows:

Cash	510,000	
Premium on Bonds Payable		10,000
Bonds Payable		500,000
(To record issuance of bonds)		

Note again that Bonds Payable is always credited for the face amount of the bonds. **Premium on Bonds Payable** is an <u>adjunct account</u>, added to Bonds Payable (two credits are added together). Right after issuance, the balance sheet presentation of the bond is:

Long-term liabilities:	
Bonds payable	$500,000
Add: Premium on bonds payable	10,000
	$510,000

The **$510,000 is the carrying (or book) value of the bonds**.

The **premium** is a <u>reduction in the cost of borrowing and reduces bond interest expense over the life of the bonds</u>. Just as discount is amortized, so, too, is premium amortized. Amortization of the premium decreases the amount of interest expense reported each period. The **total cost of borrowing** in this example can be computed as follows:

Principal at maturity	$500,000
Annual interest payments:	
$500,000 X 10% = $50,000	
$50,000 X 5 years	250,000
Cash paid to bondholders	750,000
Cash received from bondholders	510,000
Total cost of borrowing	$ 240,000

SO6.   Describe the entries when bonds are redeemed.

6

⋏ **At maturity, the book value of bonds equals the face value**, and the journal entry to redeem the bonds involves a debit to Bonds Payable and a credit to Cash.

⋏ If **bonds are redeemed before maturity**, then the carrying value must be eliminated, cash paid must be recorded, and a gain or loss on redemption must be recognized. If $500,000 of bonds with a carrying value of $496,000 are purchased by the corporation at 101, then the following entry is required:

Bonds Payable	500,000	
Loss on Redemption	9,000	
Discount on Bonds Payable		4,000
Cash		505,000
(To record redemption of bonds)		

Discount is computed as follows: $500,000 – $496,000
Cash is computed as follows: $500,000 X 101%
Loss is computed as follows: $505,000 – $496,000

SO7. Identify the requirements for the financial statement presentation and analysis of liabilities.

⋏ **Current liabilities** are the first category under Liabilities on the balance sheet. Each of the principal types is listed separately, and important data relating to them are disclosed in the notes to the financial statements.

⋏ A **common method of presenting current liabilities** is to list notes payable first, followed by accounts payable, followed by other items in order of their magnitude.

⋏ **Long-term liabilities** are reported in a separate section of the balance sheet, immediately following current liabilities.

⋏ It is very **important to have adequate disclosure about debt.** Disclosure can be on the balance sheet, with detailed data in the notes to the financial statements. On the statement of cash flows, information about the principal of debt is in the "Financing activities" section, while information about interest expense is in the "Operating activities" section.

⋏ It is also important to assess a company's ability to pay its current and long-term obligations. **Liquidity ratios** measure the short-term ability of a company to pay its maturing obligations. The **current ratio** (current assets divided by current liabilities) is one measure of liquidity.

⋏ **Many companies keep few liquid assets on hand** because they cost too much to hold, and, thus, a company must rely on other sources of liquidity. A **bank line of credit** is a prearranged agreement between a company and a lender that permits a company to borrow up to an agreed-upon amount.

⋏   **Solvency ratios** <u>measure the ability of a company to survive over a long period of time</u>. One solvency ratio is **debt to total assets**, computed by <u>dividing total liabilities by total assets</u>. Another is the **times interest earned ratio**, computed by <u>dividing income before interest expense and income tax by interest expense</u>. This ratio computes how many times the company has earned its interest payments in an accounting period, thus providing an indication of a company's ability to meet interest payments as they come due.

⋏   A **concern for analysts when evaluating a company** is <u>whether all liabilities have been recorded</u>. **Off-balance sheet** financing is an <u>attempt to borrow funds in such a way that the obligations are not recorded</u>. An example of such an unrecorded liability is a **contingency**, an <u>event with an uncertain outcome</u>. A classic example of a contingent liability is a lawsuit; other contingencies are product warranties and environmental problems. If it is <u>probable</u> that the contingency will occur and the company can <u>reasonably estimate</u> the amount of the expected loss, then the <u>company must accrue the loss</u> by debiting a loss or expense account and crediting a liability account. If <u>both conditions are not met,</u> then the <u>company must disclose the loss in the notes to the financial statements</u>. Another example of off-balance-sheet financing results from **lease transactions**. Because a lease liability increases a company's total liabilities, companies try to <u>structure a lease agreement so that an asset and a liability for the use of an asset do not appear on the balance sheet</u>. Such off-balance-sheet financing must be considered by a person who is analyzing a company.

SO8. Apply the straight-line method of amortizing bond discount and bond premium.
      (This objective is discussed in Appendix 10A in your text.)

⋏   The **straight-line method of amortization** results in constant amortization and interest expense numbers, but <u>interest expense as a percentage of carrying value varies</u>, thereby not completely satisfying the matching principle.

⋏   **Consider the bond issued at a discount in SO5.** This is a $500,000, 5-year, 10% bond issued at 96 on January 1, 2010. The discount, therefore, is $20,000 ($500,000 X 4%). Using straight-line amortization, **the following entry is written on July 1, 2010**:

Bond Interest Expense	27,000	
Cash		25,000
Discount on Bonds Payable		2,000

(To record payment of interest and
amortization of discount)

Cash is computed as follows: $500,000 X 10% X 6/12
Discount is computed as follows: $20,000 ÷ 10 interest payment periods (the bond is a 5-year bond which pays interest twice a year)
Bond Interest Expense is simply the sum of the two credits. **With straight-line amortization, you solve for the Discount and Cash (or Interest Payable) and plug the number for Interest Expense.**

On **December 31, 2010, the following entry is written**:

Bond Interest Expense	27,000	
Bond Interest Payable		25,000
Discount on Bonds Payable		2,000
(To accrue interest and		
amortization of bond discount)		

These **same two entries will be written over the next 4 years**, eventually reducing the balance in the Discount account to zero. On the maturity date, the carrying value of the bonds will be $500,000, their face value, which is correct because that is the amount that must be paid back on that date.

Now **consider the bond issued at a premium in SO5**. This is a $500,000, 5-year, 10% bond issued at 102 on January 1, 2010. The premium, therefore, is $10,000 ($500,000 X 2%). Using straight-line amortization, the **following entry is written on July 1, 2010**:

Bond Interest Expense	24,000	
Premium on Bonds Payable	1,000	
Cash		25,000
(To record payment of interest and		
amortization of bond premium)		

Cash is computed as follows: $500,000 X 10% X 6/12
Premium is computed as follows: $10,000 ÷ 10 interest payment periods (the bond is a 5-year bond which pays interest twice a year)
Bond Interest Expense is simply the difference between the cash and the premium. **With straight-line amortization, you solve for the Premium and Cash (or Interest Payable) and plug the number for Interest Expense.**

On **December 31, 2010, the following entry is written**:

Bond Interest Expense	24,000	
Premium on Bonds Payable	1,000	
Bond Interest Payable		25,000
(To accrue interest and		
amortization of bond premium)		

These **same two entries will be written over the next 4 years**, eventually reducing the balance in the Premium account to zero. Once again, on the maturity date the carrying value of the bonds will be $500,000, their face value, which is correct because that is the amount that must be paid back on that date.

SO9.   Apply the effective-interest method of amortizing bond discount and bond premium. (This objective is discussed in Appendix 10B in your text.)

ᴧ   A second method of amortization, the **effective-interest method**, results in varying amounts of amortization and interest expense, but interest expense as a percentage of carrying value remains constant, thereby satisfying the matching principle.

ᴧ   The **effective-interest method** is reasonably easy to do if you remember two things. The first is that the **carrying value of a bond** is equal to the face amount of the bond less any discount or plus any premium. The second thing to remember is the following formula:

Bond interest expense = Bond carrying value X effective interest rate

ᴧ   Consider the following example. On January 1 a company issues $100,000 of bonds, due in 5 years, with interest payment dates of January 1 and July 1 and a face rate of interest of 8%. At the time of issuance, the effective rate of interest is 10%. The bonds sell for $92,278, resulting in a discount of $7,722. The journal entry for July 1, the first interest payment date, is:

Bond Interest Expense	4,614	
Discount on Bonds Payable		614
Cash		4,000

Bond Interest Expense = $92,278 X 5% (The effective rate of interest is 10% per year, or 5% each 6 months)
Cash = $100,000 X 8% X 1/2 year
Discount = Bond Interest Expense – Cash
With effective-interest amortization, you solve for Bond Interest Expense and Cash (or Interest Payable) and plug the number for Discount.

On December 31 the company must write adjusting entries, even though the very next day, January 1, is an interest payment date. The following entry is written on December 31:

Bond Interest Expense	4,645	
Discount on Bonds Payable		645
Bond Interest Payable		4,000

The new balance in the discount account after the July 1 entry is $7,108 ($7,722 – $614), giving a new carrying value of $92,892 ($100,000 – $7,108).

Bond Interest Expense = $92,892 X 5%

ᴧ   Consider another example using the same bond, but now assume that the effective rate of interest is 6%. The company receives $108,530 for the bond, resulting in a premium of $8,530. The journal entry for July 1, the first interest payment date, is:

Bond Interest Expense	3,256	
Premium on Bonds Payable	744	
Cash		4,000

Bond Interest Expense = $108,530 X 3%
Premium = Cash – Bond Interest Expense
Remember, **with effective-interest amortization, you solve for Bond Interest Expense and Cash (or Interest Payable) and plug the number for Premium**.

The journal entry on December 31 is:

Bond Interest Expense	3,234	
Premium on Bonds Payable	766	
Bond Interest Payable		4,000

The new balance in the Premium account after the July 1 entry is $7,786 ($8,530 – 744), giving a new carrying value of $107,786.

Bond Interest Expense = $107,786 X 3%

SO10. Describe the accounting for long-term notes payable.
(This objective is discussed in Appendix 10C in your text.)

⋏ A **long-term note payable** has a term that exceeds one year. Such a note may be secured by a **mortgage**, which pledges title to specific assets as security for the loan. If an individual purchases a home, then he or she will have a mortgage note payable. Each payment on the mortgage will consist of principal and interest. In the beginning of the life of the mortgage, the payment will be mostly interest; as the term progresses, that reverses, and the payment becomes mostly payment on the principal.

⋏ A **mortgage** is initially recorded at face value with a debit to Cash and a credit to Mortgage Notes Payable. The journal entry on each payment date is:

Interest Expense
Mortgage Notes Payable
    Cash

Interest Expense is computed by multiplying the principal balance by the interest rate. The difference between cash paid and the interest expense is the reduction in the principal balance, accomplished by the debit to Mortgage Notes Payable.

CHAPTER SELF-TEST

As you work the exercises and problems, remember to use the **Decision Toolkit** discussed and used in the text:

1. <u>Decision Checkpoints</u>: at this point you ask a question.

2. <u>Info Needed for Decision</u>: you make a choice regarding the information needed to answer the question.

3. <u>Tool to Use for Decision</u>: at this point you review just what the information chosen in step 2 does for the decision-making process.

4. <u>How to Evaluate Results</u>: you perform evaluation of information for answering the question.

Note: The notation (SO1) means that the question was drawn from study objective number one.

Matching

Please write the letters of the following terms in the spaces to the left of the definitions.

a.	Carrying value	g.	Market interest rate
b.	Contingencies	h.	Mortgage
c.	Contractual interest rate	i.	Off-balance sheet financing
d.	Current ratio	j.	Premium (on a bond)
e.	Discount (on a bond)	k.	Times interest earned ratio
f.	Face value		

_____ 1.   (SO7)   A measure of a company's liquidity.

_____ 2.   (SO7)   A measure of a company's long-term solvency.

_____ 3.   (SO7)   Intentional effort by a company to structure its financing arrangements so as to avoid showing liabilities on its books.

_____ 4.   (SO5)   Occurs when the contractual interest rate of a bond is lower than the market interest rate.

_____ 5.   (SO4)   Rate used to determine the amount of interest the borrower pays and the investor receives.

_____ 6.   (SO10) A type of long-term note payable that pledges title to specific assets as security for the loan.

_____ 7.   (SO7)   Events with uncertain outcomes.

_____ 8.   (SO4)   The rate investors demand for loaning funds to the corporation.

_____ 9.   (SO4)   Amount of principal due at a bond's maturity date.

_____ 10.   (SO5)   Bond payable less its discount or plus its premium.

Multiple Choice

Please circle the correct answer.

1. (SO1)   Which of the following is a criterion for the classification of a liability as current?
    a.   It is a debt that can be paid from existing current assets.
    b.   It is a debt that can be paid through the creation of other current liabilities.
    c.   It must be paid within one year or the operating cycle, whichever is longer.
    d.   All of the above are criteria for the classification of a liability as current.

2. (SO2)   A corporation issued a $50,000, 9%, 4-month note on July 1. If the corporation's year-end is September 30, then the adjusting entry for interest on that date is:

a.	Interest Expense	1,125	
	Notes Payable		1,125
b.	Interest Expense	1,125	
	Interest Payable		1,125
c.	Interest Expense	1,500	
	Notes Payable		1,500
d.	Interest Expense	1,500	
	Interest Payable		1,500

3. (SO2)   When the corporation in number 2 pays the amount due on the maturity date, the journal entry will include a:
    a.   debit to Notes Payable for $51,500.
    b.   credit to Cash for $50,000.
    c.   debit to Interest Expense for $1,500.
    d.   debit to Interest Payable for $1,125.

4. (SO3)   A company's cash register tape shows $1,284 for the day: This number includes the 7% sales tax. The dollar amount of sales is:
    a. $1,284.
    b. $1,200.
    c. $1,194 (rounded).
    d. $84.00.

5. (SO3)   On December 30, 2010, a company issued a note payable of $50,000, of which $10,000 is repaid each year. What is the proper classification of this note on the December 31, 2010, balance sheet?
    a. $10,000 current liability; $40,000 long-term liability.
    b. $50,000 current liability.
    c. $50,000 long-term liability.
    d. $10,000 long-term liability; $40,000 current liability.

6.   (SO7) Which is a very common way to present current liabilities on the balance sheet?
      a.   Notes payable are listed first.
      b.   Current maturities of long-term debt are listed first.
      c.   By order of magnitude.
      d.   By order of maturity date.

7.   (SO7) Dividing current assets by current liabilities yields the:
      a.   debt to total assets ratio.
      b.   times interest earned ratio.
      c.   acid-test ratio.
      d.   current ratio.

8.   (SO4) Bonds that are issued against the general credit of the borrower are called:
      a.   unsecured bonds.
      b.   secured bonds.
      c.   term bonds.
      d.   callable bonds.

9.   (SO4) A corporation issues $1,000,000 of 8%, 5-year bonds. The 8% rate of interest is called the _____ rate.
      a.   yield
      b.   effective
      c.   market
      d.   contractual

10.   (SO4) The current market value of a bond is equal to the:
      a.   present value of the principal only.
      b.   present value of the principal and the interest payments.
      c.   present value of interest payments only.
      d.   face value of the principal only.

11.   (SO5) When the contractual rate of interest exceeds the market rate of interest, the bond sells at:
      a.   face value.
      b.   a discount.
      c.   a premium.
      d.   some amount other than those listed above.

12.   (SO5) Sosa Corporation issued bonds with a face value of $400,000 and a contractual rate of interest of 6% at 99 on July 1. The bonds mature in 10 years. What is the total cost of borrowing for Sosa Corporation?
      a. $640,000.
      b. $400,000.
      c. $244,000.
      d. $240,000.

13. (SO8) Bonds with a face value of $800,000 and a contractual rate of interest of 8% sold at 98 on January 1. Interest is payable on July 1 and January 1, and the bonds mature in 10 years. On July 1 the dollar amount of discount to be amortized, using straight-line amortization, is:
    a. $ 800.
    b. $1,600.
    c. $2,000.
    d. $2,400.

14. (SO5) When computing the carrying or book value of bonds payable:
    a. premium is subtracted from and discount is added to bonds payable.
    b. discount is subtracted from and premium is added to bonds payable.
    c. both discount and premium are subtracted from bonds payable.
    d. both discount and premium are added to bonds payable.

15. (SO8) Terra Corporation issued 5-year bonds with a face value of $500,000 at 99 on January 1, 2010. The company uses straight-line amortization of discount and premium. What is the carrying value of the bonds on the December 31, 2010, balance sheet?
    a. $496,000.
    b. $499,000.
    c. $500,000.
    d. $501,000.

16. (SO8) Bonds with a face value of $600,000 and a contractual rate of interest of 8% sold at 102 on January 1. Interest is payable on July 1 and January 1, and the bonds mature in 10 years. On July 1 the journal entry to pay interest and record straight-line amortization will include a:
    a. credit to Cash for $23,400.
    b. debit to Premium on Bonds Payable for $1,200.
    c. credit to Premium on Bonds Payable for $600.
    d. debit to Bond Interest Expense for $23,400.

17. (SO8) Bonds with a face value of $800,000 and a contractual rate of interest of 9% sold at 97 on January 1. Interest is payable on July 1 and January 1, and the bonds mature in 5 years. On July 1 the journal entry to pay interest and record straight-line amortization will include a:
    a. credit to Discount on Bonds Payable for $4,800.
    b. debit to Discount on Bonds Payable for $2,400.
    c. debit to Bond Interest Expense for $36,000.
    d. credit to Discount on Bonds Payable for $2,400.

18. (SO6) Bonds payable with a face value of $200,000 and a carrying value of $196,000 are redeemed prior to maturity at 102. There is a:
    a. loss on redemption of $4,000.
    b. gain on redemption of $4,000.
    c. loss on redemption of $8,000.
    d. gain on redemption of $8,000.

15

19. (SO7) A company's total debt is $250,000 while its total assets are $500,000. Income before interest expense and income tax is $300,000, and interest expense is $30,000. The company's times interest earned ratio is:
   a.   10 times.
   b.   2 times.
   c.   50%.
   d.   10%.

20. (SO7) Rouse Company is being sued by a customer. At the balance sheet date, Rouse's attorneys feel that it is probable that the company will lose the lawsuit and that a reasonable estimate of the loss is $50,000. On the balance sheet date Rouse should:
   a.   not disclose the lawsuit because a jury has not yet ruled.
   b.   disclose the lawsuit in the notes to the financial statements.
   c.   accrue the loss by debiting an expense and crediting a liability.
   d.   ask for a second opinion from an outside firm of attorneys.

21. (SO9) On January 1 Alexia Corporation issued $100,000 of 11% bonds, due in 10 years, with interest payment dates of January 1 and July 1. The effective rate of interest on that date was 10%. Alexia received $105,901 for the bonds. The journal entry on the July 1 interest payment date will include a:
   a.   credit to Cash for $11,000.
   b.   credit to Bond Interest Expense for $5,295.
   c.   debit to Premium on Bonds Payable for $205.
   d.   credit to Premium on Bonds Payable for $205.

22. (SO9) On January 1 Xio Corporation issued $200,000 of 7% bonds, due in 5 years, with interest payment dates of January 1 and July 1. The effective rate of interest on that date was 8%. Xio received $191,888 for the bonds. The journal entry on the July 1 interest payment date will include a:
   a.   debit to Bond Interest Expense for $7,676.
   b.   credit to Cash for $14,000.
   c.   debit to Discount on Bonds Payable for $676.
   d.   credit to Premium on Bonds Payable for $676.

23. (SO10) Which of the following is true with respect to mortgage notes payable?
   a.   Each payment consists of only principal.
   b.   Each payment consists of only interest.
   c.   The interest component of each payment increases as the term of the note progresses.
   d.   The interest component of each payment decreases as the term of the note progresses.

Problems

1. Please record for Jansen Corporation journal entries concerning the following current and long-term liabilities:

    a. On May 1 the corporation issued a 6-month, 12% note in the amount of $20,000. Please record the adjusting entry for interest on June 30. (SO2)

    b. On June 1 the corporation received $12,000 in advance from a customer who is renting a small building from Jansen for 12 months. Please record the adjusting entry on June 30. (SO3)

    c. On July 1 the corporation sold $400,000 of 10%, 5-year bonds at 101. The bonds pay interest every January 1 and July 1. (SO5)

    d. On November 1 the corporation paid the amount due on the $20,000 note payable in letter "a" above. (SO2)

    e. On December 31, the company recorded the adjusting entry concerning the transaction in "b." (SO3)

    f. On December 31, the corporation recorded the adjusting entry for interest and straight-line amortization of the bond issued in "c." (SO8)

Date	Account Titles	Debit	Credit

2.   Please refer to The Bon-Ton Stores, Inc. financial statements at the end of this study guide for information for answering the following questions. Don't forget to use the **Decision Toolkit** approach for help in the problem-solving.

   a. Does Bon-Ton have any contingencies? (SO7)

   b. What is Bon-Ton's long-term debt in 2007, and how much did it increase or decrease from the previous year? (SO7).

c. In 2007 and 2006 what percentage of total liabilities are current liabilities? (SO1)

d. Does it seem likely that Bon-Ton has the ability to survive over a long period of time? (SO7)

SOLUTIONS TO SELF-TEST

Matching

1.	d		6.	h
2.	k		7.	b
3.	i		8.	g
4.	e		9.	f
5.	c		10.	a

Multiple Choice

1. d
2. b $50,000 X 9% X 3/12
3. d   The journal entry is:

Notes Payable	50,000	
Interest Payable	1,125	
Interest Expense	375	
Cash		51,500

4. b $1,284 ÷ 107% = $1,200
5. a   The $10,000 is a current maturity of long-term debt.
6. a

7. d Debt to total assets is total debt divided by total assets. Times interest earned is income before interest expense and income taxes divided by interest expense. The acid-test ratio is cash, short-term investments, and net receivables divided by current liabilities.

8. a Secured bonds are secured by some sort of collateral, term bonds are due at a specific future date, and callable bonds may be repurchased by the issuing corporation before the maturity date.

9. d Yield, effective, and market rates are different terms for the same thing.

10. b Bonds involve two streams of cash flows: principal and interest.

11. c If the rates are the same, then the bond sells at par value. If the contractual rate is lower than the market rate, then the bond sells at a discount.

12. c

Principal at maturity	$400,000
Annual interest payments:	
$400,000 X 6% = $24,000	
$24,000 X 10 years	240,000
Cash paid to bondholders	$640,000
Cash received from bondholders	396,000
Total cost of borrowing	$244,000

13. a The journal entry is:

Bond Interest Expense	32,800	
Discount on Bonds Payable		800
Cash		32,000

Discount amortized = $16,000 ÷ 20 interest payment periods

14. b Premium is added to bonds payable; discount is subtracted from bonds payable.

15. a $500,000 x 99% = $495,000; so there is a $5,000 discount. One thousand dollars per year will be amortized ($5,000 ÷ 5 years). At December 31, 2010, the balance in the Discount account will be $4,000 ($5,000 – $1,000), and the carrying value will be $496,000, the bond less the discount.

16. d The journal entry is:

Bond Interest Expense	23,400	
Premium on Bonds Payable	600	
Cash		24,000

Premium = $12,000 ÷ 20 interest payment periods
Cash = $600,000 X 8% X 6/12
Bond Interest Expense = $24,000 - $600

17. d The journal entry is:

Bond Interest Expense	38,400	
Discount on Bonds Payable		2,400
Cash		36,000

Discount = $24,000 ÷ 10 interest payment periods
Cash = $800,000 X 9% X 6/12
Bond Interest Expense = $36,000 + $2,400

18. c The company had to pay $204,000 for bonds with a carrying value of $196,000. The difference between these two numbers is a loss on redemption.

19. a   The ratio is computed by dividing income before interest expense and income tax by interest expense. In this case, $300,000 ÷ $30,000 = 10 times.

20. c   It is simply disclosed in the notes if both conditions (reasonable estimate and probable) are not met. Only if the possibility of loss is remote does the company do nothing.

21. c   The journal entry is:

Bond Interest Expense	5,295	
Premium on Bonds Payable	205	
Cash		5,500

Cash = $100,000 X 11% X 1/2 year
Bond Interest Expense = $105,901 X 10% X 1/2 year
Premium = $5,500 - $5,295

22. a   The journal entry is:

Bond Interest Expense	7,676	
Discount on Bonds Payable		676
Cash		7,000

Cash = $200,000 X 7% X 1/2 year
Bond Interest Expense = $191,888 X 8% X 1/2 year
Discount = $7,676 - $7,000

23. d   Each payment consists of both principal and interest, and the interest component decreases as the term of the note progresses.

Problems

1. a. June 30

Interest Expense	400	
Interest Payable		400

(To record interest on note:
$20,000 X 12% X 2/12)

b. June 30

Unearned Revenue	1,000	
Rent Revenue		1,000

(To record revenue earned:
$12,000 X 1/12)

c. July 1

Cash	404,000	
Bonds Payable		400,000
Premium on Bonds Payable		4,000

(To record sale of bonds at premium)

d. Nov. 1

Notes Payable	20,000	
Interest Payable	400	
Interest Expense	800	
Cash		21,200

(To record payment on note)

e.	Dec. 31	Unearned Revenue	6,000	
		Rent Revenue		6,000
		(To record revenue earned:		
		$12,000 X 6/12)		

f.	Dec. 31	Bond Interest Expense	19,600	
		Premium on Bonds Payable	400	
		Bond Interest Payable		20,000
		(To accrue bond interest and		
		amortization)		

Premium = $4,000 ÷ 10 interest payment periods
Bond Int. Payable = $400,000 X 10% X 6/12
Bond Int. Expense = $20,000 - $400

2. Dollar amounts are in thousands.

a. To answer this question, you must read the notes to the financial statements beginning on page F-7 of the company's 2007 10-K on the following Web site: http://investors.bonton.com/annuals/cfm. (The notes begin immediately following the consolidated statements of cash flows.) Note 14 is entitled "Commitments and Contingencies" and discusses lease commitments and contingencies related to the company's acquisition of Carson Pirie Scott.

b. Bon-Ton's long-term debt in 2007 is $1,259,113 ($1,079,841 + $67,217 + $112,055), a 1.3% (rounded) decrease from 2006's level ($1,276,008 − $1,259,113 = $16,895 ÷ $1,276,008).

c. In 2007 the percentage is 26.1% ($445,457 ÷ $1,704,570). In 2006 the percentage is 28.7% ($512,395 ÷ $1,788,403).

d. To answer this question, you must compute the debt to total assets ratio, calculated by dividing total liabilities by total assets.

2007: 82% ($1,704,570 ÷ $2,067,631)
2006: 84% ($1,788,403 ÷ $2,134,799)

This means that Bon-Ton has $.82 and $.84, respectively, of debt for every dollar of assets.

This ratio indicates the proportion of total assets financed by creditors. Creditors must be paid regardless of what kind a year a company has; so, the higher the ratio, the riskier the financing strategy. In each year creditors contributed over 80% of the financing, meaning that stockholders' equity contributed less than 20%. While Bon-Ton probably has the wherewithal to survive over the long term, a good strategy would be to seek to lower this ratio. The ratio also should be compared with the industry average to see whether Bon-Ton's ratio is in line with its competitors' ratios.

CHAPTER **11**

Reporting and Analyzing Stockholders' Equity

CHAPTER OVERVIEW

In this chapter you will learn about advantages and disadvantages of the corporate form of business organization. You'll learn about the issuance and repurchase of stock and about the mechanics of cash and stock dividends. After reviewing retained earnings, you will learn how to prepare a comprehensive stockholders' equity section of the balance sheet. Finally, you'll learn how to measure corporate performance using various ratios.

REVIEW OF SPECIFIC STUDY OBJECTIVES

⋏   A **corporation** is created by law and thus is a legal entity with most of the rights and privileges of a person.

⋏   **Corporations** may be classified in two ways: by purpose, such as for-profit or not-for-profit (charitable or medical organizations), and by ownership (publicly held, which may have thousands of stockholders, and privately held, which have few stockholders and generally do not offer stock for sale to the public).

SO1.   Identify and discuss the major characteristics of a corporation.

⋏   The following are **characteristics of a corporation**:

1.   **Separate legal existence,** which means that a corporation acts under its own name and has most of the same rights as does a person. It may buy,

own, or sell property, borrow money, enter into contracts, and sue or be sued, and it pays its own taxes.

2. **Limited liability of stockholders,** which means that the <u>liability of stockholders is generally limited to the amount of their investment</u>. Stockholders' personal assets are not at risk unless fraud has occurred.

3. **Transferable ownership rights**, which means that a <u>stockholder may buy or sell stock without approval of the corporation or other shareholders</u>.

4. **Ability to acquire capital**, resulting from the <u>issuance of its stock</u>.

5. **Continuous life**, which means that the <u>life of the corporation is not affected by the withdrawal, death, or incapacity of a stockholder, employee, or officer</u>.

6. **Management that is separate from the owners**, meaning that <u>stockholders manage the company indirectly through the board of directors</u>. While professional managers may be hired, some view the separation of ownership and management in a negative fashion. The **chief executive officer** has overall responsibility for managing the business. The **controller** is the chief accounting officer, concerned with maintaining the accounting records and a system of internal control and preparing financial statements, tax returns, and internal reports. The **treasurer** maintains custody of the corporation's funds. The Sarbanes-Oxley Act requires the board of directors to monitor management's actions more closely.

7. **Government regulation**, both <u>by state and federal governments</u>, which can be burdensome from both time and money standpoints.

8. **Additional taxes**, resulting from the fact that the <u>corporation pays taxes on its income and stockholders pay taxes on dividends received from the corporation</u>.

⋏ Characteristics 1 through 5 are viewed as advantages; characteristics 6 through 8 are viewed as disadvantages.

⋏ A **corporation** is <u>formed by grant of a state charter</u>. While a corporation may practice in many states, it is incorporated in only one state, presumably one with laws favorable to existing management. After receiving its charter, the corporation establishes by-laws for conducting its affairs.

⋏ A **corporation may sell ownership rights** in the form of shares of stock, and if it has only one class of stock, then that class is **common stock**. <u>Each share of stock has the following rights</u>:

1. The **right to participate in management** by electing the board of directors and voting on matters requiring shareholder approval.

2. The **right to share in corporate earnings** through receipt of dividends.

3. The **right to maintain the same percentage ownership when new shares of stock are issued** (called the preemptive right, eliminated by many corporations because they view it as unnecessary and cumbersome).

4. The **right to share in distribution of assets upon liquidation of the corporation**.

↗ A **stock certificate** is a <u>printed or engraved form which is proof of stock ownership</u>. Currently, stock purchases or sales are "book transactions," and owners rarely hold the stock certificates. Instead, brokerage firms store the certificates for the stockholders.

↗ **Authorized stock** is just that: <u>shares of stock that the company may sell as authorized by the state which grants the corporate charter</u>. If a company wishes to sell more than the authorized amount, then it must change its charter. No formal journal entry is required for authorized shares, but the <u>number of shares authorized must be disclosed in the stockholders' equity section of the balance sheet</u>.

↗ A **corporation may sell its stock** <u>either directly to investors or indirectly through an investment banking firm</u>. Shares are traded on national stock exchanges, such as the New York Stock Exchange (the "Big Board"), or on 13 regional exchanges. Stock may also be traded on the NASDAQ national market.

↗ **Par value stock** is <u>capital stock that has been assigned a value per share in the corporate charter</u>. Par value is an **arbitrary amount that has absolutely nothing to do with the fair market value of the stock**. Stock with a par value of a nickel may sell for $100 per share on a given trading day.

↗ **No-par value stock** is <u>capital stock that has not been assigned a value in the corporate charter</u>. In some states the board of directors is allowed to assign a **stated value** to no-par stock.

↗ A **critical point to remember** is that <u>legal capital per share always establishes the credit to the Common Stock account</u> when shares of stock are issued.

SO2. Record the issuance of common stock.

↗ Remember that **stockholders' equity in a corporation** consists of <u>two parts</u>:

1. <u>Paid-in (contributed) capital</u>, the amount paid in to the corporation by stockholders in exchange for shares of ownership; and
2. <u>Retained earnings (earned capital)</u>, held for future use in the business.

↗ The **issuance of common stock** <u>affects only paid-in capital accounts</u>. Cash proceeds from the sale of stock may be equal to, greater than, or less than par value. Regardless of the dollar amount of the cash proceeds, <u>Common Stock is always credited for the number of shares sold times the par value</u>. If 100 shares of $5 par value common stock are sold for $5 per share, then the journal entry is:

```
Cash    500
        Common Stock                                  500
(To record sale of 100 shares of $5 par
 value stock for $5 per share)
```

If another 100 shares of $5 par value common stock are sold for $7 per share, then the journal entry is:

```
Cash                                      700
        Common Stock                                  500
        Paid-in Capital in Excess
            of Par Value                              200
(To record sale of 100 shares of $5 par
 value stock for $7 per share)
```

Note that <u>in each case, Common Stock is credited for the number of shares sold, 100, times the par value of $5</u>.

A   If no-par value stock with a stated value is sold, then the transaction is treated in the same fashion as the par value stock transaction. The only difference is that the term "Par Value" is replaced with the term "Stated Value."

SO3.   Explain the accounting for the purchase of treasury stock.

A   **Treasury stock** is a <u>corporation's own stock that has been reacquired by the corporation and held in its treasury for future use</u>.

A   **Reasons for purchasing treasury stock** include the following:

1.   To <u>reissue the shares to employees under bonus and stock compensation plans</u>.
2.   To <u>enhance the stock's market value</u> (the fewer the shares in the marketplace, the more valuable they are).
3.   To <u>use the shares in the acquisition of other companies</u>.
4.   To <u>reduce shares outstanding</u>, thereby increasing earnings per share.
5.   To <u>eliminate hostile shareholders</u> by buying them out.

A   The **cost method** is generally used to account for the purchase of treasury stock. The account Treasury Stock is debited and Cash is credited for the cost of the shares purchased: par value does not enter into the computation. If the shares are later reissued, then Treasury Stock will be reduced by the cost of the shares sold. If a company reacquires 1,000 of its $4 par value shares for $10 per share, then the journal entry is:

```
Treasury Stock                            10,000
        Cash                                          10,000
(To reacquire 1,000 shares at
```

$10 per share)

    ⋏   **Treasury Stock** is <u>deducted from total paid-in capital and retained earnings in the stockholders' equity section of the balance sheet</u>. The total number of shares issued, or sold, does not change, but the total dollar amount of stockholders' equity decreases, as does the number of shares outstanding (shares that have been sold and are still held by stockholders).

    ⋏   Despite the fact that it has a debit balance, **Treasury Stock is not an asset**. As noted above, it is <u>shown on the balance sheet as a reduction of stockholders' equity</u>.

SO4.   Differentiate preferred stock from common stock.

    ⋏   **Preferred stock** has contractual provisions that give it <u>preference or priority over common stock in certain areas</u>, usually in relation to dividends and to assets in the event of liquidation. Preferred stock often has no voting rights. If a corporation issues 500 shares of its $20 par value preferred stock for $30 per share, then the journal entry is:

Cash	15,000	
Preferred Stock		10,000
Paid-in Capital in Excess of		
Par Value—Preferred		5,000
(To record sale of 500 shares of stock		
at $30 per share)		

Note that Preferred Stock is credited for the number of shares issued times the par value, and the Paid-in Capital is labeled "Preferred" to differentiate it from Paid-in Capital in Excess of Par Value—Common.

    ⋏   **Preferred stock** is <u>listed before common stock on the balance sheet</u> because of its preferences in the areas of dividends and liquidation.

    ⋏   **Preferred stock has priority over common stock in the matter of dividends**. This does not guarantee that preferred shares will always receive the dividend. The **dividend amount** is <u>stated as a percentage of the par value or as a specified amount</u>. The stock can be listed as 10%, $50 Par Value Preferred, meaning that each share receives 10% of $50, or $5, per share, per year. Alternatively, the stock can be listed as $5 Preferred, $50 Par Value.

    ⋏   If preferred stock is **cumulative**, then <u>any dividend that has not been declared and paid is not forever lost</u>. When the corporation has money again for dividends, it must first pay the prior year's or years' dividends before the current year's dividends are paid. Preferred dividends not declared in a given period are called <u>dividends in arrears</u> and <u>should be disclosed in the notes</u> to the financial statements. Dividends in arrears are <u>not a liability</u>: no obligation exists until the board of directors declares the dividend. If a corporation pays its preferred shareholders $10,000 a year in dividends and has not paid dividends in the past two years, and if it has $50,000 for dividend distribution in the current year, then the distribution will be:

Preferred dividends in arrears	$20,000
Preferred dividends—current year	10,000
Common stock dividends	20,000
Total dividends distributed	$50,000

The common stockholders simply receive the difference between the total of $50,000 and the $30,000 that must be distributed to the preferred stockholders.

⋏ If preferred stock is **noncumulative**, then <u>any dividend not declared and paid is forever lost</u>. Since this is very unattractive to investors, most companies do not issue noncumulative preferred stock.

⋏ **Preferred shareholders** also have a <u>preference in the event of liquidation of the corporation</u>. Creditors must be paid first, then preferred stockholders, then common stockholders. The preference may be for the par value of the shares or for a specified liquidating value.

SO5. Prepare the entries for cash dividends and understand the effect of stock dividends and stock splits.

⋏ A **dividend** is a <u>distribution by a corporation to its stockholders on a pro rata basis</u>. Dividends may be in the form of cash, property, script (promissory note to pay cash), or stock.

⋏ To pay a **cash dividend**, a corporation must have <u>retained earnings, adequate cash</u>, and <u>dividends declared by the board of directors</u>. While many companies pay a quarterly dividend, there are companies, called growth stock companies, which pay no dividends but conserve cash to finance future capital expenditures.

⋏ There are **three dates of importance for all dividends**: <u>date of declaration, date of record</u>, and <u>date of distribution (for cash dividends, called the date of payment)</u>. Journal entries are required on the first and third dates. For a **cash dividend**, the journal entry on the <u>date of declaration</u> will be as follows if a corporation declares a $.25 per share cash dividend on 100,000 shares of stock:

Cash Dividends	25,000	
Dividends Payable		25,000
(To declare a cash dividend of $.25		
per share on 100,000 shares)		

<u>Dividends Payable is a current liability</u>. At the end of the accounting period, the balance in <u>Cash Dividends, a temporary account</u>, is transferred to Retained Earnings by a closing entry.

On the **date of record**, <u>ownership of the outstanding shares is determined for dividend purposes</u>. No journal entry is required.

On the **date of payment**, the following entry is required:

Dividends Payable	25,000	
Cash		25,000

(To record payment of cash dividend)

Declaration and payment of a cash dividend reduce both stockholders' equity and total assets.

A. A **stock dividend** is a pro rata distribution of the corporation's own stock to stockholders. A stock dividend results in a decrease in retained earnings and an increase in paid-in capital. Total stockholders' equity will remain the same because dollar amounts are simply transferred from retained earnings to paid-in capital accounts. A stock dividend is interesting because an investor really receives nothing extra on the day he receives the shares of stock: His ownership percentage has not changed. In the future, however, if the stock price rises, he will have more shares of stock on which there is share price appreciation.

A. **Corporations issue stock dividends for various reasons**:

1. To satisfy stockholders' dividend expectations without spending cash.
2. To increase the marketability of the stock by reducing the price per share.
3. To emphasize that a portion of equity has been permanently reinvested in the business and is unavailable for cash dividends.

A. A **small stock dividend** occurs when the stock distributed is less than 20%-25% of the outstanding shares, and a **large stock dividend** occurs when the stock distributed is more than 20%-25% of the outstanding shares. Fair market value is used for small stock dividends; par value is used for large stock dividends.

A. Like a stock dividend, a **stock split** involves the issuance of additional shares of stock to stockholders according to their percentage ownership. Unlike a stock dividend, however, a stock split results in a reduction in the par or stated value per share. The **purpose of a stock split** is to reduce the market value per share, thus making the stock more marketable. A corporation has 200,000 shares of $5 par value common stock outstanding; the market price of the stock is $100 per share. The corporation declares a 2-for-1 stock split. The number of shares will double to 400,000, par value will be reduced by half, to $2.50, and the market price will be reduced by half, to $50 per share. Note that the Common Stock account has $1,000,000 in it both before and after the split. A stock split has no effect on total paid-in capital, retained earnings, and total stockholders' equity, and no journal entry is required to record it.

SO6. Identify the items that affect retained earnings.

A. **Retained earnings** is net income retained in the business and part of the stockholders' claim on the total assets of the corporation. Just as net income is credited to the Retained Earnings account, so net loss is debited to the account, even if an overall debit balance in the account results. A <u>debit balance in Retained Earnings</u> is called a **deficit** and is reported as a deduction in the stockholders' equity section of the balance sheet.

⋏ The **balance in retained earnings** is generally <u>available for dividend declarations</u>. There may be **retained earnings restrictions** that <u>make a portion of the balance currently unavailable for dividends</u>. Restrictions result from legal, contractual, or voluntary causes and are <u>usually disclosed in the notes</u> to the financial statements.

SO7. Prepare a comprehensive stockholders' equity section.

⋏ **Paid-in capital and retained earnings are reported**, and the <u>specific sources of paid-in capital are identified</u>. Capital stock consists of preferred and common stock, and additional paid-in capital includes the excess of amounts paid in over par or stated value and paid-in capital from treasury stock.

On the **statement of cash flows**, <u>information regarding cash inflows and outflows resulting from equity transactions is reported in the "Financing Activities" section</u>.

SO8. Evaluate a corporation's dividend and earnings performance from a stockholder's perspective.

⋏ To **measure a corporation's dividend record**, an investor can <u>compute the payout ratio</u>.

⋏ The **payout ratio** <u>measures the percentage of earnings distributed in the form of cash dividends to common stockholders</u>. It is computed by <u>dividing total cash dividends declared on common stock by net income</u>. A company with a high growth rate typically has a low payout ratio because it reinvests earnings in the business.

⋏ To **measure a corporation's earnings performance**, an investor can <u>compute the return on common stockholders' equity ratio</u>. The **return on common stockholders' equity ratio** <u>shows how many dollars of net income were earned for each dollar of common stockholders' equity</u>. It is computed by <u>dividing net income available to common stockholders (net income minus preferred dividends) by average common stockholders' equity</u>.

⋏ **To raise capital**, a <u>corporation may issue bonds or sell common stock</u>. If a corporation issues bonds, stockholder control is not affected, tax savings result, and the return on common stockholders' equity may be higher. If a company desires to increase its return on common stockholders' equity, it can either increase its return on assets or increase its reliance on debt financing. Remember, though, that issuance of debt necessitates payment of interest at regular intervals and the repayment of principal at the maturity date.

SO9. Prepare entries for stock dividends.
(This objective is found in the Chapter 11 appendix in your text.)

Consider the **following example of a small stock dividend**. A corporation has outstanding 500,000 shares of common stock on the day on which the board of directors declares a 10% stock dividend. The fair market value of the stock is $30 per share; par value is $10 per share. Fifty thousand new shares (500,000 x 10%) will be issued. The journal entry on the **date of declaration** is:

Stock Dividends	1,500,000	
Common Stock Dividends		
Distributable		500,000
Paid-in Capital in Excess of		
Par Value—Common		1,000,000
(To declare a 10% stock dividend)		

The computations are as follows:
Stock Dividends = 50,000 shares x $30
Dividends Distributable = 50,000 shares x $10
Paid-in Capital = $1,500,000 – $500,000

Common Stock Dividends Distributable is a stockholders' equity account. If a balance sheet is prepared after the dividend declaration, then the account will appear directly under the Common Stock account. **Stock Dividends** is a temporary account which must be closed at the end of the accounting period.

On the **date of distribution**, the journal entry is:

Common Stock Dividends		
Distributable	500,000	
Common Stock		500,000
(To record payment of stock dividend)		

Chapter Self-Test

As you work the exercises and problems, remember to use the **Decision Toolkit** discussed and used in the text:

1. <u>Decision Checkpoints</u>: at this point you ask a question.

2. <u>Info Needed for Decision</u>: you make a choice regarding the information needed to answer the question.

3. <u>Tool to Use for Decision</u>: at this point you review just what the information chosen in step 2 does for the decision-making process.

4. <u>How to Evaluate Results</u>: you perform evaluation of information for answering the question.

Note: The notation (SO1) means that the question was drawn from study objective number one.

Completion

Please write in the word or words that will complete the sentence.

1. (SO1)   A _____ _____ corporation may have thousands of stockholders, and its stock is traded on a national securities market.

2. (SO1)   The amount of stock that a corporation is permitted to sell, as listed in the corporate charter, is called _____ stock.

3. (SO2)   The issuance of common stock affects only _____ _____ accounts in stockholders' equity.

4. (SO3)   A corporation's own stock that has been issued, paid for, and repurchased is called _____ stock.

5. (SO4)   _____ stockholders have the right to receive dividends before _____ stockholders do.

6. (SO5)   For dividend purposes, a corporation determines ownership of outstanding shares of stock on the date of _____.

7. (SO5)   A _____ stock dividend occurs when new shares to be issued are less than 20%-25% of the outstanding shares.

8. (SO6)   A debit balance in the Retained Earnings account is called a _____.

9. (SO7)   There are two classifications within paid-in capital: _____ _____ and _____ _____ _____ _____.

10. (SO8)   Cash dividends declared on common stock divided by net income yields the _____.

Multiple Choice

Please circle the correct answer.

1. (SO1)   Which of the following is considered to be a disadvantage of the corporate form of business organization?
    a.   Limited liability of stockholders.
    b.   Separate legal existence.
    c.   Continuous life.
    d.   State and federal government regulation.

2. (SO1)   Capital stock that has been assigned a value per share in the corporate charter is called:
    a.   legal capital stock.
    b.   par value stock.
    c.   no-par value stock.
    d.   stated value stock.

3. (SO1)   The amount per share of stock that must be retained in the business for the protection of corporate creditors is called:
    a.   legal capital.
    b.   par value.
    c.   market value.
    d.   stated value.

4. (SO2)   If 3,000 shares of $5 par value common stock are sold for $6 per share, then the journal entry includes a:
    a.   debit to Paid-in Capital in Excess of Par Value for $3,000.
    b.   debit to Cash for $15,000.
    c.   credit to Common Stock for $15,000.
    d.   credit to Common Stock for $18,000.

5. (SO2)   If the Common Stock account has a balance of $20,000, the Paid-in Capital in Excess of Par Value account has a balance of $3,000, and Retained Earnings has a balance of $40,000, then total stockholders' equity is:
    a. $63,000.
    b. $60,000.
    c. $57,000.
    d. $17,000.

6. (SO3)   A corporation sold 1,000 shares of its $2.00 par value common stock for $10.00 per share and later repurchased 100 of those shares for $12.00 per share. The journal entry for the repurchase includes a debit to:
    a.   Common Stock for $1,200.
    b.   Treasury Stock for $1,200.
    c.   Treasury Stock for $200.
    d.   Cash for $1,200.

7.   (SO3) If the Common Stock account has a balance of $20,000, the Paid-in Capital in Excess of Par Value account has a balance of $3,000, Retained Earnings has a balance of $40,000, and Treasury Stock has a balance of $1,000, then total stockholders' equity is:
a. $64,000.
b. $63,000.
c. $62,000.
d. $59,000.

8.   (SO3) Total stockholders' equity is $120,000. If the Common Stock account has a balance of $30,000, the Paid-in Capital in Excess of Par Value account has a balance of $5,000, and Retained Earnings has a balance of $100,000, then Treasury Stock must be:
a. $15,000.
b. $20,000.
c. $25,000.
d. $30,000.

9.   (SO4) A corporation has cumulative preferred stock on which it pays dividends of $20,000 per year. The dividends are in arrears for two years. If the corporation has in the current year $90,000 available for dividends, then the common stockholders will receive:
a. $20,000.
b. $30,000.
c. $40,000.
d. $60,000.

10.   (SO4) Which of the following statements is incorrect?
a.   Dividends cannot be paid on common stock while any dividend on preferred stock is in arrears.
b.   Dividends in arrears on preferred are not considered a liability.
c.   Dividends may be paid on common stock while dividends are in arrears on preferred stock.
d.   When preferred stock is noncumulative, any dividend passed in a year is lost forever.

11.   (SO5) A corporation has declared a $1.00 per share cash dividend on its outstanding 500,000 shares of common stock. The journal entry on the date of payment of the dividend includes a debit to:
a.   Dividends Payable for $500,000.
b.   Cash Dividends for $500,000.
c.   Cash for $500,000.
d.   Common Stock Dividends Distributable for $500,000.

12.   (SO5)   A corporation has declared a $.50 per share cash dividend on its outstanding 200,000 shares of common stock. The journal entry on the date of declaration of the dividend includes a <u>credit</u> to:

    a.   Cash Dividends for $100,000.

    b.   Common Stock Dividends Distributable for $100,000.

    c.   Cash for $100,000.

    d.   Dividends Payable for $100,000.

13.   (SO5)   A corporation is authorized to sell 1,000,000 shares of common stock. Today there are 500,000 shares outstanding, and the board of directors declares a 10% stock dividend. How many shares will be issued as a result of the stock dividend?

    a.   100,000.

    b.   50,000.

    c.   None. The corporation will pay the dividend in cash.

    d.   None of the above is correct.

14.   (SO5)   A corporation has outstanding 100,000 shares of $5 par value common stock with a fair market value of $80 per share. If the board of directors declares a 2-for-1 stock split, then the number of shares outstanding doubles,:

    a.   the par value remains $5, and the fair market value decreases to $40.

    b.   but the par value and the fair market value remain the same.

    c.   the par value decreases to $2.50, and the fair market value decreases to $40.

    d.   the par value decreases to $2.50, and the fair market value remains at $80.

15.   (SO6)   If a corporation has incurred a net loss, then the loss is:

    a.   debited to Retained Earnings in a closing entry.

    b.   credited to Retained Earnings in a closing entry.

    c.   debited to a paid-in capital account in a closing entry.

    d.   credited to a paid-in capital account in a closing entry.

16.   (SO6)   A retained earnings restriction:

    a.   makes a portion of the balance of retained earnings unavailable for dividends.

    b.   may arise from legal, contractual, or voluntary causes.

    c.   generally is disclosed in the notes to the financial statements.

    d.   All of the above are correct.

17. (SO7) A corporation shows the following account balances:

Retained Earnings	$300,000
Treasury Stock	10,000
Common Stock Dividends Distributable	20,000
Paid-in Capital in Excess of Par Value	55,000
Common Stock	200,000

What is total stockholders' equity?
a. $585,000.
b. $575,000.
c. $565,000.
d. $545,000.

18. (SO7) A corporation shows the following account balances:

Retained Earnings	$400,000
Treasury Stock--Common	20,000
Common Stock Dividends Distributable	40,000
Paid-in Capital in Excess of Par Value--Common	55,000
Treasury Stock—Preferred	30,000
Common Stock	200,000
Preferred Stock	180,000
Paid-in Capital in Excess of Par Value—Preferred	60,000

What is total stockholders' equity?
a. $885,000.
b. $925,000.
c. $935,000.
d. $985,000.

19. (SO8) Consider the following data for a corporation:

Net income	$800,000
Preferred stock dividends	$50,000
Market price per share of stock	$25
Average common stockholders' equity	$4,000,000
Cash dividends declared on common stock	$20,000

What is the payout ratio?
a   2.5%.
b.   4.0%.
c.   40%.
d.   250%.

20. (SO8) Using the data in number 19, what is the return on common stockholders' equity?
a.   21.25%.
b.   20.00%.
c.   19.50%.
d.   18.75%.

21.   (SO9) The board of directors of a corporation declares a 5% stock dividend while there are 20,000 shares of $10 par value common stock outstanding. On this day the fair market value of the stock is $40 per share. The journal entry to declare the stock dividend includes a:
a.   debit to Stock Dividends for $10,000.
b.   credit to Paid-in Capital in Excess of Par Value for $10,000.
c.   credit to Common Stock Dividends Distributable for $40,000.
d.   credit to Common Stock Dividends Distributable for $10,000.

22.   (SO9) Please use the information in number 21. The journal entry on the date of distribution of the stock dividend includes a:
a.   credit to Stock Dividends for $10,000.
b.   credit to Common Stock for $10,000.
c.   debit to Common Stock for $10,000.
d.   credit to Common Stock Dividends Distributable for $10,000.

Problems

1.   Windsor Corporation shows the following data:

Common stock, $5 par value, 500,000 shares	
authorized, 300,000 shares issued and outstanding	$1,500,000
Paid-in capital in excess of par value	200,000
Retained earnings	3,200,000

REQUIRED: Please journalize the following transactions:

a. Sold 10,000 shares of stock for $9 per share (SO2).
b. Declared and distributed a 15% stock dividend. The fair market value of the stock on this date was $12 per share (SO9). (Two entries required)
c. Sold 8,000 shares of stock for $15 per share (SO2).
d. Declared a 2-for-1 stock split. On this date the fair market value of the stock is $18 per share (SO5).
e. Declared and paid a $.10 per share cash dividend (SO5). (Two entries required)

Date	Account Titles	Debit	Credit

2. Please refer to The Bon-Ton Stores, Inc. financial statements at the end of this study guide for information for answering the following questions. Don't forget to use the **Decision Toolkit** approach for help in the problem-solving.

   a. What type of stock does Bon-Ton have? What is the par value of each type of stock? (SO1, SO2)

   b. On what other financial statements is there information about stock? (SO1, SO2)

c. Does the company hold any treasury shares? (SO3)

d. What is the return on common shareholders' equity for Bon-Ton in 2007? (SO8)

e. What portion of its earnings did Bon-Ton pay out in dividends in 2007? (SO8)

SOLUTIONS TO SELF-TEST

Completion

1. publicly held
2. authorized
3. paid-in capital
4. treasury
5. Preferred, common
6. record
7. small
8. deficit
9. capital stock, additional paid-in capital
10. payout ratio

Multiple Choice

1.	d	The other three are considered to be advantages.
2.	b	There is no such thing as legal capital stock. No-par stock is just that: stock without a par value. Stated value stock is no-par stock assigned a stated value by the board of directors.
3.	a	Par value is an arbitrary amount listed in the corporate charter, and market value is the selling price of a share of stock on a given day. Stated value is a value assigned to no-par stock by the board of directors.
4.	c	The journal entry is:

```
Cash                                        18,000
      Common Stock                                   15,000
      Paid-in Capital in Excess of P.V.               3,000
```

5.	a	$20,000 + $3,000 + $40,000
6.	b	The journal entry is:

```
Treasury Stock                              1,200
      Cash                                           1,200
```

7.	c	$20,000 + $3,000 + $40,000 – $1,000
8.	a	$30,000 + $5,000 + $100,000 - $120,000
9.	b	Preferred receives $20,000 for each of the past two years and $20,000 in the current year for a total of $60,000; common receives the difference of $90,000 and $60,000.
10.	c	Dividends may not be paid on common stock as long as preferred dividends are in arrears.
11.	a	The journal entry is:

```
Dividends Payable                          500,000
      Cash                                          500,000
```

12.	d	The journal entry is:

```
Cash Dividends                             100,000
      Dividends Payable                             100,000
```

13.	b	500,000 shares x 10% = 50,000 new shares
14.	c	With a 2-for-1 stock split, the par value and fair market value of the stock are both reduced by half.
15.	a	A loss reduces Retained Earnings, requiring a debit to that account, and it is never closed to a paid-in capital account.
16.	d	
17.	c	$300,000 – $10,000 + $20,000 + $55,000 + $200,000
18.	a	$400,000 + $40,000 + $55,000 + $200,000 + $180,000 + $60,000 - $20,000 - $30,000
19.	a	$20,000 ÷ $800,000
20.	d	($800,000 - $50,000) ÷ $4,000,000

21. d The journal entry is:

Stock Dividends	40,000	
Common Stock Div. Distributable		10,000
Paid-in Capital in Excess of P.V.		30,000

    20,000 x 5% = 1,000 new shares
    Stock Dividends = 1,000 x $40 fair market value
    C.S. Div. Distributable = 1,000 x $10 par value
    Paid-in Capital = $40,000 - $10,000

22. b The journal entry is:

Common Stock Div. Distributable	10,000	
Common Stock		10,000

Problems

1.

a.

Cash	90,000	
Common Stock		50,000
Paid-in Capital in Excess of		
Par Value		40,000
(To record issuance of stock—10,000		
shares at $9 per share)		

b.

Stock Dividends	558,000	
Common Stock Div. Distributable		232,500
Paid-in Capital in Excess of		
Par Value		325,500
(To record declaration of stock dividend)		

Common Stock Dividends Distributable	232,500	
Common Stock		232,500
(To distribute stock dividend)		

310,000 shares x 15% = 46,500 new shares

Stock Dividends = 46,500 x $12 fair market value per share
Div. Distributable = 46,500 x $5 par value
Paid-in Capital = $558,000 – $232,500

c.

Cash	120,000	
Common Stock		40,000
Paid-in Capital in Excess of		
Par Value		80,000
(To record issuance of stock—8,000		
shares at $15 per share)		

d. No entry required. The number of shares outstanding at this point, 364,500, doubles to 729,000. The fair market value and the par value will be cut in half, $9 and $2.50, respectively.

e.   Cash Dividends   72,900
                Dividends Payable   72,900
       (To declare a $.10 per share cash
        dividend)

       Dividends Payable   72,900
                Cash   72,900
       (To pay the cash dividend)

       729,000 shares x $.10 per share.

2.   All dollar amounts are in thousands.

a.   To answer this question, you must read the balance sheet. Bon-Ton lists preferred stock
       with a $0.01 par value; interestingly, no shares of the preferred have been issued, or sold. It
       lists a type of common stock with a $0.01 par value and a Class A common stock, also with
       a $0.01 par value.

b.   Other than activity from stock options and stock awards to company employees, there has
       been no activity in the common stock accounts. This information is disclosed on the
       statement of shareholders' equity. The earnings per share ratio appears on the company's
       income statements.

c.   Yes. On Bon-Ton's balance sheet in the shareholders' equity section, the dollar amount of
       the 337,800 shares of treasury stock for each year ($1,387) is deducted to arrive at total
       shareholders' equity.   Note that the company uses the cost method. There is also a column
       for treasury stock on the statement of shareholders' equity.

d.   To answer this question, you must compute the return on common stockholders' equity
       ratio which shows how many dollars of net income were earned for each dollar invested by
       common stockholders and is computed by dividing net income less preferred stock
       dividends by average common stockholders' equity. Bon-Ton has issued no preferred stock
       and, therefore, there are no preferred stock dividends. Average stockholders' equity is
       computed by adding 2007 and 2006 shareholders' equity at year-end and dividing the sum
       by 2: ($363,061 + $346,396) ÷ 2 = $354,729 (rounded). The computation is then: net
       income of $11,562 ÷ $354,729 = 3.3% (rounded). In 2007, for every dollar common
       stockholders invested in Bon-Ton, they earned approximately $.03. Remember that one
       ratio by itself doesn't give sufficient information: it must be compared to industry averages
       or to the company's ratio over several accounting periods.

e.   To answer this question, you must compute the dividend payout ratio: total cash dividends
       declared on common stock divided by net income. Total cash dividends declared can be
       found on the statement of cash flows in the financing activities section, and net income is
       found on the income statement. Since Bon-Ton has only common stock issued, the
       dividends listed on the statement of cash flows must be applicable to common stock. So

the ratio becomes: $3,438 ÷ $11,562 = 29.7%. This means that for every dollar of net income, Bon-Ton paid out approximately $.30.

CHAPTER 12

Statement of Cash Flows

CHAPTER OVERVIEW

In this chapter you will learn about the statement of cash flows, including the three types of activities of a business, the primary purpose of the statement, and how to prepare the statement using the direct or the indirect method. You'll learn how to evaluate a company using the statement of cash flows and about the impact of the product life cycle on a company's cash flows.

REVIEW OF SPECIFIC STUDY OBJECTIVES

SO1.   Indicate the usefulness of the statement of cash flows.

↑   The **information in a statement of cash flows** should help users of the statement assess the <u>entity's ability to generate future cash flows</u>, its <u>ability to pay dividends and meet obligations</u>, the <u>reasons for the difference between net income and net cash provided or used by operating activities</u>, and the <u>cash investing and financing transactions during the period</u>.

↑   The **statement answers the following questions**:
1.   Where did cash come from?
2.   What was cash used for?
3.   What was the change in the cash balance?

SO2.   Distinguish among operating, investing, and financing activities.

↑   **Operating activities**, the <u>most important category</u> because it shows the cash provided or used by company operations, include the <u>cash effects of transactions that create revenues and expenses</u> and thus enter determination of net income.

⋏   **Investing activities** include <u>purchasing and disposing of investments and productive long-lived assets using cash</u> and <u>lending money and collecting the loans.</u>

⋏   **Financing activities** include <u>obtaining cash from issuing debt and repaying the borrowed amounts</u> and <u>obtaining cash from stockholders, repurchasing shares, and paying them dividends.</u>

⋏   In general:
   Operating activities involve <u>income statement items and current assets and current liabilities.</u>
   Investing activities involve <u>investments and other long-term asset items.</u>
   Financing activities involve <u>long-term liabilities and stockholders' equity items.</u>

⋏   A **company may also have significant noncash activities,** such as the <u>issuance of common stock for the purchase of assets</u>, the <u>conversion of bonds into common stock</u>, the <u>issuance of debt to purchase assets</u>, and the <u>exchange of plant assets.</u> These are **not reported in the body of the statement of cash flows** but instead are in a <u>separate schedule at the bottom of the statement</u> or <u>in a separate note or supplementary schedule to the financial statements.</u> Reporting of such activities satisfies the full disclosure principle.

⋏   With respect to **format of the statement**, <u>cash flows from operating activities are reported first, followed by cash flows from investing and financing activities.</u> Individual inflows and outflows from investing and financing activities are reported separately, not netted against each other. Net cash provided or used by each class of activities is reported; the three numbers are totaled to show the net increase or decrease in cash for the period; and the net increase or decrease is added to or subtracted from the beginning cash balance to yield the ending cash balance. Significant noncash activities are shown separately at the bottom of the statement.

SO3.   Explain the impact of the product life cycle on a company's cash flows.

⋏   The **product life cycle** is a <u>series of phases experienced by all products.</u>

   1.   The **introductory phase** occurs when the company is purchasing fixed assets and beginning to produce and sell.
   2.   The **growth phase** occurs while the company strives to expand production and sales.
   3.   The **maturity phase** occurs when sales and production level off.
   4.   The **decline phase** is marked by falling sales due to weak consumer demand.

⋏   A company can be characterized as being in one phase because the majority of its products are in a particular phase.

1. In the **introductory phase**, cash from operations is negative, cash from investing is negative, and cash from financing is positive. The company spends to purchase productive assets by issuing stock or debt but is not generating significant cash from operations.

2. In the **growth phase**, cash from operations is less than net income, cash from investing is negative because of asset acquisitions, and cash from financing is positive.

3. In the **maturity phase**, cash from operations and net income are approximately the same, and the company can start to retire debt or buy back stock.

4. In the **decline phase**, cash from operations decreases, cash from investing may be positive as the firm sells off excess assets, and cash from financing may be negative as the company buys back stock and retires debt.

⋏ The **statement of cash flows** is not prepared from the adjusted trial balance. The preparer must adjust the effects of the use of accrual accounting to determine cash flows.

⋏ **Information for preparation of the statement** comes from three sources: comparative balance sheets, the current period income statement, and selected additional information.

⋏ The **three steps in the preparation of the statement** are as follows: determine the net cash provided or used by operating activities by converting net income from an accrual basis to a cash basis; analyze changes in noncurrent asset and liability accounts and record as investing and financing activities, or as significant non-cash transactions; and compare the net change in cash with the change in the cash account reported on the balance sheet to make sure the amounts agree..

⋏ In the **operating activities section**, accrual basis net income is converted to cash basis net income. Either the **indirect or the direct method (discussed in the appendix to chapter 12 in your text) can be used** to accomplish this conversion: Both methods arrive at the same number, just in different ways. The **indirect method is used by 99% of companies** because it is easier to prepare and focuses on the differences between net income and net cash flow from operating activities. While the FASB prefers the direct method, it allows either approach. If the direct method is used, however, then net cash flow from operating activities using the indirect method must be reported in a separate schedule.

SO4. Prepare a statement of cash flows using the indirect method.

⋏ Use of the **indirect method** affects only the operating activities section of the statement. The investing and the financing activities sections are prepared in the same way under both methods. **Accrual basis net income is converted to cash basis net income** by adjusting it for items that affected reported net income but did not affect cash. There are various expenses and losses that reduce net income but which do not involve cash and revenues and gains that increase net income but which do not involve cash. The expenses and losses are added back to net income, and the revenues and gains are subtracted from net income to convert it to net cash provided by operating activities.

⅄   Your textbook's discussion of the individual mechanics is very solid and clear, and the following is a **summary of conversion to net cash provided by operating activities with respect to current assets and current liabilities**:

Account	Add to Net Income	Deduct from Net Income
Accounts receivable	Decrease	Increase
Inventory	Decrease	Increase
Prepaid expenses	Decrease	Increase
Accounts payable	Increase	Decrease
Accrued expenses payable	Increase	Decrease

⅄   **Noncash charges that must be added back to accrual basis net income** include depreciation expense, intangible asset amortization expense, and loss on sale of assets. These items all reduce net income but have nothing to do with cash, and they must be added back to produce net cash flows from operating activities.

⅄   **Noncash credits that must be deducted from accrual basis net income** include gain on sale of assets. This item increases net income but has nothing to do with cash flow, and it must be deducted to produce net cash flows from operating activities.

⅄   The noncash charges and credits are frequently listed as the first adjustments to net income.

⅄   The **investing activities section** deals with long-term assets, and the **financing activities section** deals with long-term debt and stockholders' equity items. All items are to be listed separately, not netted against one another. For example, if a company purchases one asset for $80,000 and sells another asset for $20,000, each cash flow must be listed, not just the net outflow of $60,000.

SO5.   Use the statement of cash flows to evaluate a company.

⅄   While traditional ratios are based on accrual basis accounting, **cash-based ratios are gaining acceptance among analysts**.

⅄   **Free cash flow** is computed by subtracting capital expenditures and dividends paid from cash provided by operations. It is a measure of a company's ability to generate sufficient cash to finance new fixed assets. Analysts often estimate the capital expenditures amount by using the reported expenditures for the purchase of new fixed assets shown in the investing activities section of the statement of cash flows.

⅄   A **traditional measure of liquidity (a company's ability to meet its immediate obligations) is the current ratio**: current assets divided by current liabilities. A disadvantage of this ratio is that it uses only year-end balances. A ratio that partially corrects this problem is the **current cash debt coverage ratio**: cash provided by operations divided by average current liabilities. Cash provided by operations involves the entire year and is often considered a better representation of liquidity on the average day. In general, if the value of this ratio falls below .40 times, it necessitates additional investigation of a company's liquidity.

⅄   A **measure of solvency (the ability of a company to survive over the long term) that uses cash figures** is the **cash debt coverage ratio**: cash provided by operations divided by average total liabilities. It indicates a company's ability to repay its liabilities from cash generated by operations. In general, if the value of this ratio falls below .20 times, it necessitates additional investigation.

SO6.   Prepare a statement of cash flows using the direct method. (This objective is discussed in the Chapter 12 appendix in your text.)

⅄   Use of the **direct method** affects only the operating activities section of the statement. The investing and the financing activities sections are prepared in the same way under both methods. Under the direct method, **net cash provided by operating activities** is computed by adjusting each item in the income statement from the accrual basis to the cash basis. Only major classes of operating cash receipts and cash payments are reported. An **efficient way to apply the direct method** is to analyze the revenues and expenses reported in the income statement in the order in which they are listed.

⅄   Your textbook's discussion of the individual mechanics is very solid and clear, and the following is a **summary of the formulas for computing the various cash inflows and outflows in order to arrive at net cash provided by operating activities**:

Revenues from sales
Deduct: Increase in accounts receivable OR
Add: Decrease in accounts receivable
Cash receipts from customers

Purchases**
Deduct: Increase in accounts payable OR
Add: Decrease in accounts payable
Cash payments to suppliers

**To solve for purchases:
Cost of goods sold
Deduct: Decrease in inventory OR
Add: Increase in inventory
Purchases

Operating expenses
Deduct: Decrease in prepaid expenses OR
Add: Increase in prepaid expenses AND
Deduct: Increase in accrued expenses payable OR
Add: Decrease in accrued expenses payable
Cash payments for operating expenses

Income tax expense
Deduct: Increase in income taxes payable OR
Add: Decrease in income taxes payable
Cash payments for income taxes

⋏ The **following do not appear on a statement of cash flows under the direct method because they are noncash charges**: depreciation expense, loss on sale of assets, intangible asset amortization expense, and depletion expense. A gain on sale of assets likewise will not appear because it is a noncash credit.

⋏ **Net income is not reported in the statement of cash flows under the direct method.** In the operating activities section, cash payments are subtracted from cash receipts to arrive at net cash provided by operating activities.

⋏ The **investing activities section** deals with long-term assets, and the **financing activities section** deals with long-term debt and stockholders' equity items. All items are to be listed separately, not netted against one another. For example, if a company purchases one asset for $80,000 and sells another asset for $20,000, each cash flow must be listed, not just the net outflow of $60,000.

Chapter Self-Test

As you work the exercises and problems, remember to use the **Decision Toolkit** discussed and used in the text:

1. Decision Checkpoints: at this point you ask a question.

2. Info Needed for Decision: you make a choice regarding the information needed to answer the question.

3. Tool to Use for Decision: at this point you review just what the information chosen in step 2 does for the decision-making process.

4. How to Evaluate Results: you perform evaluation of information for answering the question.

Note: The notation (SO1) means that the question was drawn from study objective number one.

Completion

Please write in the word or words that will complete the sentence.

1. (SO1) The usefulness of a statement of cash flows is to _____ _____, among other things, about an entity's ability to generate future cash flows.

2. (SO2) The issuance of long-term bonds for cash is an example of a/an _____ activity.

3. (SO2) Significant _____ activities are not reported in the body of the statement of cash flows.

4. (SO3) All products go through a series of phases called the _____ _____ _____.

5. (SO3) During the _____ phase of a company, cash from operations decreases, and the firm sells off excess assets and buys back stock and retires debt.

6. (SO4) With the _____ method of preparing the statement of cash flows, net income is adjusted for items that did not affect cash.

7. (SO4) With the indirect method of preparing the statement of cash flows, _____ expense is an example of noncash charge that is added back to net income.

8. (SO6) If a company uses the _____ method of preparing the statement of cash flows, then net income is not reported in the operating activities section.

9. (SO6) If a company uses the direct method of preparing the statement of cash flows, then _____ _____ do not appear in any section.

10. (SO5) If cash provided by operations is $200,000 and average current liabilities are $125,000, then the current cash debt coverage ratio is _____.

Multiple Choice

Please circle the correct answer.

1. (SO2) What type of activity is the purchase of a piece of equipment?
    a. Operating activity.
    b. Investing activity.
    c. Financing activity.
    d. Balance sheet activity.

2. (SO2) Which of the following is the most important category of activity for a business?
    a. Operating activity.
    b. Investing activity.
    c. Financing activity.
    d. Income statement activity.

3.   (SO2) Mach Corporation uses the indirect method when preparing its statement of cash flows. Which of the following will appear in the operating activities section of the statement?
a.   Sale of a parcel of land.
b.   Payment of cash dividends.
c.   Retirement of a long-term note payable.
d.   Increase in accounts receivable.

4.   (SO2) Blass Corporation uses the indirect method when preparing its statement of cash flows. Which of the following will appear in the investing activities section of the statement?
a.   Purchase of a piece of equipment.
b.   Decrease in prepaid expenses.
c.   Sale of a long-term bond payable.
d.   Increase in inventory.

5.   (SO2) Which of the following statements is correct?
a.   Significant financing and investing activities that do not affect cash are never reported in a company's annual report.
b.   Significant financing and investing activities that do not affect cash are reported in the body of the statement of cash flows.
c.   Significant financing and investing activities that do not affect cash are reported either in a separate schedule at the bottom of the state of cash flows or in a separate note or supplementary schedule to the financial statements.
d.   Significant financing and investing activities that do not affect cash are always reported on the company's income statement.

6.   (SO3) During the introductory phase of a company, which of the following is expected?
a.   Cash from operations is positive.
b.   Cash from investing is positive.
c.   Cash from financing is negative.
d.   Cash from operations is negative.

7.   (SO3) During the growth phase of a company, which of the following is expected?
a.   Cash from investing is negative.
b.   Cash from investing is positive.
c.   Cash from financing is negative.
d.   Cash from operations is more than net income.

8.   (SO3) In which phase of the product life cycle are cash from operations and net income approximately the same?
a.   Decline phase.
b.   Maturity phase.
c.   Growth phase.
d.   Introductory phase.

9.   (SO3)   Which of the following is a source of information for preparation of the statement of cash flows?
   a.   Comparative balance sheet.
   b.   Current period income statement.
   c.   Selected additional information.
   d.   All of the above are needed for preparation of the statement.

10.   (SO4)   If the indirect method is used for preparation of the statement of cash flows, then a decrease in accounts receivable is accounted for as a(n):
   a.   cash inflow in the investing activities section.
   b.   cash inflow in the financing activities section.
   c.   addition to net income in the operating activities section.
   d.   deduction from net income in the operating activities section.

11.   (SO4)   If the indirect method is used for preparation of the statement of cash flows, then an increase in prepaid expenses is accounted for as a(n):
   a.   cash inflow in the investing activities section.
   b.   cash inflow in the financing activities section.
   c.   addition to net income in the operating activities section.
   d.   deduction from net income in the operating activities section.

12.   (SO4)   If the indirect method is used for preparation of the statement of cash flows, then a gain on sale of equipment is accounted for as a(n):
   a.   deduction from net income in the operating activities section.
   b.   addition to net income in the operating activities section.
   c.   cash inflow in the financing activities section.
   d.   cash inflow in the investing activities section.

13.   (SO4)   If a company purchases land through the issuance of long-term bonds, then this is accounted for as a(n):
   a.   operating activity.
   b.   investing inflow.
   c.   financing outflow.
   d.   significant noncash investing and financing activity that merits disclosure.

14.   (SO6)   A company has $200,000 of net income, $500,000 of revenues from sales, and an increase in accounts receivable of $50,000. If the company uses the direct method of preparing the statement of cash flows, then cash receipts from customers total:
   a. $500,000.
   b. $450,000.
   c. $300,000.
   d. $150,000.

15. (SO6) A company has cost of goods sold of $300,000, an increase in inventory of $100,000, and an increase in accounts payable of $30,000. If it uses the direct method of preparing the statement of cash flows, then purchases total:
    a. $400,000.
    b. $370,000.
    c. $300,000.
    d. $200,000.

16. (SO6) A company has cost of goods sold of $300,000, an increase in inventory of $100,000, and an increase in accounts payable of $30,000. If it uses the direct method of preparing the statement of cash flows, then cash payments to suppliers total:
    a. $400,000.
    b. $370,000.
    c. $300,000.
    d. $200,000.

Please use the following data to answer questions 17 and 18.

Clark Corporation shows the following:

Cash provided by operations	$500,000
Capital expenditures	125,000
Dividends	40,000
Average total liabilities	300,000

17. (SO5) What is the company's free cash flow?
    a. $335,000.
    b. $375,000.
    c. $415,000.
    d. $500,000.

18. (SO5) What is Clark's cash debt coverage ratio?
    a. .25 times.
    b. .60 times.
    c. 1.67 times.
    e. 4.00 times.

Problems

1. The following are comparative balance sheet data for Knowl Corporation for the years 2011 and 2010:

Knowl Corporation
Comparative Balance Sheet Data
December 31, 2011 and 2010

	2011	2010
Cash	$ 3,600	$ 2,300
Accounts Receivable	3,500	2,600
Inventory	3,200	3,800
Equipment	3,800	3,400
Accumulated Depreciation	(2,400)	(2,340)
Long-Term Investments	2,600	2,840
	$14,300	$12,600
Accounts Payable	$ 2,400	$ 1,800
Accrued Liabilities	400	500
Bonds Payable	2,800	3,100
Common Stock	3,800	3,400
Retained Earnings	4,900	3,800
	$14,300	$12,600

Selected data from the income statement include net income of $2,140 and depreciation expense of $60. Cash dividends declared and paid totaled $1,040.

REQUIRED: Using the indirect method, please prepare a statement of cash flows for Knowl Corporation for the year ended December 31, 2011 (SO4). For long-term assets, long-term liabilities, and common stock, assume that an increase or decrease in these accounts involved a cash transaction.

Knowl Corporation
Statement of Cash Flows
For the Year Ended December 31, 2011

2. Please refer to The Bon-Ton Stores, Inc. financial statements at the end of this study guide for information for answering the following questions. Don't forget to use the **Decision Toolkit** approach for help in the problem-solving.

   a. What method does Bon-Ton use in its preparation of the statement of cash flows? (SO4)

   b. What is Bon-Ton's free cash flow in 2007? (SO5)

   c. In 2007 did the company generate sufficient cash from operating activities to meet its current obligations? (SO5)

   d. Does it seem that Bon-Ton will be able to survive over the long term? (SO5)

SOLUTIONS TO SELF-TEST

Completion

1.	provide information	7.	depreciation or amortization
2.	financing	8.	direct
3.	noncash	9.	noncash charges
4.	product life cycle	10.	1.6 times ($200,000 ÷ $125,000)
5.	decline		
6.	indirect		

Multiple Choice

1.   b   Operating activities deal with income statement items and with current assets and current liabilities. Financing activities deal with long-term liabilities and with stockholders' equity items. "Balance sheet activity" is a fabricated term.

2.   a   It is critical that a company generate its cash flow from operations, generally considered to be the best measure of a company's ability to generate enough cash to continue as a going concern.

3.   d   Sale of land is an investing activity (assumed here to be sold at cost so that there is no gain or loss), while payment of cash dividends and retirement of long-term debt are financing activities.

4.   a   Decrease in prepaid expenses and increase in inventory are operating activities, while sale of the long-term bond payable is a financing activity.

5.   c   Significant noncash activities <u>are</u> reported but not in the body of the statement of cash flows. They do not appear on the income statement.

6.   d   In the introductory phase the company does not generate positive cash from operations. Cash from investing is negative, and cash from financing is positive.

7.   a   Cash from investing is negative, and cash from financing is positive. Cash from operations is less than net income.

8.   b   During the maturity phase, cash from operations and net income are approximately the same.

9.   d   The information for the preparation of the statement of cash flow comes from three sources; comparative balance sheets, the current income statement, and additional information.

10.   c   A change in a current asset is an operating activity, not an investing or a financing activity. The decrease in receivables is not a deduction from net income.

11.   d   A change in a current asset is an operating activity, not an investing or a financing activity. The increase in prepaid expenses is not an addition to net income.

12.   a   The gain on sale of a fixed asset is a noncash credit that must be deducted from accrual basis net income to arrive at cash provided or used by operating activities.

13. d   Cash is not involved in this transaction; therefore, it is not an operating, an investing, or a financing activity. It is a noncash transaction.
14. b $500,000 – $50,000
15. a $300,000 + $100,000
16. b $300,000 + $100,000 – $30,000
17. a $500,000 – $125,000 – $40,000
18. c $500,000 ÷ $300,000

Problems

1.

Knowl Corporation
Statement of Cash Flows
For the Year Ended December 31, 2011

Cash flows from operating activities
  Net income $2,140
  Adjustments to reconcile net income to net
    cash provided by operating activities:
      Depreciation expense $ 60
      Decrease in inventory   600
      Increase in accounts payable   600
      Increase in accounts receivable   (900)
      Decrease in accrued liabilities   (100)   260
  Net cash provided by operating activities   2,400

Cash flows from investing activities
  Sale of long-term investments   240
  Purchase of equipment   (400)
  Net cash used by investing activities   (160)

Cash flows from financing activities
  Issuance of common stock   400
  Retirement of bonds payabldù(300)
  Payment of cash dividends   (1,040)
  Net cash used by financing activities   (940)

Net increase in cash   1,300
Cash at beginning of period   2,300
Cash at end of period $3,600

Without other information available, the assumption is that the increase in Equipment is due to a cash purchase. The decrease in Long-Term Investments is attributed to a sale of these for cash. The decrease in Bonds Payable is attributed to a retirement of some bonds, and the increase in Common Stock is assumed to be from a sale of stock for cash. The increase of $1,100 in Retained Earnings is due to net income of $2,140 less dividends declared and paid of $1,040.

2.   Dollar amounts are in thousands.

a.   To answer this question you must look at the operating activities section of the statement of cash flows. In this section, net income is listed first, and adjustments are made to arrive at cash flows from operating activities. This indicates that Bon-Ton uses the indirect method. If the direct method is used, then net income does not appear on the statement. Net cash provided by operating activities is computed by adjusting each item in the income statement from the accrual basis to the cash basis.

b.   To compute free cash flow, the sum of capital expenditures and dividends paid is subtracted from cash provided by operations (found on the statement of cash flows). Capital expenditures are found in the investing activities section of the statement of cash flows, while dividends can be found in the financing activities section of that statement.

Cash provided by operations	$135,564
Less: capital expenditures	−109,659
Less: dividends paid	−3,438
Free cash flow	$22,467

Significant free cash flow indicates greater potential to finance new investment and to pay additional dividends. Bon-Ton did generate enough cash flow in 2007 for both activities.

c.   To answer this question you must compute the current cash debt coverage ratio, calculated by dividing cash provided by operations by average <u>current</u> liabilities. For Bon-Ton, average current liabilities are $478,926 [($445,457 + $512,395) ÷ 2]. The ratio, therefore, is $135,564 ÷ $478,926, or .28 times (rounded). This indicates that the company has $.28 of cash from operating activities for every dollar of average current liabilities. Remember that the ratio must be compared with something for it to have value, either with Bon-Ton's ratios from prior years or with industry averages (typically there are no industry averages for the cash-based ratios). This ratio is a measure of liquidity based on cash basis figures, not on accrual basis figures.

d.   To answer this question you must compute the cash debt coverage ratio, calculated by dividing cash provided by operations by average <u>total</u> liabilities. For Bon-Ton, average total liabilities are $1,746,487 [($1,704,570 + $1,788,403) ÷ 2]. The ratio, therefore, is $135,564 ÷ $1,746,487, or .08 times (rounded). This indicates that the company has $.08 of cash from operating activities for every dollar of average total liabilities. Again, this ratio must be compared either with prior years' ratios or the industry average for it to have value, but it certainly does seem to be a weak ratio, one that the company should focus on improving.

CHAPTER **13**

Financial Analysis: The Big Picture

CHAPTER OVERVIEW

This chapter is essentially a capstone chapter for the textbook. You will learn about several new items: sustainable income and irregular items such as discontinued operations and extraordinary items; changes in accounting principle; comprehensive income; and horizontal and vertical analysis. You'll revisit ratios learned in prior chapters, focusing on what the ratios indicate, and learn about the limitations of financial analysis. Finally, you'll study the concept of quality of earnings.

REVIEW OF SPECIFIC STUDY OBJECTIVES

SO1.   Understand the concept of sustainable income.

    ⋏   **Sustainable income** is <u>net income adjusted for irregular items</u>. It is the most likely level of income to be obtained in the future, to the extent that this year's net income is a good predictor of future years' net income.

SO2.   Understand how irregular items are presented.

    ⋏   There are **two types of irregular items**: <u>discontinued operations and extraordinary items</u>. Both items are **reported net of income taxes**. If there is an extraordinary loss of $100,000 and the tax rate is 30%, then the loss is reported at its net amount of $70,000 (the $30,000 of income taxes is actually a tax savings in the case of a loss).

    ⋏   **Discontinued operations** refer to the <u>disposal of a significant segment of a business, such as the elimination of a major class of customers or an entire activity</u>.

The income statement should report income from continuing operations and income (or loss) from discontinued operations. (It is important to distinguish infrequently occurring items from routine, recurring operations, and, in general, it makes sense to eliminate all irregular items in estimating future sustainable income.) The **income (loss) from discontinued operations consists of the income (loss) from operations and the gain (loss) on disposal of the segment**. Remember that both the operating income or loss and the disposal gain or loss are reported net of income taxes.

∧ **Extraordinary items** are events and transactions that meet two conditions: they are unusual in nature and infrequent in occurrence. The "unusual" and "infrequent" conditions are necessarily influenced by the judgment of the accountants dealing with the items. Extraordinary items are reported net of income taxes in a separate section of the income statement immediately below discontinued operations. If a transaction meets only one of the criteria, then it is treated as a line item in the upper half of the income statement under Other Expenses and Losses or Other Revenues and Gains: it is shown at the gross amount, not net of tax. It will go into the determination of income from continuing operations, and income taxes are calculated for that number.

∧ A **change in accounting principle** occurs when the principle used in the current year is different from the one used in the preceding year. Remember that consistency is desirable but that changes can be made as long as management can show that the new principle is preferable to the old principle and the effects of the change are clearly disclosed in the income statement. **Examples** of changes include changes in the method used for depreciation and in the method used for inventory costing. A company reports a change in principle retroactively: Both the current and any previous periods reported are reported on the face of the statement using the new principle.

SO3. Explain the concept of comprehensive income.

∧ There is currently a **proliferation of items that bypass the income statement**. You have studied unrealized gains and losses on available-for-sale securities that appear in the stockholders' equity section of the balance sheet. Excluding such items from the income statement reduces the volatility of net income due to fluctuations in fair value but still informs the user of the gain or loss that would be incurred if the securities were sold at fair value. To address concerns of analysts and users about these items which do not appear on the income statement, the **FASB requires that a company must report not only net income but also comprehensive income**, which includes all changes in stockholders' equity during a period except those resulting from investments by stockholders and distributions (dividends) to stockholders. One format for the presentation of comprehensive income is to present a combined statement of income and comprehensive income. On such a statement, after net income is computed, any comprehensive income items are added to or subtracted from the net income number to arrive at comprehensive income.

SO4.   Describe and apply horizontal analysis.

    ⋏   **For data to be meaningful, they must be compared to something.** Comparisons may be:

        1.   <u>Intracompany comparisons</u>. Comparisons may be made within a company on a year-to-year basis to detect changes in financial relationships and significant trends. "Intra" is a Latin preposition which means "within."

        2.   <u>Intercompany comparisons</u>. Comparisons with other companies provide insight into a company's competitive position. "Inter" is a Latin preposition which means "between."

        3.   <u>Industry comparisons</u>. Comparisons with industry averages provide information about a company's relative position within the industry.

    ⋏   **Three basic tools** are used in <u>financial statement analysis: horizontal analysis, vertical analysis</u>, and <u>ratio analysis</u>.

    ⋏   **Horizontal (or trend) analysis** is a <u>technique for evaluating a series of financial statement data over a period of time</u>. Its **purpose** is to <u>determine the increase or decrease that has taken place, expressed as either an amount or a percentage</u>.

    ⋏   A company has net sales of $100,000 in 2009, $110,000 in 2010, and $116,000 in 2011. The **formula for computing changes since the base period** is:

$$\frac{\text{Current-Year Amount} - \text{Base-Year Amount}}{\text{Base-Year Amount}}$$

In our example, $10,000 ÷ $100,000 = 10% increase in 2010's net sales over 2009's. For the year 2011:

$$\frac{\$116,000 - \$100,000}{\$100,000} = 16\%$$

Note that the base year amount is always $100,000. Net sales in 2011 have increased by 16% over 2009's net sales, not over 2010's net sales.

    ⋏   An **advantage of horizontal analysis** is that it <u>helps to highlight the significance of a change by reducing the change to a percentage</u>. Sometimes it is difficult to see the magnitude of a change when only the dollar amount is examined.

    ⋏   **Several complications can arise using horizontal analysis.** If an item has no value in a base year or preceding year and a value in the next year, then no percentage change can be computed. If a negative number appears in the base year or preceding year and a positive amount exists the next year, or vice versa, then no percentage change can be computed.

SO5.   Describe and apply vertical analysis.

⅄ **Vertical (or common-size) analysis** is a <u>technique for evaluating financial statement data that expresses each item in a financial statement as a percent of a base amount</u>. On the balance sheet, assets are usually expressed as a percentage of total assets, and liability and stockholders' equity items are usually expressed as a percentage of total liabilities and stockholders' equity. On the income statement, items are usually expressed as a percentage of net sales.

⅄ When comparative balance sheets and income statements are presented, **vertical analysis shows not only the relative size of each category in each year on the balance sheet and on the income statement but also the percentage change in the individual items on the two financial statements**.

⅄ If current assets are $2,200 and total assets are $9,000, then current assets are 24.4% of total assets ($2,200 ÷ $9,000).

⅄ Just as is true with horizontal analysis, an **advantage of vertical analysis** is that it <u>helps to highlight the significance of a change by reducing the change to a percentage</u>. It also helps when making comparisons between companies of different sizes.

SO6. Identify and compute ratios used in analyzing a firm's liquidity, solvency, and profitability.

⅄ **Ratios can be classified into three types**: <u>liquidity</u>, which measure the short-term ability of the company to pay its debts and to meet unexpected needs for cash; <u>solvency</u>, which measure a company's ability to survive in the long term; and <u>profitability</u>, which measure the income or operating success of a company for a given period of time.

⅄ A **single ratio is not meaningful but must be compared with something**. As noted above, there may be <u>intracompany comparisons</u>, <u>intercompany comparisons</u>, and <u>comparisons with industry averages</u>.

⅄ The following are **liquidity ratios**:

1. **Current ratio**, computed by <u>dividing current assets by current liabilities</u>. If the current ratio is 1.25 to 1, then the company has $1.25 of current assets for every $1.00 of current liabilities.

2. Working capital is computed by subtracting the Current liabilities from the Current assets. Hopefully, the Current assets exceed the Current liabilities.

3. **Current cash debt coverage ratio**, computed by <u>dividing cash provided by operations by average current liabilities</u>. Instead of using in the numerator and denominator balances from just one point in time, this ratio uses numbers covering a period of time and thus may provide a better representation of liquidity. If the ratio is .5 to 1, then the company has $0.50 of cash provided by operations for every $1.00 of current liabilities. This ratio is cash basis, not accrual basis.

4. **Receivables turnover ratio,** computed by <u>dividing net credit sales by average gross receivables</u>. This ratio measures the number of times, on average, receivables are collected during the period. If the ratio is 12.5 times, then the company collects its receivables 12.5 times during the accounting period.

5. **Average collection period**, computed by <u>dividing 365 days by the receivables turnover ratio</u>. Using the 12.5 times from the previous ratio, the average collection period for this company is 29.2 days (365 ÷ 12.5). The general rule is that the collection period should not greatly exceed the credit term period (the time allowed for payment).

6. **Inventory turnover ratio**, computed by <u>dividing cost of goods sold by average inventory</u>. If the ratio is 8 times, then the company sold its inventory 8 times during the accounting period. Since the business of a merchandiser is to sell inventory, this ratio is very closely monitored. If it shows significant change in either direction, then action is taken. This ratio varies widely among industries.

7. **Days in inventory**, computed by <u>dividing 365 days by the inventory turnover ratio</u>. Using the 8 times from the previous ratio, the average days in inventory number is 46.5 days. The company takes approximately 46 days to sell its inventory.

A   The following are **solvency ratios**:

1. **Debt to total assets ratio**, computed by <u>dividing total liabilities by total assets</u>. It measures the percentage of the total assets provided by creditors and provides some indication of the company's ability to withstand losses without impairing the interests of its creditors. If the ratio is 65%, then creditors have provided financing sufficient to cover 65% of the company's total assets. The higher the percentage of liabilities to total assets, the greater the risk that the company may be unable to pay its debts; therefore, creditors usually like to see a low ratio. The <u>debt to equity ratio</u> shows the relative use of borrowed funds compared with resources invested by the owners.

2. **Times interest earned ratio**, computed by <u>dividing income before interest expense and income taxes by interest expense</u>. It indicates the company's ability to meet interest payments as they come due. If the ratio is 13 times, then the company has income before interest and taxes that is 13 times the amount needed for interest expense.

3. **Cash debt coverage ratio**, computed by <u>dividing cash provided by operations by average total liabilities</u>. It indicates a company's ability to repay its debts from cash generated from operating activities without having to liquidate the assets used in its operations. If the ratio is .24, then net cash generated from 1 year of operations is sufficient to pay off 24% of the company's total liabilities. This ratio is cash basis, not accrual basis.

4. **Free cash flow**, computed by <u>subtracting the sum of capital expenditures and dividends paid from cash provided by operations</u>. It indicates the cash available for paying dividends or expanding operations.

The following are **profitability ratios** (profitability is used frequently as the ultimate test of management's operating effectiveness):

1. **Return on common stockholders' equity ratio**, computed by <u>dividing income available to common stockholders (net income – preferred stock dividends) by average common stockholders' equity</u>. It shows how many dollars of net income were earned for each dollar invested by the owners. Two factors affect this ratio: the return on assets ratio and the degree of leverage.

2. **Return on assets ratio**, computed by <u>dividing net income by average total assets</u>. It measures the rate earned on each dollar invested in assets. **Leveraging** (or trading on the equity at a gain) means that the <u>company has borrowed money by issuing bonds or notes at a lower rate of interest than it is able to earn by using the borrowed money</u>: the company borrows at 10% but is able to earn 15%. Note that the opposite could be true: the company borrows at 10% but is able to earn only 8%. This is called trading on the equity at a loss. Two factors affect this ratio: the profit margin ratio and the asset turnover ratio.

3. **Profit margin ratio**, computed by <u>dividing net income by net sales</u>. This is a measure of the percentage of each dollar of sales that results in net income. If the ratio is .12, then each dollar of sales results in $.12 of net income. High-volume enterprises (grocery stores) generally have low profit margins, whereas low-volume enterprises (jewelry stores) usually have high profit margins. Two factors strongly influence this ratio, one of which is the gross profit rate.

4. **Asset turnover ratio**, computed by <u>dividing net sales by average total assets</u>. It measures how efficiently a company uses its assets to generate sales. This ratio varies widely among industries.

5. **Gross profit rate**, computed by <u>dividing gross profit by net sales</u>. It indicates a company's ability to maintain an adequate selling price above its costs. The more competition in an industry, the lower the gross profit rates. If the gross profit rate is .58, then each dollar of net sales generates gross profit of $.58.

6. **Earnings per share (EPS)**, computed by <u>dividing income available to common stockholders (net income – preferred stock dividends) by the average number of outstanding common shares</u>. It is a measure of the net income earned on each share of common stock. If earnings per share is $2.05, then $2.05 of net income was earned on each share of common stock.

7.   **Price-earnings ratio**, computed by <u>dividing the market price per share of stock by earnings per share</u>. It measures the ratio of the market price of each share of common stock to the earnings per share. If the price-earnings ratio is 23, then each share of stock sold for 23 times the amount that was earned on each share.

8.   **Payout ratio**, computed by <u>dividing cash dividends declared on common stock by net income</u>. It measures the percentage of earnings distributed in the form of cash dividends. Growth companies have low payout ratios because they reinvest earnings in the business.

⋏   **Availability of information** is not a problem in financial statement analysis. The goal is to perform relevant analysis and select pertinent comparative data. The goal is to know what ratio will give the answer to the question being asked.

SO7.   Understand the concept of quality of earnings.

⋏   **Quality of earnings** <u>indicates the level of full and transparent information provided to financial statement users</u>. Analysts and other users of financial statements certainly prefer a high quality of earnings.

⋏   **Factors affecting quality of earnings** include the following:

1.   **Alternative accounting methods**. Variations among companies in the application of GAAP can impede comparability and reduce quality of earnings.

2.   **Pro forma income**. In addition to income reported according to GAAP, some companies are reporting pro forma income, <u>a measure that usually excludes items that the company thinks are unusual or nonrecurring</u>. Because there are no rules governing pro forma income reporting, companies take a lot of leeway in what they include or exclude. Therefore, many analysts and investors are critical of this measure because it often makes companies look better than they really are.

3.   **Improper recognition**. Because of the huge pressure to meet earnings expectations, managers are sometimes guilty of manipulating the earnings numbers. One type of manipulation is <u>improper revenue recognition</u>: recognizing revenue "before its time." Some companies use channel stuffing, which involves selling far more product to their customers then the customers can use in the current accounting period. This makes the current period look good but can bode disaster for future periods if goods are returned or if customers don't order more product because they already have too much. <u>Improper capitalization of expenses</u> is another gimmick used by management to make results look better than they are. Instead of showing expenses as expenses, these managers debit them to an asset account and write them off slowly over future periods. <u>Failure to report all liabilities</u> is another way to make earnings results look better than they are.

    4. **Price-earnings ratio.** This ratio is computed by dividing earnings per share into the stock price per share. A low P-E ratio often means that investors think a company's future earnings will not be strong and sometimes reflects the market's belief that a company has poor quality earnings.

Chapter Self-Test

As you work the exercises and problems, remember to use the **Decision Toolkit** discussed and used in the text:

    1. <u>Decision Checkpoints</u>: at this point you ask a question.

    2. <u>Info Needed for Decision</u>: you make a choice regarding the information needed to answer the question.

    3. <u>Tool to Use for Decision</u>: at this point you review just what the information chosen in step 2 does for the decision-making process.

    4. <u>How to Evaluate Results</u>: you perform evaluation of information for answering the question.

Note: The notation (SO1) means that the question was drawn from study objective number one.

Matching

Please write the letters of the following terms in the spaces to the left of the definitions.

a. Asset turnover ratio	g. Leveraging
b. Cash debt coverage ratio	h. Price-earnings ratio
c. Current cash debt coverage ratio	i. Profit margin ratio
d. Earnings per share	j. Return on common stockholders' equity ratio
e. Free cash flow	
f. Horizontal analysis	k. Vertical analysis

_____ 1. (SO6) Cash provided by operations divided by average total liabilities.

_____ 2. (SO4) A technique for evaluating a series of data over a period of time to determine the increase or decrease that has taken place, expressed as either an amount or a percentage.

_____ 3. (SO6) Income available to common stockholders divided by average common stockholders' equity.

_____ 4. (SO6) Income available to common stockholders divided by the weighted average common shares outstanding.

_____ 5. (SO6) Net sales divided by average total assets.

_____ 6. (SO5) A technique for evaluating data that expresses each item in a financial statement as a percent of a base amount.

_____ 7. (SO6) Cash provided by operations minus the sum of capital expenditures and dividends paid.

_____ 8.   (SO6)   Market price of a share of stock divided by the stock's earnings per share.

_____ 9.   (SO6)   Cash provided by operations divided by average current liabilities.

_____ 10.   (SO6)   Net income divided by net sales.

Multiple Choice

Please circle the correct answer.

1.   (SO1)   Net income adjusted for irregular items is called:
   a.   sustainable income.
   b.   comprehensive income.
   c.   quality income.
   d.   accrual income.

2.   (SO2)   To be classified as extraordinary, an item must:
   a.   result from an act of God.
   b.   be only unusual in nature.
   c.   be only infrequent in occurrence.
   d.   be both unusual in nature and infrequent in occurrence.

3.   (SO2)   Discontinued operations and extraordinary items appear on the:
   a.   income statement as part of income from continuing operations.
   b.   income statement net of income taxes, below "Income from Continuing Operations."
   c.   income statement at their gross amount, below "Income from Continuing Operations."
   d.   balance sheet in the stockholders' equity section.

4.   (SO2)   A corporation shows income from continuing operations of $175,000. It has an extraordinary gain of $50,000, and its tax rate is 30%. What is the corporation's net income?
   a. $225,000.
   b. $210,000.
   c. $140,000.
   d. $125,000.

5.   (SO3)   Income that includes all changes in stockholders' equity during a period except those resulting from investments by stockholders and distributions to stockholders is called:
   a.   net income.
   b.   income from continuing operations.
   c.   comprehensive income.
   d.   bottom line net income.

6. (SO3) A company has net income of $200,000. Its portfolio of available-for-sale securities has a cost of $50,000 and a market value at the end of its accounting period of $54,000. What is the company's comprehensive income?
   a. $254,000.
   b. $250,000.
   c. $204,000.
   d. $200,000.

7. (SO4) Which of the following is a type of comparison providing decision usefulness of financial information?
   a. Industry averages.
   b. Intercompany basis.
   c. Intracompany basis.
   d. All of the above provide decision usefulness.

8. (SO4) Total current liabilities are $10,000 in 2009, $18,000 in 2010, and $22,000 in 2011. What is the percentage increase from 2009 to 2011?
   a. 22% (rounded).
   b. 80%.
   c. 120%.
   d. It cannot be computed from the data given.

9. (SO5) Consider the following data for Elizabeth Corporation:

Net sales	$100,000
– Cost of goods sold	30,000
Gross profit	70,000
– Operating expenses	50,000
Net income	$ 20,000

Performing vertical analysis and using net sales as the base, what percentage of net sales is cost of goods sold?
   a. 20%.
   b. 30%.
   c. 70%.
   d. 333% (rounded).

10. (SO5) Consider the following data for Soledad Corporation:

Cash	$ 30,000
Accounts receivable	125,000
Inventory	200,000
Prepaid assets	20,000
Total current assets	$375,000

Performing vertical analysis and using total current assets as the base, what percentage of total current assets is inventory?
   a.   214% (rounded).
   b.   188% (rounded).
   c.   53% (rounded).
   d.   47% (rounded).

11. (SO6) Measures of a company's ability to survive over a long period of time are called:
   a.   liquidity ratios.
   b.   solvency ratios.
   c.   profitability ratios.
   d.   acid-test ratios.

12. (SO6) _____ is frequently used as the ultimate test of management's operating effectiveness.
   a.   Net income
   b.   Liquidity
   c.   Solvency
   d.   Profitability

Please use the following data for 13, 14, and 15:

Current assets	150,000
Total assets	500,000
Current liabilities	125,000
Total liabilities	200,000
Net credit sales	600,000
Cost of goods sold	160,000
Average receivables	50,000
Average inventory	40,000

13. (SO6) What is the receivables turnover ratio?
   a.   3.2 times.
   b.   4.0 times.
   c.   12 times.
   d.   15 times.

11

14. (SO6) What is the inventory turnover ratio?
    a.   3.2 times.
    b.   4.0 times.
    c.   12 times.
    d.   15 times

15. (SO6) What is the debt to total assets ratio?
    a.   25.0%.
    b.   40.0%.
    c.   62.5%.
    d.   83.3%.

16. (SO6) Net sales are $6,000,000, net income is $800,000, income available to common stockholders is $700,000, and the average number of outstanding common shares is 300,000. What is the profit margin ratio?
    a.   13.3%.
    b.   11.7%.
    c. $2.67.
    d. $2.34.

17. (SO6) Net sales are $6,000,000, net income is $800,000, income available to common stockholders is $700,000, and the average number of outstanding common shares is 300,000. What is earnings per share?
    a.   13.3%.
    b.   11.7%.
    c. $2.67.
    d. $2.34.

18. (SO6) Which of the following is considered a profitability ratio?
    a.   Price-earnings ratio.
    b.   Times interest earned ratio.
    c.   Average collection period.
    d.   Current cash debt coverage ratio.

19. (SO6) Which of the following is considered a solvency ratio?
    a.   Price-earnings ratio.
    h.   Times interest earned ratio.
    c.   Average collection period.
    d.   Current cash debt coverage ratio.

Problems

1. What is meant by quality of earnings, and what are some of the factors affecting quality of earnings? (SO7)

2. Please refer to The Bon-Ton Stores, Inc. financial statements at the end of this study guide for information for answering the following questions. Don't forget to use the **Decision Toolkit** approach for help in the problem-solving.

    a. How much did Bon-Ton's cost of merchandise sold increase or decrease from 2005 to 2006? From 2005 to 2007? (SO4)

    b. What percentage of 2007's net sales is cost of merchandise sold? What percentage of 2007's total assets is current assets? (SO5)

    c. In 2007 and 2006 what percentage of each dollar of sales resulted in net income? (SO6)

d. How does the company report its comprehensive income? (SO3)

SOLUTIONS TO SELF-TEST

Matching

1.	b		6.	k
2.	f		7.	e
3.	j		8.	h
4.	d		9.	c
5.	a		10.	i

Multiple Choice

1.   a   Sustainable income does not include discontinued operations or extraordinary items.

2.   d   An act of God may be extraordinary or ordinary, and an item must be <u>both</u> unusual and infrequent to be classified as extraordinary.

3.   b   They are shown net of tax in the bottom half of the income statement, below income from continuing operations. They never appear on the balance sheet.

4.   b   The gain of $50,000 net of 30% tax of $15,000 is $35,000. The $35,000 is added to income from continuing operations of $175,000 to arrive at $210,000.

5.   c   Net income and income from continuing operations do not include such items, and "bottom line net income" is a fabricated phrase.

6.   c   The company has an unrealized gain of $4,000 ($54,000 market value –

$50,000 cost) which is added to net income of $200,000 to arrive at comprehensive income.

7.	d	Three types of comparisons improve the decision usefulness of financial information: intracompay, intercompany, and industry averages.
8.	c	($22,000 – $10,000) ÷ $10,000
9.	b	$30,000 ÷ $100,000
10.	c	$200,000 ÷ $375,000
11.	b	Liquidity refers to a company's short-term ability to pay obligations as they arise, and profitability measures the operating success of a business for a given period of time. The acid-test ratio is a measure of liquidity.
12.	d	Net income is simply the difference between revenues and expenses, and liquidity and solvency refer to the company's ability to survive on a short-term and on a long-term basis, respectively.
13.	c	$600,000 ÷ $50,000
14.	b	$160,000 ÷ $40,000
15.	b	$200,000 ÷ $500,000
16.	a	$800,000 ÷ $6,000,000
17.	d	$700,000 ÷ 300,000 shares
18.	a	Times interest earned is a solvency ratio, and average collection period and the current cash debt coverage ratio are liquidity measures.
19.	b	The price-earnings ratio is a profitability ratio.

Problems

1. Quality of earnings refers to the fact that a company's management provides full and transparent information that will not confuse or mislead users of its financial statements. Analysts sometimes feel that a company that uses conservative, as opposed to aggressive, accounting policies has a high quality of earnings. Some of the factors affecting quality of earnings are the following:

   a. Variations among companies in the application of GAAP may hamper comparability and reduce quality of earnings.
   b. The reporting of so-called pro forma income, a measure that usually excludes items that the company thinks are unusual or nonrecurring, can affect quality of earnings. Companies have a great amount of leeway in what items to include in or exclude from pro forma income, and some feel that companies choose to treat items in a way that will show the company in a very favorable light.
   c. The pressure on management to meet earnings expectations may cause managers to recognize revenue improperly, to capitalize items that should be expensed, and to omit completely some liabilities.

2. Dollar amounts are in thousands.

   a. To answer this question you must perform one type of financial statement analysis called horizontal analysis, the purpose of which is to determine the increase or decrease that has taken place, expressed as either an amount or a percentage. In this case you must compute a percentage of increase or decrease.

Cost of merchandise sold increased 158% from 2005 to 2006.
$2,118,762 - $822,171 = $1,296,591 ÷ $822,171 = 158% (rounded).

Cost of merchandise sold increased 162% from 2005 to 2007.
$2,150,131 – $822,171 = $1,327,960 ÷ $822,171 = 162% (rounded).

Note that in each case 2005 is the base year.

b.   To answer this question you must perform another type of financial statement analysis called vertical analysis in which each item in a financial statement is expressed as a percent of a base amount. On the income statement net sales is usually the base. On the balance sheet, total assets, and total liabilities and stockholders' equity are the two bases.

$2,150,131 ÷ $3,365,912 = 63.8% (rounded)
$871,908 ÷ $2,067,631 = 42.2% (rounded)

c.   To answer this question you must compute for each year the profit margin ratio, calculated by dividing net income by net sales.

In 2007: $11,562 ÷ $3,365,912 = 0.3% (rounded)
In 2006: $46,883 ÷ $3,362,279 = 1.4% (rounded)

A higher value suggests a favorable return on each dollar of sales. It would be interesting to compare Bon-Ton's numbers with those of other retail department stores.

d.   Your text notes that there are various formats for reporting comprehensive income and discusses a combined statement of income and comprehensive income. Bon-Ton does not do this, however. Instead, it includes line items for comprehensive income on its statement of shareholders' equity.

APPENDIX C

Time Value of Money

APPENDIX OVERVIEW

This appendix addresses the difference between simple interest, which is computed on principal only, and compound interest, which is computed on both principal and interest earned that has not been paid or withdrawn. Simple interest is the product of the principal, the rate, and the time, but the formula used for compound interest depends on whether you are solving for the present value or future value and whether the amount involved is a single sum or an annuity (a series of equal dollar amounts paid or received periodically).

Study Objective 1 – Distinguish Between Simple and Compound Interest

♦ Interest is payment for the use of another person's money. The amount of interest involved in any financing transaction is based on three elements:
  ▪ **Principal (p):** The original amount borrowed or invested.
  ▪ **Interest Rate (i):** An annual percentage of the principal.
  ▪ **Time (n):** The number of years that the principal is borrowed or invested.

♦ **Simple interest** is computed on the principal amount only. Simple interest is usually expressed as:

$$\text{Interest} = \text{Principal x Rate x Time}$$
$$\text{OR}$$
$$\text{Interest} = p \text{ x } i \text{ x } n$$

♦ **Compound interest** is computed on principal and on any interest earned that has not been paid or withdrawn. It is the return on (or growth of) the principal for two or more time periods.

Study Objective 2 – Solve for Future Value of a Single Amount

♦ The **future value of a single amount** is the value at a future date of a given amount invested assuming compound interest. Future value is usually expressed as:

$$FV = p \times (1 + i)^n$$

FV = future value of a single amount
p = principal (or present value)
i = interest rate for one period
n = number of periods

♦ The Future Value of 1 table is used for obtaining a factor which is multiplied by the principal to calculate the future value.

♦ Table 1 on page C4 is such a table, showing factors with 5-digit decimals.

Study Objective 3 – Solve for Future Value of an Annuity

♦ The **future value of an annuity** is the sum of all the payments (receipts) plus the accumulated compound interest on them. In computing the future value of an annuity, it is necessary to know the (1) interest rate, (2) the number of compounding periods, and (3) the amount of the periodic payments or receipts. When the periodic payments or receipts are the same in each period, the future value can be computed by using a future value of an annuity of 1 table.

♦ Calculating the future value of each individual cash flow is required when the period payments or receipts are not equal in each period.

♦ Table 2 on page C6 shows the future value of 1 to be received periodically for a given number of periods.

♦ This table assumes that each payment is made at the **end** of each period.

Study Objective 4 – Identify Variables Fundamental to Solving Present Value problems.

♦ The **present value** is based on three variables: (1) the dollar amount to be received (future amount), (2) the length of time until the amount is received (number of periods), and (3) the interest rate (the discount rate).

♦ Present value computations are used for principal and interest payments for determining the market price of bonds, as well as notes payable and lease liabilities.

Study Objective 5 – Solve for Present Value of a Single Amount

♦ If the future amount to be received in n periods is discounted at interest rate i, then the computation of a single amount to be invested is calculated as:

$$PV = FV/(1 + i)^n$$

PV = present value
FV = future value
i = interest rate
n = number of periods

♦ The present value of 1 may also be determined through tables that show the present value of 1 for n periods.

♦ Table 3 on page C8 is used to find the present value of a single amount.

Study Objective 6 – Solve for Present Value of an Annuity

♦ In computing the present value of an annuity, it is necessary to know (1) the discount rate, (2) the number of discount periods, and (3) the amount of the periodic receipts or payments. When the future receipts are the same in each period, there are two other ways to compute the present value. First, the annual cash flow can be multiplied by the sum of the three present value factors. Second, annuity tables may be used.

♦ Discounting may also be done over shorter periods of time such as monthly, quarterly, or semiannually. When the time frame is less than one year, it is necessary, to convert the annual interest rate to the applicable time frame.

♦ Table 4 on page C10 is used to find the present value of an annuity.

Study Objective 7 – Compute the Present Value of Notes and Bonds

♦ The present value (or market price) of a long-term note or bond is a function of three variables: (1) the payment amounts, (2) the length of time until the amounts are paid, and (3) the discount rate.

♦ The first variable (dollars to be paid) is made up of two elements: (1) a series of interest payments (an annuity) and (2) the principal amount (a single sum). To compute the present value of the bond, both the interest payments and the principal amount must be discounted— two different computations.

♦ When the investor's discount rate is equal to the bond's contractual interest rate, the present value of the bonds will equal the face value of the bonds.

Study Objective 8 – Use a Financial Calculator To Solve Time Value of Money Problems.

♦ Once an understanding of the basic time value of money concepts is gained, many professionals use financial calculators to solve the computations.

♦ The most common keys used for solving time value of money problems with a financial calculator include:

> ♦ N = number of periods
> ♦ I = interest rate per period (some calculators use I/YR or i)
> ♦ PV = present value (occurs at the beginning of the first period)
> ♦ PMT = payment (all payments are equal, and none are skipped)
> ♦ FV = future value (occurs at the end of the last period)

♦ Most problems give three of four variables and require solving for the remaining variable. The fifth key (key not used) is given a value of zero to ensure that this variable is not used in the computation.

♦ Financial calculators are particularly useful where interest rates and compounding periods are not presented in tables.

APPENDIX SELF TEST

As you work the exercises and problems, remember to use the **Decision Toolkit** discussed and used in the text:

1. Decision Checkpoints: at this point you ask a question.

2. Info Needed for Decision: you make a choice regarding the information needed to answer the question.

3. Tool to Use for Decision: at this point you review just what the information chosen in step 2 does for the decision-making process.

4. How to Evaluate Results: you perform evaluation of information for answering the question.

Note: The notation (SO1) means that the question was drawn from study objective number one.

Completion

Please write in the word or words that will complete the sentence.

1. (SO1) _____ interest is computed on the principal amount only.

2. (SO1) _____ interest is computed on principal and on any interest that has not been paid or withdrawn.

3. (SO3)   An _____ is a series of equal dollar amounts to be paid or received periodically.

4. (SO3)   If you wish to know how much money you will have if you invest $3,000 at the end of each year for 5 years, you must solve for the _____ value of an annuity.

5. (SO5)   If you wish to know how much to invest today so that you will have $2,000 at the end of 2 years, you must solve for the _____ value of a single amount.

Multiple Choice

Please circle the correct answer.

1.   (SO1)   What is the annual simple interest on $4,000 borrowed for 3 years at 8%?
   a. $160.
   b. $320.
   c. $480.
   d. $960.

2.   (SO2)   Erin has invested $5,000 for 5 years compounded annually at an interest rate of 9%. How much money will she have available at the end of the 5 years?
   a. $29,923.55.
   b. $19,448.25.
   c. $16,248.25.
   d. $ 7,693.10.

3.   (SO3)   Harry plans to invest $1,000 at the end of each year for 8 years with interest compounded annually at 6%. How much money will he have available at the end of the eighth year?
   a. $ 5,019.28.
   b. $ 6,209.79.
   c. $ 9,897.47.
   d. $12,750.80.

4.   (SO5)   Angela needs to have $7,000 available in 3 years. How much must she invest today, with interest compounded annually at 8%, to have that amount available when she needs it?
   a. $5,556.81.
   b. $6,013.23.
   c. $7,574.93.
   d. $8,817.97.

5. (SO7) On January 2, 2010, Culloden Corporation issued $500,000 of 9% bonds with a maturity date of January 2, 2020. The bonds pay interest each January 1 and July starting on July 1, 2010. On the sale date, the discount rate was 8%. How much did Culloden receive when it sold the bonds?
    a. $545,000.00.
    b. $533,977.42.
    c. $522,500.00.
    d. $500,000.00.

Problems

1. If Elizabeth invests $20,900 now and wants to receive $100,000 at the end of 15 years, what annual rate of interest will Elizabeth earn on her investment?

2. Boyd Corporation receives a $20,000, 8-year note bearing interest of 10% (paid annually) from a customer at a time when the discount rate is 8%. What is the present value of the note received by Boyd?

SOLUTIONS TO SELF-TEST

Completion

1. Simple
2. Compound
3. annuity
4. future
5. present

Multiple Choice

1.	b	$4,000 x .08 = $320 interest for one year
2.	d	$5,000 x 1.53862 (factor from Future Value of 1 table, 5n, 9%)
3.	c	$1,000 x 9.89747 (factor from Future Value of Annuity of 1 table, 8n, 6%)
4.	a	$7,000 x .79383 (factor from Present Value of 1 table, 3n, 8%)
5.	b	Since the bond pays interest twice each year, the 10-year period becomes 20 periods on the tables, and the 8% discount rate becomes 4%. Annual cash interest paid is $45,000 ($500,000 x 9%), but since the bond pays twice a year, $22,500 is paid each 6 months.

$500,000 x .45639 = $228,195.00
$ 22,500 x 13.59033 = $305,782.42
$533,977.42

.45639 = factor from Present Value of 1 table
13.59033 = factor from Present Value of Annuity of 1 table

Problems

1. $20,900 ÷ $100,000 = .20900.
    Using Table 1 and going across period row 15, .20900 is under the 11% column, indicating that an annual rate of interest of 11% must be earned.

2. Present value of principal to be received at maturity:
    $20,000 X PV of 1 due in 8 periods at 8%
    $20,000 X .54027 (Table 1) $10,805

    Present value of interest to be received periodically
    over the term of the note:
    $2,000 X PV of 1 due periodically for 8 periods at 8%
    $2,000 X 5.74664 (Table 2)   11,493
        Present value of note $22,298

APPENDIX D

Reporting and Analyzing Investments

CHAPTER OVERVIEW

In this chapter you will learn about the reasons for corporations' investing in stocks and debt securities and how to account for both, as well as about consolidated financial statements. You'll learn how stock and debt investments are valued and reported in the financial statements and, finally, how to distinguish between short-term and long-term investments.

REVIEW OF SPECIFIC STUDY OBJECTIVES

SO1. Identify the reasons corporations invest in stocks and debt securities.

> ⚑ **Corporations invest in debt or equity securities** for one of three reasons:
>
>   1. They <u>have excess cash</u> that they do not need for immediate purposes. Excess cash may result from seasonal fluctuations in sales or from economic cycles. Excess cash is usually invested in low-risk, highly liquid securities, most often short-term government securities.
>   2. Some companies <u>generate a significant portion of their earnings from investment income</u>.
>   3. There may be <u>strategic reasons</u>, such as a corporation's desire to establish a presence in another industry or to purchase a controlling interest in another company.

SO2. Explain the accounting for debt investments.

> ⚑ **Debt investments** are <u>investments in government and corporation bonds</u>.

⋏ **Acquisition costs** include <u>all expenditures necessary to acquire the investment, such as the price paid plus brokerage fees (commissions)</u>. If a company **purchases bonds for $60,000 plus commissions of $2,000**, then the journal entry is:

Debt Investments   62,000
       Cash   62,000
(To record purchase of bonds)

Note that <u>there is no separate account for fees or commissions</u>: the purchase price and the commissions are debited to the asset account.

⋏ When **bond interest is received**, the debit is to Cash and the credit is to Interest Revenue (an Other Revenues and Gains item on the income statement). If interest is accrued, then the entry is a debit to Interest Receivable and a credit to Interest Revenue.

⋏ When **bonds are sold**, <u>any difference between net proceeds (sales price less fees) and the cost of the bonds is recorded as a gain or loss.</u> If **bonds with a cost of $20,000 are sold for a net amount of $18,000**, then the entry is as follows:

Cash   18,000
Loss on Sale of Debt Investments   2,000
       Debt Investments   20,000
(To record sale of bonds at a loss)

The **Loss account** appears <u>on the income statement as an Other Expenses and Losses item.</u> A **gain** appears <u>on the income statement as an Other Revenues and Gains item.</u>

SO3. Explain the accounting for stock investments.

⋏ **Stock investments** are <u>investments in the capital stock of corporations.</u> An **investment portfolio** consists of <u>securities (stock and/or debt) of several different corporations.</u>

⋏ **Accounting for stock investments** is <u>based on the extent of the investor's influence over the operating and financial affairs of the issuing corporation (the investee).</u> **Guidelines are as follows:**

1. If the **investor holds less than 20% of the investee's stock**, then there is an insignificant influence on the investee, and the <u>cost method</u> is used.
2. If the **investor holds between 20% and 50% of the investee's stock**, then there is a presumption of significant influence on the investee, and the <u>equity method</u> is used.
3. If the **investor holds more than 50% of the investee's stock**, then the investor has a controlling influence, and <u>consolidated financial statements</u> are prepared.

For **holdings of less than 20%**, the cost method is used. The <u>investment is recorded at cost</u>, and <u>revenue is recognized only when dividends are received</u>. As is true for debt investments, cost includes all expenditures necessary to acquire the investments, including the price paid plus brokerage fees (commissions). If **a corporation acquires 2,000 shares of common stock at $50 per share plus $2,000 in commissions**, then the journal entry is:

Stock Investments	102,000	
Cash		102,000
(To record purchase of stock)		

Note that once again <u>there is no separate account for fees or commissions</u>: the purchase price and the commissions are debited to the asset account.

If **dividends of $3.00 per share are received**, then the journal entry is:

Cash	6,000	
Dividend Revenue		6,000
(To record receipt of dividends)		

Dividend Revenue is an <u>Other Revenues and Gains item in the income statement</u>.

If **the shares of stock are sold** for net proceeds of $105,000, then the journal entry is:

Cash	105,000	
Stock Investments		102,000
Gain on Sale of Stock		
Investments		3,000
(To record sale of stock)		

A **loss account** appears <u>on the income statement as an Other Expenses and Losses item</u>. A **gain** appears <u>on the income statement as an Other Revenues and Gains item</u>.

For **holdings between 20% and 50%**, the <u>equity method is used</u>. The <u>investment is recorded initially at cost</u> and is <u>adjusted annually to show the investor's equity in the investee</u>. The investor debits the investment account and increases revenue for its share of the investee's net income. The investor debits Cash and credits the investment account for the amount of dividends received. With this method, the **investor is essentially purchasing an interest in the investee's Retained Earnings account**. Anything which makes that account increase, such as net income, is reflected in the investor's investment account as an increase, and anything which makes that account decrease, such as net loss or payment of dividends, is reflected in the investor's investment account as a decrease.

3

Reiher Corporation purchased 40% of the common stock of Sosa Corporation for $250,000. The journal entry is:

Stock Investments	250,000	
Cash		250,000
(To record purchase of Sosa stock)		

For the year, **Sosa reported $200,000 of net income and paid dividends of $50,000**. The journal entries for Reiher are:

Stock Investments	80,000	
Revenue from Investment		
in Sosa Corporation		80,000
(To record 40% equity in Sosa's		
net income)		

Cash	20,000	
Stock Investments		20,000
(To record dividends received)		

After these entries, the **balance in Stock Investments totals $310,000**: $250,000 + $80,000 − $20,000.

SO4.   Describe the purpose and usefulness of consolidated financial statements.

> A   A **parent company** is a company that owns more than 50% of the common stock of another entity. A **subsidiary (affiliated) company** is the entity whose stock is owned by the parent company. The parent company has a **controlling interest** in the subsidiary company.

> A   **Consolidated financial statements** are prepared. These statements present the assets and liabilities controlled by the parent company and the aggregate revenues and expenses of the subsidiary companies. They are presented in addition to the financial statements for each of the individual parent and subsidiary companies.

> A   **Consolidated financial statements** are especially useful to the stockholders, board of directors, and management of the parent company.

SO5.   Indicate how debt and stock investments are valued and reported in the financial statements.

> A   **Debt and stock investments** (in which the holdings are less than 20%) are classified into three categories for purposes of valuation and reporting at a financial statement date:
> 1.   **Trading securities** are bought and held primarily for sale in the near term to generate income.
> 2.   **Available-for-sale securities** are those that may be sold in the future.

3.　　**Held-to-maturity securities** are debt securities for which the <u>investor has the intent and ability to hold to maturity</u>. Notice that **this category includes only debt securities** because stocks do not have a maturity date.

⋏　**Trading securities are reported at fair value** (called mark-to-market accounting), and <u>changes from cost are reported as part of net income</u>. Since the securities have not been sold, the changes are reported as **unrealized gains or losses**, calculated as the difference between the total cost of the securities and their total fair value. Trading securities are classified as a current asset.

Consider the **following example**. A corporation owns three trading securities with a total cost of $90,000. On the financial statements date, their total fair market value is $96,000. The journal entry to record this unrealized gain is:

Market Adjustment—Trading	6,000	
Unrealized Gain—Income		6,000
(To record unrealized gain on trading		
securities)		

Use of a Market Adjustment—Trading account enables the company to <u>maintain a record of the investment cost</u>. Since this account in this situation has a debit balance, it will be added to the investments account on the balance sheet to give the fair value of the investments. Note that is it the <u>fair value of the investments that is reported on the balance sheet</u>. The **Unrealized Gain—Income** account is <u>reported on the income statement under Other Revenues and Gains</u>.

If the investments had had a fair value of $88,000, then the journal entry would have been a debit to Unrealized Loss—Income and a credit to Market Adjustment—Trading for $2,000. The **Unrealized Loss—Income** account is <u>reported on the income statement under Other Expenses and Losses</u>. Since Market Adjustment—Trading has a credit balance, it is subtracted from the investments account on the balance sheet to give the fair value of the investments.

Both unrealized gain and loss accounts are closed at the end of the accounting period. The <u>market adjustment account is carried forward into future periods and adjusted accordingly</u>.

⋏　**Available-for-sale securities** are <u>reported at fair value with changes reported in the stockholders' equity section of the balance sheet</u>. If the intent is to sell the securities within the next year or operating cycle, then they are classified as current assets. Otherwise, they are classified as long-term assets in the investments section of the balance sheet.

Consider the **following example**. A corporation owns three securities, considered to be available-for-sale, with a total cost of $90,000. On the financial statements date, their total fair market value is $96,000. The journal entry to record this unrealized gain is:

Market Adjustment—Available-For-Sale	6,000	
Unrealized Gain or Loss—Equity		6,000
(To record unrealized gain on available-for-sale securities)		

The **Market Adjustment** account is added to the investments account to give the fair value of the investments. The **Unrealized Gain—Equity** account is added to stockholders' equity on the balance sheet, not to income on the income statement as is the case with trading securities.

If the investments had had a fair value of $88,000, then the journal entry would have been a debit to Unrealized Gain or Loss—Equity and a credit to Market Adjustment—Available-For-Sale for $2,000. The **Unrealized Loss—Equity** account is reported on the balance sheet as a contra equity account, meaning that it is subtracted from stockholders' equity. Since Market Adjustment—Available-For-Sale has a credit balance, it is subtracted from the investments account on the balance sheet to give the fair value of the investments.

The **unrealized gain or loss account is carried forward to future periods, not closed**, and is adjusted with the market adjustment account to show the difference between cost and fair value at the financial statements date.

SO6.   Distinguish between short-term and long-term investments.

- For **balance sheet** presentation, investments must be classified as either short-term or long-term.

- **Short-term investments** are those that are readily marketable (can be sold easily whenever the need for cash arises) and intended to be converted into cash within the next year or operating cycle, whichever is longer. Short-term investments are **listed immediately below Cash on the balance sheet** because of their high liquidity (nearness to cash). They are reported at fair value.

- **Long-term investments** are reported in a separate section of the balance sheet immediately below current assets. Long-term investments in available-for-sale securities are reported at fair value, and investments in common stock accounted for under the equity method are reported at equity.

- On the **income statement**, gains and losses, both realized and unrealized, as well as interest and dividend revenue, are reported in the nonoperating section. On the **balance sheet**, an unrealized gain or loss on available-for-sale securities is reported as a separate component of stockholders' equity. The latter **presentation serves two purposes**: it reduces the volatility of net income due to fluctuations in fair value, and it informs the financial statement user of the gain or loss that would occur if the securities were sold at fair value. Unrealized gains and losses on available-for-sale securities must be reported in comprehensive income.

A   On the **statement of cash flows**, information on the <u>cash inflows and outflows resulting from investment transactions is reported in the "investing activities" section</u>.

Chapter Self-Test

As you work the exercises and problems, remember to use the **Decision Toolkit** discussed and used in the text:

1. <u>Decision Checkpoints</u>: at this point you ask a question.

2. <u>Info Needed for Decision</u>: you make a choice regarding the information needed to answer the question.

3. <u>Tool to Use for Decision</u>: at this point you review just what the information chosen in step 2 does for the decision-making process.

4. <u>How to Evaluate Results</u>: you perform evaluation of information for answering the question.

Note: The notation (SO1) means that the question was drawn from study objective number one.

Matching

Please write the letters of the following terms in the spaces to the left of the definitions.

a. Available-for-sale securities

b. Consolidated financial statements

c. Controlling interest

d. Cost method

e. Equity method

f. Held-to-maturity securities

g. Long-term investments

h. Parent company

i. Short-term investments

j. Subsidiary (affiliated) company

k. Trading securities

_____ 1. (SO4) A company that owns more than 50% of the common stock of another entity.

_____ 2. (SO5) Securities bought and held primarily for sale in the near term to generate income on short-term price differences.

_____ 3. (SO4) Financial statements that present the assets and liabilities controlled by the parent company and the aggregate profitability of the affiliated companies.

_____ 4. (SO3) Method in which the investment in common stock is recorded at cost and revenue is recognized only when cash dividends are received.

_____ 5. (SO4) A company in which more than 50% of its stock is owned by another company.

_____ 6. (SO5) Securities that may be sold in the future.

_____ 7. (SO6) Investments that are not readily marketable or that management does not intend to convert into cash within the next year or operating cycle, whichever is longer.

_____ 8. (SO6) Investments that are readily marketable and intended to be converted into cash within the next year or operating cycle, whichever is longer.

_____ 9. (SO3) Method in which the investment in common stock is recorded at cost, and the investment account is then adjusted periodically to show the investor's equity in the investee.

_____ 10. (SO5) Debt securities that the investor has the intent and ability to hold to their maturity date.

Multiple Choice

Please circle the correct answer.

1. (SO2) Meyers Corporation acquired 20 of New Company's 5-year, 10%, $1,000 bonds for $22,000. In addition, brokerage fees were $500. The entry to record the acquisition of the bonds includes a debit to:
    a. Brokerage Fee Expense for $500.
    b. Debt Investments for $22,000.
    c. Debt Investments for $22,500.
    d. Cash for $22,500.

2. (SO2) Meyers Corporation sells its New Company bonds (from number 1 above) for $25,000. The journal entry to record the sale includes a:
    a. credit to Debt Investments for $25,000.
    b. credit to Cash for $25,000.
    c. debit to Gain on Sale of Debt Investments for $2,500.
    d. credit to Gain on Sale of Debt Investments for $2,500.

3. (SO3) Mack Corporation owns 10% of the common stock of Knife Corporation. When Mack receives $5,000 in cash dividends, the journal entry is:
    a. Cash   5,000
            Dividend Revenue   5,000
    b. Cash   5,000
            Stock Investments   5,000
    c. Stock Investments   5,000
            Dividend Revenue   5,000
    d. Stock Investments   5,000
            Cash   5,000

4. (SO3)   Mack Corporation owns 40% of the common stock of Knife Corporation. When Mack receives $5,000 in cash dividends, the journal entry is:

    a.   Cash   5,000
             Dividend Revenue   5,000
    b.   Cash   5,000
             Stock Investments   5,000
    c.   Stock Investments   5,000
             Dividend Revenue   5,000
    d.   Stock Investments   5,000
             Cash   5,000

5. (SO3)   Ross Corporation owns 40% of the common stock of Searcy Corporation. When Searcy reports total net income of $200,000, the journal entry on Ross's books is:

    a.   Stock Investments   80,000
             Dividend Revenue   80,000
    b.   Cash   80,000
             Stock Investments   80,000
    c.   Stock Investments   200,000
             Revenue from Investment   200,000
    d.   Stock Investments   80,000
             Gain from Investment   80,000

6. (SO4) Penny Corporation purchased 80% of the common stock of Sassy Corporation. Penny is the _____ company, and Sassy is the _____ company.
    a.   subsidiary, controlling
    b.   controlling, subsidiary
    c.   subsidiary, parent
    d.   parent, subsidiary

7. (SO4)   With respect to the Penny purchase of Sassy Corporation stock in number 6 above, which of the following is true?
    a.   Only consolidated financial statements are prepared.
    b.   Penny and Sassy each prepare their own financial statements, and consolidated financial statements are also prepared.
    c.   Penny and Sassy each prepare their own financial statements, and consolidated financial statements are not prepared.
    d.   Since Penny is the purchaser, it prepares its own financial statements, Sassy does not, and consolidated financial statements are also prepared.

8. (SO5)   A security bought and held for sale in the near term to generate income on short-term price differences is a(n):
    a.   trading security.
    b.   held-to-maturity security.
    c.   available-for-sale security.
    d.   long-term investment.

9. (SO5) Cassie Corporation has a portfolio of trading securities with a total cost of $75,000. On the financial statements date, the total fair value is $72,000. The adjusting entry is:

a.	Market Adjustment—Trading	3,000	
	Unrealized Gain—Income		3,000
b.	Market Adjustment—Trading	3,000	
	Unrealized Gain or Loss—Equity		3,000
c.	Unrealized Loss—Income	3,000	
	Market Adjustment—Trading		3,000
d.	Unrealized Gain or Loss—Equity	3,000	
	Market Adjustment—Trading		3,000

10. (SO5) Cassie Corporation has a portfolio of available-for-sale securities with a total cost of $85,000. On the financial statements date, the total fair value is $88,000. The adjusting entry is:

a.	Market Adjustment—Available-for-Sale	3,000	
	Unrealized Gain—Income		3,000
b.	Market Adjustment—Available-for-Sale	3,000	
	Unrealized Gain or Loss—Equity		3,000
c.	Unrealized Loss—Income	3,000	
	Market Adjustment—Av.-for-Sale		3,000
d.	Unrealized Gain or Loss—Equity	3,000	
	Market Adjustment—Av.-for-Sale		3,000

11. (SO5) Digger Corporation has a portfolio of trading securities with a total cost of $125,000. On the financial statements date, the Market Adjustment—Trading account has a debit balance of $5,000. How will the trading securities be reported in the current assets section of the balance sheet?
    a. Trading Securities, $130,000.
    b. Trading Securities, $125,000.
    c. Trading Securities, $120,000.
    d. Trading Securities is not a current asset: It will appear in the long-term assets section called "Investments."

12. (SO6) An unrealized gain or loss on a portfolio of trading securities is reported:
    a. in the stockholders' equity section of the balance sheet.
    b. in the current assets section of the balance sheet.
    c. as an operating item on the income statement.
    d. as a nonoperating item on the income statement.

13. (SO6) An unrealized gain or loss on a portfolio of available-for-sale securities is reported:
    a. in the stockholders' equity section of the balance sheet.
    b. in the current assets section of the balance sheet.
    c. as an operating item on the income statement.
    d. as a nonoperating item on the income statement.

14.   (SO6)   Information about the cash inflows and outflows resulting from investment transactions is reported:

    a.   on the statement of cash flows in the "Operating activities" section.

    b.   on the statement of cash flows in the "Investing activities" section.

    c.   on the income statement in the "Investing activities" section.

    d.   on the statement of cash flows in the "Financing activities" section.

Problems

1. Knowl Corporation has purchased 10% of the common stock of Georgia Corporation for $50,000 plus brokerage fees of $1,000. At the end of the accounting period, Georgia reported $300,000 of net income and paid cash dividends of $80,000.

    a. Please record Knowl Corporation's purchase of the stock and any other necessary journal entries.

Date	Account Titles	Debit	Credit

    b. Assume the same data as in "a" above, but now the stock purchased represents 30% of the common stock of Georgia Corporation. Please record the purchase of the stock and any other necessary journal entries.

Date	Account Titles	Debit	Credit

c. Knowl Corporation's portfolio of trading securities has a total cost of $225,000, and at the end of the accounting period the fair value of the total portfolio is $215,000. Please record the necessary adjusting entry.

Date	Account Titles	Debit	Credit

2. Please refer to The Bon-Ton Stores, Inc. financial statements at the end of this study guide for information for answering the following questions. Don't forget to use the **Decision Toolkit** approach for help in the problem-solving.

a. Does Bon-Ton own any subsidiary companies? (SO4)

b. What information is given about consolidation in the first note to the financial statements? (SO4)

SOLUTIONS TO SELF-TEST

Matching

1.	h		6.	a
2.	k		7.	g
3.	b		8.	i
4.	d		9.	e
5.	j		10.	f

Multiple Choice

1.	c	The journal entry is:

Debt Investments 22,500
    Cash 22,500
Brokerage fees are included in the asset account.

2.   d   The journal entry is:

Cash 25,000
    Debt Investments 22,500
    Gain on Sale of Debt Investments 2,500

3.   a   The cost method is used.

4.   b   The equity method is used.

5.   c   The equity method is used.

6.   d   "Controlling" refers to the interest the parent has in the subsidiary.

7.   b

8.   a   Held-to-maturity securities are just that: held to their maturity. Available-for-sale securities may be sold in the future. Since the security is to be sold in the near term it is not a long-term investment.

9.   c   Since the fair market value is lower than the cost, there is a loss, which is debited. Since it is a trading securities portfolio, the loss appears on the income statement.

10.   b   Since the fair market value is higher than the cost, there is a gain, which is credited. Since it is an available-for-sale securities portfolio, the gain appears in the equity section of the balance sheet.

11.   a   Since both have debit balances, they are added together to arrive at the $130,000, the fair market value of the portfolio.

12.   d   The unrealized gains or losses of trading securities appears on the income statement under "Other revenues and gains."

13.   a   It does not appear in the current assets section of the balance sheet, and it is not an income statement item.

14.   b   It does not appear on the income statement. Information about long-term assets appears in the "Investing activities" section of the statement of cash flows.

Problems

1.

a.   The cost method is used because the purchase is of 10% of the stock of Georgia Corporation. Only dividends are recognized.

Stock Investments 51,000
    Cash 51,000
(To record purchase of Georgia
 Corporation stock—10%)

Cash	8,000	
Dividend Revenue		8,000

(To record dividends:
10% x $80,000)

b.   The equity method is used because the purchase is of 30% of the stock of Georgia Corporation. Knowl's percentage of net income is recognized, as are dividends.

Stock Investments	51,000	
Cash		51,000

(To record purchase of Georgia
Corporation stock—30%)

Stock Investments	90,000	
Revenue from Investment		90,000

(To record 30% equity in Georgia
Corp. stock—$300,000 x 30%)

Cash	24,000	
Stock Investments		24,000

(To record dividends received:
30% x $80,000)

c.   An unrecognized loss of $10,000 must be recorded in the entry.

Unrealized Loss—Income	10,000	
Market Adjustment—Trading		10,000

(To record unrealized loss on
trading securities)

The word "Income" is used to indicate that the account will appear on the income statement. The word "Trading" is used to differentiate it from the Market Adjustment account for available-for-sale securities.

2.

a.   To answer this question, you must look at the titles of the financial statements and at the notes to the financial statements. The word "consolidated" is the beginning word in each financial statement title and indicates that Bon-Ton is the parent of some subsidiary companies. In various notes to the financial statements and in the audit report there are references to the company and its subsidiaries.

b.   The notes to the financial statements begin on page F-7 of the company's 2007 10-K on the following Web site: http://investors.bonton.com/annuals/cfm. (They are found immediately after the consolidated statements of cash flows.) The introduction to the first note mentions subsidiaries of 280 assorted stores. In Note 1, "Summary of Significant Accounting Policies," the first area discussed is entitled "Basis of Presentation." It mentions that the consolidated financial statements include the accounts of Bon-Ton and its subsidiaries and that all intercompany transactions have been eliminated.

SPECIMEN FINANCIAL STATEMENTS

The Bon-Ton Stores, Inc.

THE BON-TON STORES, INC.
CONSOLIDATED BALANCE SHEETS

(In thousands except share and per share data)	February 2, 2008	February 3, 2007
Assets		
Current assets:		
Cash and cash equivalents	$ 21,238	$ 24,733
Merchandise inventories	754,802	787,487
Prepaid expenses and other current assets	78,332	84,731
Deferred income taxes	17,536	17,858
Total current assets	871,908	914,809
Property, fixtures and equipment at cost, net of accumulated depreciation and amortization of $418,279 and $311,160 at February 2, 2008 and February 3, 2007, respectively	885,455	897,886
Deferred income taxes	87,357	76,586
Goodwill	17,767	27,377
Intangible assets, net of accumulated amortization of $21,917 and $12,087 at February 2, 2008 and February 3, 2007, respectively	165,872	176,700
Other long-term assets	39,272	41,441
Total assets	**$2,067,631**	**$2,134,799**
Liabilities and Shareholders' Equity		
Current liabilities:		
Accounts payable	$ 220,158	$ 209,742
Accrued payroll and benefits	49,902	68,434
Accrued expenses	166,603	178,642
Current maturities of long-term debt	5,656	5,555
Current maturities of obligations under capital leases	2,239	1,936
Income taxes payable	899	48,086
Total current liabilities	445,457	512,395
Long-term debt, less current maturities	1,079,841	1,120,169
Obligations under capital leases, less current maturities	67,217	69,456
Other long-term liabilities	112,055	86,383
Total liabilities	**1,704,570**	**1,788,403**
Commitments and contingencies (Note 14)		
Shareholders' equity		
Preferred Stock — authorized 5,000,000 shares at $0.01 par value; no shares issued	—	—
Common Stock — authorized 40,000,000 shares at $0.01 par value; issued shares of 14,614,111 and 14,469,196 at February 2, 2008 and February 3, 2007, respectively	146	145
Class A Common Stock — authorized 20,000,000 shares at $0.01 par value; issued and outstanding shares of 2,951,490 at February 2, 2008 and February 3, 2007	30	30
Treasury stock, at cost — 337,800 shares at February 2, 2008 and February 3, 2007	(1,387)	(1,387)
Additional paid-in capital	139,805	130,875
Accumulated other comprehensive income	799	1,189
Retained earnings	223,668	215,544
Total shareholders' equity	**363,061**	**346,396**
Total liabilities and shareholders' equity	**$2,067,631**	**$2,134,799**

The accompanying notes are an integral part of these consolidated financial statements.

THE BON-TON STORES, INC.
CONSOLIDATED STATEMENTS OF INCOME

(In thousands except share and per share data)	Fiscal Year Ended		
	February 2, 2008	February 3, 2007	January 28, 2006
Net sales	$ 3,365,912	$ 3,362,279	$ 1,287,170
Other income	101,747	93,531	20,425
	3,467,659	3,455,810	1,307,595
Costs and expenses:			
Costs of merchandise sold	2,150,131	2,118,762	822,171
Selling, general and administrative	1,065,753	1,056,472	407,145
Depreciation and amortization	121,125	103,189	27,245
Amortization of lease-related interests	4,978	3,720	839
Income from operations	125,672	173,667	50,195
Interest expense, net	108,165	107,143	12,052
Income before income taxes	17,507	66,524	38,143
Income tax provision	5,945	19,641	12,129
Net income	$ 11,562	$ 46,883	$ 26,014
Per share amounts —			
Basic:			
Net income	$ 0.70	$ 2.85	$ 1.61
Basic weighted average shares outstanding	16,545,101	16,430,554	16,204,414
Diluted:			
Net income	$ 0.68	$ 2.78	$ 1.57
Diluted weighted average shares outstanding	17,073,198	16,841,183	16,518,268

The accompanying notes are an integral part of these consolidated financial statements.

THE BON-TON STORES, INC.
CONSOLIDATED STATEMENTS OF SHAREHOLDERS' EQUITY

(In thousands except per share data)	Common Stock	Class A Common Stock	Treasury Stock	Additional Paid-in Capital	Deferred Compensation	Accumulated Other Comprehensive Income (Loss)	Retained Earnings	Total
BALANCE AT JANUARY 29, 2005	$136	$30	$(1,387)	$119,284	$(1,096)	$ (427)	$146,017	$262,557
Comprehensive income (Note 16):								
Net income	—	—	—	—	—	—	26,014	26,014
Change in fair value of cash flow hedges, net of tax	—	—	—	—	—	422	—	422
Total comprehensive income								26,436
Dividends to shareholders, $0.10 per share	—	—	—	—	—	—	(1,668)	(1,668)
Proceeds from stock options exercised	2	—	—	1,440	—	—	—	1,442
Issuance of stock under stock award plans	4	—	—	7,756	(7,760)	—	—	—
Share-based compensation expense	—	—	—	114	2,193	—	—	2,307
Tax benefit of stock options and restricted shares	—	—	—	1,022	—	—	—	1,022
Cancellation of restricted shares	—	—	—	(2)	—	—	—	(2)
BALANCE AT JANUARY 28, 2006	142	30	(1,387)	129,614	(6,663)	(5)	170,363	292,094
Comprehensive income (Note 16):								
Net income	—	—	—	—	—	—	46,883	46,883
Pension and postretirement benefit plans, net of tax	—	—	—	—	—	(313)	—	(313)
Change in fair value of cash flow hedges, net of tax	—	—	—	—	—	(839)	—	(839)
Total comprehensive income								45,731
Cumulative adjustment to adopt SFAS No. 158 (Note 8), net of tax	—	—	—	—	—	2,346	—	2,346
Adoption of SFAS No. 123R (Note 17)	(5)	—	—	(6,658)	6,663	—	—	—
Dividends to shareholders, $0.10 per share	—	—	—	—	—	—	(1,702)	(1,702)
Proceeds from stock options exercised	1	—	—	1,085	—	—	—	1,086
Share-based compensation expense	7	—	—	5,772	—	—	—	5,779
Excess tax benefit from share-based compensation	—	—	—	1,062	—	—	—	1,062
BALANCE AT FEBRUARY 3, 2007	145	30	(1,387)	130,875	—	1,189	215,544	346,396
Comprehensive income (Note 16):								
Net income	—	—	—	—	—	—	11,562	11,562
Pension and postretirement benefit plans, net of tax	—	—	—	—	—	3,266	—	3,266
Change in fair value of cash flow hedges, net of tax	—	—	—	—	—	(3,656)	—	(3,656)
Total comprehensive income								11,172
Dividends to shareholders, $0.20 per share	—	—	—	—	—	—	(3,438)	(3,438)
Proceeds from stock options exercised	1	—	—	603	—	—	—	604
Share-based compensation expense	—	—	—	7,965	—	—	—	7,965
Excess tax benefit from share-based compensation	—	—	—	366	—	—	—	366
Cancellation of restricted shares	—	—	—	(4)	—	—	—	(4)
BALANCE AT FEBRUARY 2, 2008	$146	$30	$(1,387)	$139,805	$ —	$ 799	$223,668	$363,061

The accompanying notes are an integral part of these consolidated financial statements.

THE BON-TON STORES, INC.
CONSOLIDATED STATEMENTS OF CASH FLOWS

(In thousands)	Fiscal Year Ended		
	February 2, 2008	February 3, 2007	January 28, 2006
Cash flows from operating activities:			
Net income	$ 11,562	$ 46,883	$ 26,014
Adjustments to reconcile net income to net cash provided by operating activities:			
Depreciation and amortization	121,125	103,189	27,245
Amortization of lease-related interests	4,978	3,720	839
Bad debt provision	—	—	1,510
Share-based compensation expense	7,965	5,779	2,307
Excess tax benefit from share-based compensation	(366)	(1,062)	—
Loss (gain) on sale of property, fixtures and equipment	281	(1,373)	237
Amortization of deferred financing costs	4,143	5,984	1,523
Amortization of deferred gain on sale of proprietary credit card portfolio	(2,414)	(2,460)	(1,346)
Deferred income tax provision (benefit)	1,378	(16,004)	(20,986)
Cancellation of restricted shares	(4)	—	(2)
Net transfers of receivables to accounts receivable facility	—	—	(244,000)
Proceeds from sale of proprietary credit card portfolio	—	—	315,445
Loss on sale of proprietary credit card portfolio	—	—	596
Changes in operating assets and liabilities, net of effect of acquisitions:			
Decrease (increase) in merchandise inventories	32,844	(28,902)	11,798
Decrease (increase) in prepaid expenses and other current assets	6,399	(22,632)	23,757
Decrease (increase) in other long-term assets	892	(3,077)	134
Decrease in accounts payable	(5,808)	(48,422)	(12,936)
(Decrease) increase in accrued payroll and benefits and accrued expenses	(25,112)	49,708	(3,684)
(Decrease) increase in income taxes payable	(33,067)	18,889	22,990
Increase in other long-term liabilities	10,768	1,675	1,363
Net cash provided by operating activities	135,564	111,895	152,804
Cash flows from investing activities:			
Capital expenditures	(109,659)	(95,209)	(28,159)
Acquisitions, net of cash acquired	(62)	(1,073,295)	(2,054)
Proceeds from sale of property, fixtures and equipment	2,807	2,516	2,514
Net cash used in investing activities	(106,914)	(1,165,988)	(27,699)
Cash flows from financing activities:			
Payments on long-term debt and capital lease obligations	(893,473)	(967,788)	(449,313)
Proceeds from issuance of long-term debt	851,309	2,048,355	312,700
Cash dividends paid	(3,438)	(1,702)	(1,668)
Proceeds from stock options exercised	604	1,086	1,442
Excess tax benefit from share-based compensation	366	1,062	—
Deferred financing costs paid	(307)	(27,839)	(336)
Increase (decrease) in bank overdraft balances	12,794	15,881	(1,067)
Net cash (used in) provided by financing activities	(32,145)	1,069,055	(138,242)
Net (decrease) increase in cash and cash equivalents	(3,495)	14,962	(13,137)
Cash and cash equivalents at beginning of period	24,733	9,771	22,908
Cash and cash equivalents at end of period	$ 21,238	$ 24,733	$ 9,771

The accompanying notes are an integral part of these consolidated financial statements.